DAPHNE

The Genus in the Wild and in Cultivation

By C. D. BRICKELL, v.m.h. and B. MATHEW

HON. EDITOR R. C. ELLIOTT, F.L.S., V.M.H.

First published 1976

First Reprint 1981

© The Alpine Garden Society,

Lye End Link, St. John's, Woking GU21 1SW,Surrey.

Printed by
L. Baker (Printers) Ltd.
71 Lombard Street, Birmingham B12 0QU

ISBN 0 900048 23 9

CONTENTS

©

	PAGE
Acknowledgements	1
Introduction	2
Historical notes	3
Taxonomy	5
Cultivation	9
Daphne troubles	15
Propagation	21
Descriptions of species and hybrids	46
List of hybrids	185
Bibliography	187
Index to *Daphne* names	188

The Alpine Garden Society acknowledges its great debt of gratitude to the Trustees of the Stanley Smith Horticultural Trust, for their munificent grant towards the publication costs of this book.

D. rodriguezii (p. 171) Fig. 1
    Photo: *H. Money-Coutts*

D. acutiloba (p. 46) Fig. 2
    Photo: *B. Mathew*

D. petraea (p. 158) Fig. 3
    Photo: *E. Hodgkin*

D. cneorum (p. 82) Fig. 4
    Photo: *A.G.S.*

Dedication

For Eliot Hodgkin
whose knowledge, enthusiasm and kindly
teaching have made this book possible.

ACKNOWLEDGEMENTS

One of the many plant enthusiasms of Eliot Hodgkin was the study and cultivation of the genus *Daphne*. For 20 years he had grown at his garden, Shelleys in Berkshire, all the *Daphne* species and hybrids he could obtain, and his knowledge of the habits and foibles of these fascinating plants was unequalled. Additionally he gathered together a very considerable amount of information on the literature of the genus which he meticulously filed and which we have been privileged to consult during the writing of this book. We gratefully acknowledge our indebtedness to him and to his wife Katharine Hodgkin, who has generously allowed us the fullest access to his papers and to the plants in the garden at Shelleys.

Similarly, Hugo Money-Coutts has provided us with much valuable information which we have used freely, whilst Mrs. K. Dryden, Ivor Barton, John Bond, Dr. G. A. C. Herklots, H. G. Hillier, Roy Lancaster, Tony Schilling, Sir Peter Smithers, Major Tom Spring-Smyth and Barry Starling have contributed most useful horticultural and botanical details, for which we offer our sincere thanks. Chris Grey-Wilson produced the cover drawing, and Pat Halliday the drawing of grafting techniques for which we are equally grateful.

To Josef Halda, and Jarmila Haldova whose delightful line-drawings appear in this work, we are indebted, particularly for information on *D. arbuscula*, but also for their account of daphnes which appeared in the Czechoslovak publication *Skalnicky* in 1972 and from an English translation of which we have extracted appropriate comments and information.

Arthur Carter has very kindly read the chapter on *Propagation* and provided extremely useful information and advice, whilst the chapter on *Daphne Troubles* has been vetted by Audrey V. Brooks and Andrew Halstead of the Wisley Staff, whose most helpful advice is duly acknowledged.

Roy Elliott deserves our sympathy and sincerest thanks for his skill in editing this account and endless patience in the face of the authors' delaying tactics, as does Dorothy Patterson, who battled with one author's scrawl successfully to produce most of the typescript.

Finally, our sincere thanks to our wives, who put up with "that other woman" about the house with only the mildest of reproaches!

1

INTRODUCTION

The original task set for us of producing a booklet on daphnes appeared relatively simple initially, but as we progressed, like Topsy, she grew and grew and the complications of taxonomy increased. It soon became obvious that the smaller format would not be satisfactory in view of the information we had compiled and although a full-scale monograph was out of the question it became apparent that sufficient material would be available to produce a more comprehensive account than had originally been envisaged.

We must emphasize that no attempt has been made to produce a botanical monograph of *Daphne*, a task which would take many years of full-time study. Our intention has been to provide, in what we hope is a readable form, as much information on the genus in cultivation as possible and to distil this with our own personal botanical and horticultural knowledge of the genus.

From the outset, it was clear that controversy and contradictions were legion in botanical and horticultural literature. The assessments we provide of the limits of the species and the garden value of individual daphnes may well meet with some disagreement—it would surprise us if they did not! It should be remembered that cultivated plants of any one species are often unrepresentative of the species as it occurs in nature, for they frequently result from no more than a few collections in the wild and so may not show the variation over the range of the species concerned. It is easy, therefore, for horticulturists to obtain a false idea of any particular species which is not infrequently represented in gardens by only a limited number of clones.

Our philosophy has been to accept nomenclatural changes when the arguments put forward seem to us logical and based on adequate research, but to maintain the *status quo* where the "sinking" of a well-known specific name may appear botanically sensible but where, at present, the evidence for so doing is inconclusive. Examples include *D. tangutica* and *D. collina*, which may well disappear botanically into *D. retusa* and *D. sericea* respectively at some future time.

The descriptions have for the most part been based on herbarium material at Kew and living material, wild and cultivated from various sources. We have been fortunate in seeing populations of a number of southern European and Turkish species in the wild and between us have grown (not always entirely successfully!) many of the daphnes described.

We have limited our account to those species and hybrids we know or believe to be in cultivation; or which may in the reasonably near future possibly be introduced. In a very few cases species are briefly described which may only be known to us from herbarium

2

specimens or from botanical descriptions. These are mostly included as reference points for those who delve into botanical literature whilst one, *D. macrantha*, is described in the hope that one day some fortunate being may again penetrate S.E. Tibet and bring to our gardens this superlative species. Diligent searchers of the *Index Kewensis* will find reference to various species, particularly from China, which do not appear in this work. Space has forced us, somewhat regretfully, to omit these and also to exclude reference to closely related genera such as *Stellera*, *Thymelaea* and *Wikstroemia*.

Botanical groupings into sections or other divisions have been avoided in view of the lack of information on certain species and nomenclatural complications which require a great deal of further work. No key to the species and hybrids has been provided for the same reason.

Concerning details of cultivation there are many opinions, and indeed various ways of growing a particular daphne successfully. Again we have, wherever possible, relied on our own experience attempting to avoid dogmatic statements and bearing in mind all the time that even in the same garden microclimatic conditions may vary. Basically cultivation details refer to growing daphnes in Britain, and will certainly require adaptation for other countries and climates.

Our purpose throughout is to stimulate interest in this most attractive genus which is much less widely grown than the beauty and ease of cultivation of many of its members deserve.

HISTORICAL NOTES

The elusive nymph Daphne, a daughter of the river god, Peneios, is reputed to have escaped the persistent and certainly dishonourable attentions of the god Apollo only after Zeus (or perhaps her father) took pity on her plight and transferred her from the animal to the plant kingdom by transforming her in mid-flight to a small tree.

Alas for legend, this plant known to the Greeks as Daphne was in fact *Laurus nobilis*, the Bay Tree, famed as the source of foliage for the victors' wreaths in the Games and known to us now mainly for its use in flavouring stews and other culinary delights. At one time *Laurus nobilis* was planted at the entrance to the sanctuary of Apollo at Delphi, the foliage being used by his high priestess on ceremonial occasions.

It is a pleasant but misconceived idea that *Daphne jasminea*, which clings to rock faces close to the holy shrine at Delphi, was the plant associated with the legend, but to gardeners it would be much more appropriate that one of the most beautiful members of this attractive genus should have been cast in the star role rather than the more mundane Bay Tree.

3

It is also sometimes stated that the spurge laurel, *D. laureola*, was the plant concerned, but this is unlikely as it is relatively uncommon in Greece, whereas *Laurus nobilis* is abundant and certainly the leaves usually depicted on Apollo's headband appear to be of this species.

The name *Daphne*, although normally considered to be of Greek origin, may be derived from an Indo-European root meaning "odour"—this would be understandable as many species have characteristically sweet-smelling flowers. Robert Graves makes an interesting reference to the origin of the name in *The Greek Myths* (Vol. 1 pp. 76-82) 1955.

Apart from legend, Theophrastus (*Enquiry into Plants;* Sir Arthur Hort's translation) gives us some early information on daphnes which he called *kneoron*.

D. gnidium, in the form of its fruits, was used as an emetic "Cnidian berry". He described the fruits as "round, red in colour, larger than that of pepper, and far stronger in its heating power; wherefore when it is given as a pill (for it is given to open the bowels) they knead it up in a piece of bread or dough; otherwise it burns the throat". Apparently an uncomfortable but effective relief for constipation!

D. oleoides was also known to Theophrastus who distinguished it from *D. gnidium* in growth and leaf characters as well as scent, stating also that the root was long, tough and pliant, being used "for binding and putting round things, like withy".

Parkinson in his *Paradisus* of 1629 describes two forms of *D. mezereum* which were grown at that time as *Chamaelaea Germanica*, one pale red fading white, the other deep red, whilst he also refers to *Chamaelaea Alpina*, the Mountaine Spurge Olive from Italy. This is said to be the *Chamaelaea Alpina incana* of Lobel and the *Chamaelaea secunda* of Clusius, and is described by Parkinson as evergreen with flowers of a light blush colour, with little or no scent and fruits at first "of an excellent red colour, which afterwards turn black". As an evergreen it could scarcely be *D. alpina* and there must remain a degree of uncertainty as to the identity of this plant at present, for the chief contenders, *D. collina* and *D. oleoides*, both have orange-red, ripe fruits. Parkinson also refers to *D. laureola*, although only in passing, but his *Cneorum Matthioli* or Small Rocke Roses matches *D. cneorum* well and he also mentions an albino.

Gerard (*Historie of Plants*, 1633) figures *D. mezereum* as the German Olive Spurge also using the names *Chamaelaea Germanica* and Dutch Mezereon. He was familiar with it in cultivation from Europe, but did not apparently know of its occurrence wild in Britain. Spurge Laurel, *D. laureola*, was also well-known to Gerard, who figures it both in flower and fruit, commenting on its "vertues" which include purging phlegmatic humours, drawing water from the

4

head, and provoking vomit! Similar properties are attributed to *D. gnidium*, called Spurge Flax by Gerard, and seeds of both species appear to have been used in abortion although the poisonous properties of the plants must have made their use in medicine somewhat hazardous.

By 1731, when the first edition of Miller's *Gardeners' Dictionary* appeared, no further species appear to have been brought into English gardens although the white-flowered *D. mezereum* is listed, as well as striped-leaved forms of this species and *D. laureola*—perhaps early records of virus symptoms! Miller included all these species and garden forms in the genus *Thymelaea* and by 1740 when Volume 2 was published he listed no less than thirty-four additional species under *Thymelaea*. It is not easy to equate these with *Daphne* species known today but at least twelve can be recognised immediately as belonging to genera other than *Daphne* and probably only five true daphnes were then grown. By the advent of the *Species Plantarum* (1753) where Linnaeus described ten *Daphne* species (some in fact referable to *Thymelaea*), *D. alpina*, *D. pontica* and *D. indica* could be added to the list of daphnes known to the botanical world. Later editions of Miller's *Gardeners Dictionary* include (under *Daphne* not *Thymelaea*) *D. laureola*, *D. mezereum*, *D. alpina*, *D. pontica*, *D. cneorum* and *D. gnidium* as being grown in gardens. Jumping to 1811, Aiton's *Hortus Kewensis* adds *D. odora* and *D. collina* to the list cultivated. In the late 18th and first half of the 19th centuries several of the eastern daphnes, including *D. genkwa* and forms of *D. odora*, arrived, whilst further European and Asiatic species—*D. altaica*, *D. oleoides*, *D. sericea* and *D. striata* among them—found their way into our gardens about the same period.

Slowly the list grew: *D. blagayana* and *D. petraea* appeared in the 1870's, and Asiatics like *D. aurantiaca*, *D. giraldii*, *D. retusa* and *D. tangutica* in the early part of this century. *D. bholua* and *D. glomerata* arrived just prior to the Second World War, and even during the last twenty or so years *D. euboica*, *D. jasminea* and *D. jezoensis* have arrived to stimulate further our interest in this fascinating group of plants.

TAXONOMY

The family Thymelaeaceae to which the genus *Daphne* belongs, is a very natural group with no close affinities. Willis (1973) allows 50 genera containing about 500 species from both temperate and tropical regions, with a high concentration in Africa. In this book we are able to cover the daphnes known to be in cultivation, with brief descriptions in a few instances of species likely to be of interest to horticulturists. Members of related genera, such as *Dais*, *Dendrostellera*, *Dirca*, *Edgeworthia*, *Gnidia*, *Ovidia*, *Passerina*, *Pimelia*, *Stellera*, *Thymelaea* and *Wikstroemia* are sometimes cultivated, but in most cases (*Stellera*, perhaps, excepted) are of less value to most gardeners.

5

Some authorities have expressed doubt concerning the maintenance of *Daphne* and *Wikstroemia* as separate genera. In this work we follow authors such as Rehder in treating the genera separately, as, without a thorough taxonomic study of the family as a whole, it would be impossible to offer a constructive opinion.

DAPHNE Linnaeus. The genus contains approximately 70 species which are mainly concentrated in Europe and temperate and subtropical Asia, with a few representatives in North Africa. All are shrubs varying considerably in habit from the prostrate *D. jasminea* to the upright *D. bholua* which may reach ten or more feet in height in the wild. The stems contain tough fibres and both wood and bark of some species, notably *D. bholua* and its relatives, have been used for making ropes and paper. The wood of most daphnes has a characteristic foetid odour.

The leaves, which are sessile or only shortly stalked, may be evergreen or deciduous and are normally alternate, except in *D. genkwa* where the majority (although not all) of the leaves are in opposite pairs and in *D. aurantiaca* where apparently the leaves are always opposite. They may be completely glabrous to densely hairy, but appear very seldom to be toothed or divided, though they are slightly toothed in *D. rodriguezii*.

The flowers, borne singly, in short racemes or in axillary or capitate clusters, are usually hermaphrodite, but in some species (*D. laureola*, *D. odora*, *D. oleoides* and probably others) dimorphism occurs and some plants tend to "maleness" whilst others are more female in character. Money-Coutts has observed populations of both *D. laureola* (in Sicily) and *D. oleoides* (in Crete) which showed this tendency, but further study of the genus as a whole is required to determine the significance of these characters.

The individual flowers lack petals and each consists of a fleshy calyx-tube with four spreading lobes which are quite frequently hairy outside and may be greenish-white, pink, purple, yellow or orange in colour. There are eight stamens arranged in two whorls of four, and more or less included within the tube. The ovary has a single locule and ovule, the style being very short or lacking and topped by a capitate stigma. Nectar is present at the base of the ovary within the tube, attracting long-tongued insects for pollination purposes. In many cases the flowers are pleasantly and often strongly scented, but in some species (such as *D. oleoides*) this character is not always immediately apparent, and appears to vary under different atmospheric conditions and possibly also the time of day. This variation could well account for some of the discrepancy in accounts in the literature on this point.

The fruit is usually a fleshy berry containing a single seed, but may sometimes be enclosed by the persistent calyx and less succulent. The colour of the fruits may be red, orange, yellow or black.

6

We have not attempted to subdivide *Daphne* for the purposes of the descriptive accounts of the species and hybrids, preferring an alphabetical scheme which we believe to be more helpful in this instance.

Botanical subdivision of the genus may perhaps be useful to those interested in the relationships of different species, although inevitably different authorities disagree on the best system to be used. The most recent botanical study of the genus, and that only of the section *Daphnanthes*, was by Keissler in 1898. Nitsche in 1907 (*Beitrage der Gattung Daphne*) and Domke in 1934 (*Untersuchungen über die systematische u. geographische Gliederung der Thymelaeaceae*) contribute further studies but no really satisfactory infra-generic classification has yet been developed, mainly because our knowledge of many species particularly from the Far East is poor.

The following Sectional and Sub-sectional divisions (basically those of Keissler) provide a guide to the relationship of the species.

SECTION MEZEREUM Spach.
   D. jezoensis, D. kamtschatica, D. koreana, D. mezereum,
   D. pseudomezereum, D. rechingeri.

SECTION GENKWA Benth. et Hook.
   D. genkwa.

SECTION LAUREOLA Spach.
   D. albowiana, D. glomerata, D. laureola, D. pontica.

SECTION ERIOSOLENA Blume.
   D. aurantiaca.

SECTION DAPHNANTHES C. A. Meyer
   Subsection Alpinae
      D. alpina, D. altaica, D. caucasica, D. giraldii, D. sophia.
   Subsection Oleoides
      D. baksanica, D. euboica, D. gnidioides, D. jasminea,
      D. kosaninii, D. linearifolia, D. mucronata, D. oleoides,
      D.rodriguezii (?), *D. stapfii, D. transcaucasica.*
   Subsection Gnidium
      D. gnidium.
   Subsection Cneorum
      D. arbuscula, D. cneorum, D. juliae, D. petraea, D. striata.
   Subsection Daphnanthoides
      D. acutiloba, D. bholua, D. grueningiana, D. kiusiana,
      D. longilobata, D. luzonica, D. miyabeana, D. odora,
      D. papyracea, D. retusa, D. shillong, D. sureil,
      D. taiwaniana, D. tangutica.
   Subsection Collinae
      D. blagayana, D. collina, D. macrantha, D. sericea.

It should be emphasized that the placement of species within the above categories is one of convenience rather than one based on

7

scientific assessment. As one instance, there is controversy between various authors over the placement of the species grouped here under *Section Daphnanthes, Subsection Alpinae* which have also been placed under *Section Laureola*. Without a considerable amount of research we would not offer an opinion as to the correct infrageneric classification and for this same reason have made no attempt to provide Sectional characters.

POISONOUS AND MEDICINAL PROPERTIES

Although only a limited number of species have been investigated, it is known that *D. mezereum, D. laureola, D. gnidium, D. cneorum* and *D. odora* contain chemicals which are poisonous to both livestock and human beings. Various glucosides (notably Daphnin) and an acrid resin (Mezerein) have been isolated from most parts of the plants and apparently impart a bitter, unpleasant and burning taste if chewed. Linnaeus certainly knew of the poisonous properties of *D. mezereum* (q.v.) and there are several documented cases of poisoning by the fruits of this species which have, on occasion, been mistaken for redcurrants and were at one time apparently used (unwisely!) as substitutes for pepper in Europe. The symptoms include intense irritation and burning pains in the mouth and stomach, gastro-enteritis and convulsions which in severe cases may be followed by death. In cases of suspected *Daphne* poisoning immediately call a doctor. If one is not quickly available, give the patient an emetic followed by a demulcent (mixed eggs, sugar and milk is recommended) to relieve the irritation.

Luckily, the unpleasant taste of the fruit (and other parts) of daphnes is sufficient deterrent in the majority of instances to prevent more than the odd fruit being eaten by even the most inquisitive child or animal. Although it is important to be aware of the poisonous properties of daphnes, it is equally important to keep a sense of proportion and not banish all daphnes to the bonfire purely because of their poisonous properties. Be very careful, particularly when there are young children about, but remember also that very large numbers of our garden plants are poisonous to some extent.

As is often the case with plants containing poisons, use has also been made of daphnes in medicine, mainly from decoctions of the bark and roots of *D. mezereum* and *D. laureola*, which retain their properties even when dried. At one time it was thought to be a cure for cancer, whilst worms, toothache, rheumatism and various skin diseases are purported to have been alleviated by the use of Mezereon, the pharmaceutical name for the dried bark of various species. In addition, application to the skin causes blisters to appear, and possibly it was used in the Middle Ages by professional beggars to raise sores on their bodies aimed at loosening the purse strings of the gullible!

Nowadays, although Mezereon is still recognised in the *British Pharmaceutical Codex*, its use in medicine is negligible.

8

CULTIVATION IN THE OPEN GARDEN

One of the factors which make *Daphne* such a fascinating genus to gardeners is that no two authorities appear to agree on any aspect of their cultivation. Contradictory and often dogmatic statements on position, soil, feeding and virtually any other detail of cultivation can be found for almost all the species or hybrids known in gardens.

In our own experience we have found very few daphnes particularly difficult to grow, although some certainly require more attention than others. Many of them can be grown in ordinary garden soil without any special attention, apart from the common courtesies which one would afford to shrubs such as roses as to site and soil preparation. Commonsense in the choice of site would, one hopes, prevent a species such as *D. petraea* being grown in the herbaceous border, but such reputedly difficult species as *D. arbuscula* and *D. blagayana* can be quite happy in a small shrub border provided simple rules of good cultivation are observed.

On the other hand it is much less easy to maintain species like *D. striata* and *D. genkwa* in prime condition for long periods and these mavericks in the genus represent a challenge to which enthusiasts are quick to respond when they can obtain plants of the species concerned.

That daphnes are sometimes unpredictable in their behaviour we would not deny, and their perversity has been emphasised by both Dr. Amsler (1953) and Eliot Hodgkin (1961) in their excellent accounts in the *R.H.S. Journal*. In the chapter "Daphne Troubles" we put forward a variety of reasons for the sudden demise of daphnes which is frequently mentioned by growers, but would emphasise again that most can be grown without difficulty in any garden where a well-drained soil and an open position can be provided.

The following details of cultivation are expanded where necessary in the accounts for each species described.

Soil Conditions

(A) ACID OR ALKALINE?

It has been stated that species such as *D. odora*, *D. retusa* and *D. genkwa* (and by one author, *D. arbuscula* and *D. blagayana*) must have acid conditions to grow well, but such statements are not borne out when the facts are investigated. Even *D. genkwa*, reported as a calcifuge by many, grows naturally in limestone areas, and in the wild most daphnes occur on neutral or alkaline soils. Plants obtained from some nurserymen, particularly of species like *D. cneorum*, may be grown in a peat-mix which can mislead a would-be grower into believing that acid conditions are

9

necessary. This is certainly not the case and Farrer, not unexpectedly, has an appropriate comment on *D. cneorum* as it occurs in nature—"its yard-long rat-tail of nude, yellow tap-root runs down into stuff that is nothing other than fine white limestone debris."

In cultivation daphnes are generally tolerant of a wide range of pH, and, even in conditions of considerable alkalinity or acidity, can be grown perfectly satisfactorily provided drainage and feeding requirements are met.

(B) DRAINAGE

All daphnes require a well-drained soil, and some insist upon it. The rock-dwellers such as *D. petraea* and *D. jasminea* push their roots deep into cliffs and crevices in their natural habitat where the sharpest of drainage prevails and they expect similar treatment in cultivation. Some of the woodlanders like *D. pontica* and *D. laureola* are more easy-going, but none long tolerate soils where the drainage is impeded to any extent.

A mistake that is sometimes made, however, is to provide a medium which is sharply drained but has poor moisture retaining qualities. One of the most common methods of killing daphnes is to plant them in a soil or compost of this type which dries out rapidly, leaving the feeding roots short of moisture unless natural or artificial watering occurs. If some of the feeding roots are killed by drought the plant is immediately under stress and may itself quickly die.

It is important to make sure that sufficient humus is present in the soil or compost to maintain a reasonable moisture level around the plants' roots without in any way impeding drainage and causing stagnation. Obviously the method of achieving this in the open garden will depend on the basic soil type. In sandy or chalky soils which are normally well-drained but deficient in humus, it is usually unnecessary to add further drainage materials; but ample humus— peat, leaf-mould, spent hops, mushroom compost, well-rotted manure or garden compost, separately or in any combination— are all suitable and should be thoroughly mixed with the soil of the planting area.

On heavier soils drainage may be a problem. In addition to digging in ample humus to assist flocculation of the clay particles, it is as well to include a proportion of coarse grit to improve the drainage further. Lime may also be usefully applied (3—4 oz. per sq. yd.) on acid clays (unless the neighbours are calciphobes), serving a similar purpose to the humus. As will be appreciated these comments apply equally to the preparation of the ground for planting almost any shrubs, but we include them here to emphasise that many daphnes require no more coddling than roses or hebes.

Aspect

In nature many daphnes grow in full sun, and in almost all cases it is better to give them open, unshaded positions in the garden, provided, and it is an important proviso that they do not dry out at the roots. Some such as *D. laureola* and *D. pontica* occur naturally in or at the edge of woodlands, and it is preferable to offer them a similar garden habitat although both are tolerant enough for more open situations unless totally sun-baked. Certain of the high mountain species are used to a high degree of atmospheric humidity from mist following high day-time temperatures, conditions not always easy to reproduce in most gardens.

Luckily most of these are tolerant of cultivation and any difficulties can usually be overcome by providing a cool root-run and slight shade during the hottest part of the day. It must be remembered that many mountain plants, although apparently living in the most spartan of habitats, have their roots in cool conditions, comfortably buried in stones and leaf-detritus, receiving ample moisture from snow-melt early in the season and from evening mists later on. "Open aspect in a well-drained soil" does *not* mean dry soil in the hottest area one can find.

Feeding

Thorough initial soil preparation, followed by an annual spring mulch of well-rotted humus, will normally be sufficient to keep the plant healthy for some years. In sandy and chalky soils, which are frequently less well endowed with plant food than clay soils, an occasional dressing of bone meal and a foliar feed can be beneficial, the latter to be applied as the young growth is developing. No elaborate programme of feeding is otherwise necessary, but if a plant should show signs of lack of food give the root-ball a thorough watering, apply a mulch of well-rotted humus (in that order) and spray on a foliar feed two or three times during the growing season to provide a quick boost to growth. Plant foods given as foliar sprays in this way are quickly absorbed by the leaves and can be very valuable in reviving plants where for some reason root action is poor.

Watering

If preparation of the planting position has been carried out properly and annual mulches given, watering, additional to natural rainfall, should only be necessary in exceptionally dry spells. Make sure, however, that the root-ball of any daphne being planted is moist right through. Failure to establish any plant can result from not taking this elementary precaution, but it is surprising how often it is forgotten and it is much more difficult to wet the root-ball thoroughly once planting has taken place.

Daphnes abominate dry conditions, with a few exceptions, and one of the most frequent factors contributing to die-back in mature

11

plants is dryness at the roots. Ball-watering of large plants is a useful precaution in dry periods, particularly in sandy or chalky soils and at the first signs of distress in a daphne always investigate root-dryness first.

Remember that, although the soil surface may appear damp, underneath where the feeder roots are attempting to take up water and nutrients it may be bone-dry. Thorough soaking is essential to prevent the plant being severely checked and perhaps dying back.

Transplanting

Daphnes are usually said to be difficult to transplant successfully, and certainly this operation should not be undertaken if it can be avoided. Nevertheless it is possible to transplant quite large daphnes provided that lifting is carried out properly and aftercare is not neglected.

If there is any choice, transplanting is best undertaken during early spring when there is an upsurge in the plant's metabolic activities as the season's growth begins. Daphne roots are usually rather thick and fleshy with relatively little fibre, and it is not always easy to dig them up with a good root ball, particularly on sandy soils. It is essential, however, to disturb the root system as little as possible, and time and trouble at this stage can reduce the aftercare required considerably. Dig carefully round the plant to be moved so that the root ball is at least the circumference of the top-growth and preferably more. The depth of the cut will depend on the size of the plant, but always allow at least a spade's depth. Use a spade, not a fork, which is more likely to loosen the soil around the roots. Then undercut the plant about half way and slip a piece of sacking (or polythene) under the cut. Undercut the remaining section and gently ease the sacking beneath the plant so that the root-ball can be enclosed in the sacking, which is then tied at the neck and the plant carefully removed. Never pick up the plant by its neck or branches as this immediately causes strain on the root-ball which will probably crumble. Use the sacking to carry the plant to its new position, which should be prepared previous to transplanting if possible. After placing the plant at the correct depth in the prepared hole, remove the sacking from the plant carefully so that the minimum of disturbance occurs and plant in the normal way. Do not leave the sacking under the plant as is sometimes recommended as it will hinder further root development.

Once transplanting has taken place, water-in thoroughly and make sure that the plant never dries out, particularly in the early stages of re-establishment; foliar feed several times during the season. With this treatment there should be no real problems in moving most daphnes unless they are very large. No doubt there are instances of large daphnes being transplanted perfectly well without the preparations just described, but care always pays.

12

We have successfully transplanted fairly large specimens of the following: *D.* x *burkwoodii* 'Somerset'; *D. caucasica; D. cneorum* 'Eximia'; *D. mezereum* forms; *D. odora* 'Aureo-marginata'; *D. longilobata; D. retusa;* and *D. tangutica.*

In the A.G.S. *Bulletin* there are additional records of *D. arbuscula, D. collina* and *D. petraea* 'Grandiflora' being moved as fairly large plants with good success. Mrs. K. Dryden has successfully transplanted a venerable 34-year-old *D. mezereum.*

Pruning

The old maxim "when in doubt don't" applies very definitely, in our view, to the pruning of daphnes. Dr. Amsler (1953) mentions "ruthlessly pruning" *D.* x *burkwoodii* 'Somerset', when it outgrew its position, without losing the plant but we would regard this treatment as only to be tried in exceptional circumstances. As a general rule, apart from initial shaping by judicious pinching out of the young growths of such species as *D. cneorum* which tend to legginess from rooted cuttings, pruning should only involve removing any wayward or unhealthy growth which appears.

Most species and hybrids are naturally neat in habit, but if for some reason it is necessary to remove a branch from a mature plant, make sure that the cut surface is quickly covered with a bitumen wound-paint which should minimise risk of fungal infection, particularly by *Botrytis* (see p. 18). Quite frequently one reads or hears the statement that to cut a mature daphne is to kill it. All that this usually means is that a branch has been cut out and the plant has later died, almost certainly *not* because it was pruned, but through one of the causes suggested on pp. 18 and 19.

Longevity of Daphnes

"Daphnes are short-lived plants in cultivation" is a generalisation one often sees in horticultural literature, but even a reasonably cursory search indicates that such statements are only half-truths, particularly when "short-lived" remains undefined! Most daphnes, provided they are hardy, can be expected to live twenty or more years given reasonable care and attention. It is only when troubles such as neglect, virus and die-back affect them that they deteriorate into the lamented "miffs" of the literature, and in an attempt to counteract the impression often given that all daphnes are difficult and unlikely to survive long the following records of longevity are given, taken either from garden literature or our own knowledge.

D. arbuscula 17 years old (Mrs. K. Dryden, 1976)

D. bholua 15 years old (Wisley, 1976); 14 years old (Spring-Smyth 1976)

D. blagayana "5 yds across after 14 years from a cutting"; 15 years old (Mrs. K. Dryden, 1976)

D. x *burkwoodii* 'Somerset' 17 years old (Wisley, 1976)

D. cneorum 17 years old (Mrs. K. Dryden, 1976)

D. cneorum 'Eximia' 18 years old (Wisley, 1976)

D. collina 30+ years old (Lady Drury, 1975)
D. glomerata 11 years old (Mrs. Hodgkin, 1976)
D. x *hybrida* 11 years old (Mrs. Hodgkin, 1976)
D. jasminea 11-12 years old (Mrs. K. Dryden, 1975)
D. laureola ssp. *philippi* 15 years old (Wisley, 1976)
D. x *mantensiana* 14 years old (Mrs. Hodgkin, 1976)
D. mezereum and var. *alba*. Both over 20 years old (Wisley, 1976) 41 years old (Mrs. K. Dryden, 1976)
D. odora 'Aureo-marginata' 18 years old (Wisley, 1976)
D. oleoides "Over 14 years old"; 20 years old (Mrs. Hodgkin, 1976)
D. petraea An ancient plant 40 years old in R. B. Cooke's garden grown out of doors; from Co. Dublin a plant purchased in 1938 and planted out in 1945 was 17 in. across in 1965; over 20 years old in the open (Dr. Amsler, 1953); 25+ years (Joe Elliott, 1976)
D. pontica over 25 years old (Mrs. Hodgkin, 1976)
D. retusa 40 years old at Highdown, Goring, (on chalk, in spite of its reputation as a calciphobe!).
D. tangutica over 16 years old (Wisley; and Mrs. Hodgkin, 1976)

As will be appreciated, the ages given here can only be rough guides to the longevity of the daphnes listed and only plants which have lived 10 or more years have been included. We fully realise that the list is incomplete and that there may be many older specimens than those quoted of which we are unaware. Any further information will be most welcome.

CULTIVATION IN POTS

As long ago as 1843, *D. odora* and *D. cneorum* in their various forms were widely grown both in Britain and in France as florists' plants, and were particularly valued in the conservatories and greenhouses of the day for their intensely fragrant blooms.

Contradictions as to cultural procedure, particularly the best soil mixture, can be found in the *Gardeners' Chronicle* and *The Garden* for that period, indicating that gardeners then were just as wedded to their 'pet' composts as some are today.

A great deal of unwarranted mystique envelopes the use of potting mixtures and the "cookery-book proportions" of compost ingredients so often recommended for individual species grown in pots are quite unnecessary in the vast majority of cases. Many daphnes can be grown as alpine house plants very successfully—one only has to visit the various A.G.S. Shows to marvel at the expertise of the grower and the age of the plants of *D. petraea* 'Grandiflora', *D. arbuscula* and *D. jasminea* shown by some exhibitors. Certainly more attention to detail may be required in growing them in pots rather than in the open, but happily there is an excellent A.G.S. Guide, *Alpines in Pots* by Roy Elliott, which provides admirable guidance on the subject. We need do no more than recommend that the excellent advice given in this publication be followed by those setting out to grow their daphnes for the alpine house.

Daphne oleoides (p. 152)   *Photo: H. Money-Coutts*

Daphne jezoensis (p. 119)   *Photo: T. Rokujo*

Daphne altaica (p. 79)

Photos: E. Hodgkin

Daphne sophia (p. 80)

DAPHNE TROUBLES

Under this euphemistic heading we include attack by pests, diseases (including virus) and "sudden death", that notorious, oft-quoted phenomenon which is reported to afflict so many daphnes.

When compared with other shrubby genera, daphne troubles are few, the most serious enemies being aphids which transmit most of the debilitating virus diseases mentioned below.

Major Troubles

Virus Diseases

Cucumber Mosaic, Alfalfa Mosaic and Bean Yellow viruses which are aphid-borne and Arabis Mosaic virus which is spread by eelworms have been isolated from various daphnes and cause unsightly mottling and often distorted foliage. Serious weakening and eventual death of affected plants occurs and plants which definitely show virus symptoms should be burnt immediately. The symptoms can be masked to a certain extent by foliar feeding, but it is pointless to waste time and money in this way as virus-infected plants are a menace not only to other daphnes but to many different plants which are subject to the same viruses.

Some success has been reported in eliminating virus by heat-treating infected material of *D. odora* in the U.S.A. Problems in propagation with treated material were experienced and re-infection by aphid vectors occurred at an early stage after virus-free material was planted out.

Prevention is therefore more important than attempts to cure virus diseases so:—

DO NOT propagate vegetatively from infected plants as the virus will inevitably be passed on. It is particularly important, of course, not to propagate grafting stocks from cuttings of virus-infected plants.

DO NOT handle other plants after touching infected plants or using a knife to prune or propagate from an infected plant. Sap-inoculation of viruses often occurs in this way. Wash and disinfect your hands and knives if virus-infection is suspected.

The "DONT'S" may appear over-fussy, but it is surprising how many plants are infected by virus by this means—even by professional propagators who should know better.

Some of the transmitting agents, various aphid species such as *Myzus persicae*, can be controlled without too much difficulty by regular spraying with contact or systemic insecticides but it must be remembered that control chemicals are constantly under review by manufacturers and up-to-date advice should always be sought.

Aphids, however, are sucking insects and although killed by insecticides it is important to realise that an aphid carrying virus can pass it on merely by inserting its sucking organ (the stylus) into plant cells. The fact that very soon afterwards it may be killed

15

by the systemic insecticide it has sucked up is of little comfort if the virus infection has already been passed on.

Arabis Mosaic virus, unfortunately, is even more difficult to control than aphid-borne viruses. It is transmitted by the eelworm vector *Xiphenema diversicaudatum* which is known to be widespread in soils in the southern half of England and which has also been recorded as far north as Dundee. It is found mostly in cultivated soils and is probably present, therefore, in the gardens of some housing estates built on the sites of old grassland or deciduous woods. If virus symptoms appear on a plant in a fairly new garden, it is advisable to discard both the plant and the soil in which it is growing, as there is no effective method at the moment by which an amateur can control any eelworm vectors which may be present in the garden.

General garden hygiene and in particular the limiting of aphid populations on other plants is also of obvious importance as well as the elimination of plants other than daphnes which are infected with virus. Every effort should also be made to keep gardens weed-free as weeds can be a major source of Cucumber Mosaic virus infection.

As far as is known, these virus diseases are not seed-transmitted in daphnes, but Cucumber Mosiac virus can be transmitted in the seed of certain weeds, including chickweed. If there is any choice, therefore it is far better to avoid risk and use seed only from virus-free plants—a counsel of perfection as we fully realise.

The following species are most seriously affected by virus diseases:-

1. *D. odora* and its forms (usually by a mixture of both Arabis and Cucumber Mosaic virus) which show the disease by a "pinching" and narrowing of the leaves accompanied by pale green or yellowish mottling or streaking of the normally dark green surface. The older leaves drop, young foliage is clustered at the shoot tips which are often stunted; flowering is also much reduced.

2. *D. laureola* and *D. pontica*. Virus symptoms are similar to those described for *D. odora*.

3. *D. mezereum*. The most commonly grown and most frequently affected species. Virus symptoms in Britain usually show as pale green or sometimes creamy mottling on the leaves which are often reduced in size. Leaf-fall also tends to be earlier in virus-infected plants and may be preceded by curling of the foliage.

In Holland, at Boskoop, disease on *D. mezereum* characterised by the development of small yellow streaks and spotting of the foliage was attributed to virus infection following a thorough investigation. It seems likely that different viruses or combinations of viruses can cause a variety of mottling, streaking and spotting of the foliage, but as far as we know a thorough study of the problems has yet to be undertaken.

D. mezereum appears to be particularly prone to virus attack from the seedling stage onwards, and although infected plants will

16

quite frequently continue to flower for a number of years they are a sorry sight in leaf and gradually deteriorate. Sudden death on the bonfire is better than a lingering, unhygienic existence for such plants.

No definite records of virus disease attacking other *Daphne* species have been traced but almost certainly relatives of *D. mezereum* (*D. pseudomezereum*, *D. jezoensis* and *D. kamtschatica*), *D. odora*, *D. laureola* and *D. pontica* are liable to succumb.

PREVENTION

Even on the more leathery-leaved species, the young growth—particularly the shoot tips and the under-surfaces of the leaves—can frequently be infested with aphids, which are easily overlooked. It is important early in the season, as young growth begins, to spray with a systemic insecticide to minimise the possibility of virus infection by aphids.

A number of systemic sprays to control aphids based on the chemicals Dimethoate and Formothion are available and are particularly suitable as they are absorbed by the plant and remian effective for several weeks, thus obviating the need to spray every few days.

CONTROL

Once plants have been infected with virus there is no satisfactory cure, and, as has already been stated, they should be burnt immediately and the surrounding soil discarded, particularly in a new garden.

Leaf-spots

The fungus *Marssonina daphnes*, first reported in Scotland in 1908 and in England in 1934, causes a leaf-spot on *D. mezereum* which is now widespread. It is characterised by numerous brown spots on the leaf-surfaces and petioles accompanied by early defoliation. Frequently the disease remains unnoticed until the leaves drop prematurely, and weaken the plant, which may well die if control measures are not taken before further attack by the leaf-spot fungus occurs. It is also prevalent on *D. mezereum* in Germany and perhaps elsewhere on the Continent, and is known to occur in the U.S.A. It has not so far apparently been recorded on daphnes other than *D. mezereum*.

The fungus, *Gloeosporium mezerei*, first reported in 1890 on *D. mezereum* is almost certainly identical with *M. daphnes*.

CONTROL

Spraying with Bordeaux mixture as the leaves develop in spring or with a dithiocarbamate fungicide such as maneb or zineb is the best preventive measure, but if the attack is only slight it is possible, if wearisome, to pick off and burn infected leaves. In severe cases, the diseased leaves which have fallen should be raked up and burnt.

Grey Mould (*Botrytis cinerea*)

Most gardeners associate the familiar grey mould disease with lettuce and many other non-woody plants, but seldom realise that it can quietly but devastatingly affect some shrubs. Undoubtedly it is one cause of branch die-back and sometimes death in daphnes, the spores (which are air-borne) entering perhaps through a pruning wound or frost-damaged, precocious growth, and quickly forming dense mats of greyish fungal threads which girdle and kill affected branches. The sudden collapse of daphnes, so frequently bemoaned by growers, can on occasion be traced to the insidious spread of grey mould on the main stem which, once girdled, is incapable of maintaining the essential passage of food and water between the roots and the foliage. In many cases it is probable that other factors, particularly dryness at the roots, contribute to the demise. In an interesting article on *Daphne* in the *Gardeners Chronicle* for September 27, 1967, Miss M. G. Hodgman mentions a link between resistance to grey mould on lettuce and the provision of sufficient water to maintain leaf turgidity, surmising that shortage of water and attack by grey mould on daphnes could also be linked.

PREVENTION

Ensure that the plants do not become dry at the roots and that plants are growing vigorously. If pruning is necessary, make certain that the wounds are covered immediately with a bitumen wound-paint such as "Arbrex".

CONTROL

If die-back in some branches occurs, these should be cut out well below any stained wood (which may indicate the presence of an attacking fungus) and immediately covered with wound-paint.

Progressive die-back and "sudden death"

One might flippantly attribute "sudden death" to the capriciousness of the fair sex, *Daphne* being a feminine genus, but it is a worrying problem for growers and one which has never been investigated fully or explained satisfactorily.

Almost certainly, there is no single cause and "sudden deaths" are probably due to a combination of different but associated factors—and not always the same factors at that!

It is frequently asserted that daphnes are not long-lived plants and after a few years die naturally, but this is too facile an explanation and certainly untrue in some cases (see p. 13 under *Longevity of Daphnes*). Equally, the explanation that their profuse flowering habit gradually reduces their vigour is an unlikely one, although it is true that weak plants may bloom abundantly just before dying, in a last ditch effort to produce offspring. In such cases the weakness is usually due to other causes, not to over-production of bloom.

Our own observations suggest that any of the following factors could be involved in varying combinations:—

(a) Poor nutrition (lack of either some major or trace element or both).

(b) Dryness at the roots, particularly in spring.

(c) Poor drainage.

(d) Virus attack.

(e) Grey mould (*Botrytis cinerea*) entering through wounds.

(f) Leaf spot attack.

(g) Frost damage to young growth.

(h) Use of weak, starved, pot-bound or diseased stocks for grafting.

(i) Incompatibility of stock and scion (unproven).

(j) Lack of hardiness of the stock.

(k) The use of stock of a woodland species more sensitive to drought than the species grafted on to it (e.g. the use of *D. laureola* as a stock for *D. sericea*).

(l) Poor planting (either too deep or with the roots not spread out).

It has also been suggested that there may be some symbiotic association with certain fungi and lack of the correct fungus in the area in which daphnes are planted would result in less vigorous plants. There appears to be no evidence to support this suggestion but it is a theory which might bear investigation in the future.

Minor Troubles

Root, Stem and Crown Rots

BLACK ROOT ROT caused by *Thielaviopsis basicola* has occasionally been reported on *D. mezereum* in Britain but it is not a serious threat.

RHIZOCTONIA (probably *R. solani*) was reported to have affected cuttings on two occasions in Britain, in one case the cuttings were being propagated under mist.

PYTHIUM species have been isolated as causes of root rots on daphnes in New Zealand (species not stated but possibly *D. odora*).

PHYTOPHTHORA PARASITICA is known to have caused root and stem rots on *D. odora* in California, the condition being aggravated by poor drainage. Artificial inoculation of *D. cneorum* with the same fungus caused the death of the plants within a month, but luckily *Phytophthora* does not yet appear to have gained a serious foothold on daphnes in Britain.

CROWN AND STEM ROTS caused by various fungi have been recorded in the U.S.A., particularly of plants grown in shade.

Diseases caused by these root and stem rot fungi are most frequent on young stock and are usually encouraged by poor hygiene. Use of sterilised soil in the cutting and potting composts should minimise possible attack. Watering young plants with Cheshunt Compound, captan or zineb is a useful precaution.

Crown gall. This is caused by *Agrobacterium tumefaciens*, and occurs occasionally on *D. mezereum* in Britain and on the Continent, being characterised by small aerial galls on the shoots. This disease does not appear to be widespread and it is usually sufficient to cut out diseased shoots. Seriously infected plants should be burnt as there is no satisfactory control known.

Honey fungus (*Armillariella* (*Armillaria*) *mellea*). In areas where honey fungus is prevalent it is a threat to almost any woody or herbaceous plant and control is by no means easy. This root parasite should always be considered as a possible cause of death whenever a shrub dies back rapidly. The main diagnostic symptom to look for is a sheet of white fan-shaped fungal growth beneath the bark of roots and the main stem of the shrub at and just above ground level. Dead and dying plants affected by this fungus should be dug out, together with as many of the roots as possible, and burnt.

Wilt caused by *Verticillium dahliae*. This has been reported on daphnes in England and Holland. There is no known control for this disease and any plant showing a progressive wilting of shoots should be destroyed.

Blast or Bacterial Spot caused by *Pseudomonas synisintae*. This has been recorded in New Zealand on *D. odora rubra*. Raised black spots appear on the undersurfaces of the leaves, which gradually turn yellow and drop. To date this disease has not been recorded on daphnes in Britain. It has been found that regular spraying with Bordeaux mixture provides satisfactory control.

Insect pests. Apart from aphids, these are few, and although occasionally some caterpillar damage to the leaves occurs, routine spraying to control aphids should prevent damage from other pests.

Although this section on troubles contains information on most of the afflictions of the genus, do not be discouraged by the thought that all your daphnes will succumb immediately!

The minimum of sensible precautions is necessary and only occasionally are the minor troubles likely to cause problems. Good garden hygiene should be observed, the plants should be fed properly and not allowed to dry out (or become stagnant) at the roots, and spraying against aphids and leaf spots should be carried out.

You may well grow good daphnes without these simple precautions, but commonsense dictates that they should be undertaken. Remember too that advice on such problems is constantly under review, particularly as regards sprays. The Advisory Service run by the Scientific staff at the Royal Horticultural Society's Garden, Wisley, provides up-to-date advice on a very wide range of horticultural matters, and can be consulted about horticultural problems which may occur. But do not forget to send an S.A.E. for the reply!

PROPAGATION

Daphnes may be propagated successfully by a number of methods: from seed, by layering and by grafting, or from stem, and less often, from root or leaf-bud cuttings.

We have dealt with propagation in some detail in the hope that the comments we make will help to clarify the incomplete, dogmatic and often contradictory statements on propagation which are to be found in many publications. Although a considerable amount has been written on propagation, relatively little accurate research has been carried out to substantiate the statements made. Many are undoubtedly based on long practical experience, but equally much of what is written is not!

Our comments, unless otherwise stated, are based on our own experience of *Daphne* propagation and the successful establishment of the resulting plants. We hope that some who read this book will be stimulated into trying the techniques suggested and improving upon them. Many of the propagation techniques described are, of course, applicable to numerous other plants.

Unfortunately, few *Daphne* species or hybrids are readily available through trade sources, due mainly to the length of time which is needed to produce a marketable plant and to the relatively limited demand. Several daphnes which are readily increased by seed (for example *D. mezereum*, *D. laureola* and *D. pontica*), or which strike easily from cuttings (*D.* x *burkwoodii* clones, *D. odora* 'Aureomarginata' and *D. cneorum* forms), are offered reasonably frequently but only one or two specialist nurseries list a wider range— and then it may be necessary to go on a waiting list before some of the choicer daphnes can be obtained.

For gardeners who want to grow the less common daphnes, the alternatives are either a long (and ultimately expensive) wait until plants of the particular species or hybrid become available from a specialist nursery, or an attempt to propagate for themselves using material from plants growing in friends' gardens or from seed offered occasionally in various specialist lists.

The challenge of raising one's own plants is formidable for the amateur, but the satisfaction of obtaining relatively cheaply a plant of *Daphne petraea* 'Grandiflora' which does not try to become partly deciduous (sometimes attributed to the nursery practice of grafting on to stock of *D. mezereum*) is very considerable. With patience, care, and the help of generous friends, it should be possible for most gardeners to propagate virtually all the *Daphne* species and hybrids in cultivation by the methods described in this chapter. Of necessity only general descriptions of the propagating methods recommended can be given but in cases where specialist techniques may be used these are mentioned under the description of the species or hybrid concerned or referred to in the bibliography.

21

Seed

If seed is available it affords the best method of increasing many daphnes, but regrettably not all the species produce seed freely in cultivation. A list of those known to do so is to be found on p. 26. A considerable amount of advice is offered in books on propagation as to the best time or times for sowing daphne seed and the correct composts to use. As yet no thorough investigation of the germination mechanisms appears to have been carried out and the advice given in various publications is conflicting.

In our experience the following factors appear to be of importance but should not be accepted without question for all species.

1. Virus. Cucumber Mosaic and other viruses which afflict *D. mezereum*, *D. odora* and *D. laureola* in particular, are not known to be seed-borne. It is always wise, however, to take seed from healthy plants if there is any choice.

2. A number of seeds of woody plants require periods of exposure to low temperatures (usually just above freezing) in *moist* (not dry) conditions before germination can occur and this process is known as *stratification*. Undoubtedly seed of several *Daphne* species requires stratification, allowing essential internal changes in metabolism to take place which would not occur unless the seeds were subjected to the appropriate cold spell. A simple method of achieving this is to put the seed between layers of moist peat or moist sand in a container and place it (in our cases, wives willing!) in an ordinary domestic refrigerator. Many seeds stored dry in a refrigerator retain their viability well, but it must be emphasized that the stratification process requires that, in addition to the appropriate cold periods, the seeds must be able to take in sufficient water and air to enable the necessary chemical changes to be initiated. No accurate information is yet available on the length or temperatures of the stratification period required for individual daphnes, and this may well vary from species to species. A three-month cold period before the seeds are sown in the normal way should, however, prove sufficient in most instances.

Stratification is not essential for seed of all species. At Wisley, fresh seed of *D. bholua* sown in June 1974 germinated within six weeks and older (1973-gathered) dry-stored seed of *D. gnidium* and *D. acutiloba* (possibly *D. longilobata*) sown in March 1974 took eight weeks to germinate.

As a general rule we would suggest that daphne seeds are stratified unless the species are not hardy in Britain—and even then it may well be that, although tender in cultivation here, in their native habitat the species concerned are subject to cold conditions and that their tenderness is due to other factors.

3. Daphne seed is probably best gathered slightly *before* the berry appears fully mature and frequently, if the fleshy portion of the berry is removed and the seed sown immediately, a high germination

22

rate may be expected the following spring. If seed is left until fully mature and then cleaned and sown, a few seedlings may appear the following spring but often the seed will remain dormant for a further year or more. This is a useful device, often chemically or physically controlled, by which nature ensures that not all her eggs are in one basket, the delayed germination giving the greatest chance of the species surviving if disaster befalls the seedlings in the first or even second years.

D. mezereum provides an excellent example. If seed is cleaned and sown in June, when the berries are apparently not fully ripe, germination the following spring is frequently as high as 90—100%, whereas seed which is not sown until August or September of the same year may often germinate erratically over a 2—3 year period. It is worth noting (regretfully!) that the berries of *Daphne mezereum* and other species are greedily sought after by birds and, if one is lucky, self-sown seedlings may appear the following spring somewhere in the garden, or, if one is less fortunate, in a neighbour's garden. It is possible that the absorption into the bird's stomach of the fleshy portions surrounding the seed prevents the mechanism for inhibiting germination coming into action and may also scarify the seed coat which could also encourage the germination processes to begin. However, if the culprits are greenfinches the seeds themselves are split—see further under *D. mezereum*.

It is probable that the fleshy covering of the seed of some *Daphne* species contains a germination inhibitor, but it must be emphasized again that only a limited amount is known about the germination of daphne seeds and the observations made so far may well require modifying when further study of the interactions of temperature and chemical changes within the seed is made.

4.   Dry storage of daphne seed (except possibly in a refrigerator) is *not* recommended as in many cases it appears that the viability of the seeds is appreciably reduced. Unfortunately, seed obtained from various specialist lists has frequently been stored dry for some months before distribution, which probably accounts for the erratic and often poor germination attributed to daphnes.

Seed of most daphnes is stated to lose its viability fairly quickly, but there are cases known where seed several years old has been germinated successfully. Halda provides an example of 4-year old seed of *D. retusa* (wild collected) giving 50% germination, but no mention is made of storage conditions. If storage is necessary, our advice would be to do so in a domestic refrigerator in moist sand, first removing the fleshy portion surrounding the seed which is liable to become mouldy in some cases. Accurate experimental work is still required to determine the optimum storage conditions for seed of the various species.

5. Composts. Recommendations are legion, from a peaty soil mixed with coal-dust to pure sand! It is doubtful whether any of the various soil recipes suggested have any advantage over John Innes Seed Compost, provided this contains good quality ingredients and is correctly mixed. Certainly in our experience very satisfactory results have been obtained by using this medium when sowing seed of a wide range of *Daphne* species. Unfortunately many commercial offerings under the name "John Innes Seed Compost" bear little resemblance to the original and should be avoided like the plague. Alternatives include the multitude of soil-less composts which are discussed by Dr. Good in his valuable commentary on seed composts in the A.G.S. *Bulletin* (Vol. 42, pp. 322-332). Our preference is for J.I. Seed Compost, *provided* that it is properly constituted. As J.I. composts contain ground chalk, seed of the few *Daphne* species which are reputed to dislike lime are probably best sown in a mixture similar to J.I. seed compost from which the chalk has been omitted (J.I. Acid or "A" Compost) As it is seldom available commercially this usually means mixing the compost oneself or choosing a peat-based soil-less compost No comparative tests have been made (as far as we can trace) to indicate whether or not the ground chalk in the J I. seed composts is sufficient to affect either the germination or the subsequent growth of *Daphne* seedlings. Certainly seeds of *D. retusa* and *D. tangutica*, both reputed to dislike lime, have been germinated and the seedlings grown on successfully in J.I. composts at Wisley, so it is probably that the plants themselves are unaware of their reputation! If, however, one ever managed to obtain seed of *D. genkwa*, it might be wise to use an acid seed compost as this species is said to be a lime-hater.

6. Containers and seed-sowing. Although daphnes can be raised from seed sown in the open ground or in a simple seed frame, it is normally more convenient to use small clay or plastic pots for seed-sowing. Few amateurs require more than a dozen or so seedlings of any one species, unless they are raising larger numbers for use as grafting stocks, so $2\frac{1}{2}$ in., 3 in. or $3\frac{1}{2}$ in. pots are usually sufficiently large for the purpose, remembering also that standardisation of pot-size for seed-sowing of alpines, bulbs and small shrubs is well worthwhile, and that more care is required when using plastic pots to ensure that drainage and moisture retention are properly balanced.

There are many excellent (and sometimes contradictory!) articles in the A.G.S. *Bulletin* and other publications which describe sowing techniques in detail. Provided one standardises the technique, ensuring efficient drainage and aeration for the seeds to germinate and develop into healthy seedlings, it matters little which method is used for daphnes. With clay pots, a basal crock covered by up to $\frac{1}{2}$ in. of coarse (about $\frac{3}{16}$ in.) grit and topped up with J.I. Seed Compost to within $\frac{1}{4}$—$\frac{1}{2}$ in. of the top of the pot before sowing the seed proves perfectly satisfactory. If plastic pots with small drainage holes are used, the basal crock is unnecessary, but in our experience it is advisable to modify the compost by mixing in up to one third by bulk of additional drainage material—angular grit about $\frac{1}{16}$–$\frac{1}{8}$ in. in size is suitable.

Once the cleaned seed has been sown, cover it with a thin layer of compost and fill the pot to the rim with $\frac{3}{16}$–$\frac{1}{4}$ in. chippings. Some growers do not bother to cover the seeds with compost, merely covering with chippings—both methods seem effective. Label appropriately, water the seed pots thoroughly and plunge in a simple frame using sand, ash or chippings as the plunging medium, and hopefully await germination. An additional precaution is to cover the pots with wire to prevent rodents eating the seed. The seed pots can then be left to the elements, covering being unnecessary except during hot spells in spring and summer when shading by laths or netting may be needed to prevent too rapid drying of the compost, which must be avoided. The relatively large chippings suggested allow ample aeration and drainage around the seeds and are not washed away by heavy rain as may occur with fine grit. If plunging is not possible, more care must be taken to prevent the seed and compost from drying out. Use of plastic pots will help as the compost will dry out more slowly and plunging is then less necessary.

It is worth remembering that daphne seed is generally poisonous (although the "flesh" does no harm to birds) and it is advisable to make sure that they are kept out of children's reach if there is any delay in sowing.

7. Aftercare. Most daphnes do not like root disturbance, and if germination occurs in spring and the seedlings have developed their first true leaves, they are best pricked off singly into 3 in. pots as soon as they can be easily handled, using J.I. No. 1 Compost or the acid equivalent. Some authorities recommend a compost containing more humus but no comparative tests have been made and John Innes No. 1, or a slight modification of it, has proved perfectly adequate with all the species listed at the end of this section.

Once the seedlings have been potted up, thoroughly watered and kept in a cool, moist atmosphere for a few days, the pots should be plunged in an uncovered frame which should be shaded in hot weather.

Occasionally germination occurs in autumn or during mild spells in winter. If so, the pots of seedlings are best transferred to a covered cold frame until spring to protect them from severe weather. The seedlings can then be potted individually in April and treated in the same way as spring-germinated daphnes.

The plants are kept in the plunge-frames until the following spring and the plants should then be transferred to their permanent quarters in the garden unless growth has been slow or pot-grown daphnes are required.

Two further points should be borne in mind. Some daphnes can quickly develop into gawky, straggling plants if left to their own devices. Hard though it may seem, those beautiful young shoots should be stopped (pinched back) at an early stage to ensure that the plants develop a strong framework and do not become the "tufted walking sticks" one sometimes sees. This treatment is usually unnecessary, and perhaps harmful with slow-growing, compact species like *D. retusa* and *D. collina*, but is useful for those of more wayward habit.

Secondly the question of feeding. Most daphnes grow sedately, and normally additional feeding of young plants is unlikely to hurry the process along without adversely altering the habit of the plant. Slow-release balanced artificial fertilisers like "Osmocote", "Vitax" and other similar products have produced excellent results commercially when used to feed container-grown plants, and it is quite possible that their use in the potting compost in small quantities—they are expensive—would be beneficial to the young seedlings.

To sum up:

(1) Gather, clean off the fleshy portion and sow seed slightly *before* apparently ripe (usually late summer or early autumn) if possible.

(2) If this is not possible, stratify the cleaned seed for about 3 months as soon as it is obtained (except for species known to be or suspected of being tender) and then sow in the normal way.

(3) Once germination occurs pot off into 3 or 3½ in. pots in spring (March-April) when the seedlings are at the 2 or 3 leaf stage. Pricking-out or potting the seedlings in autumn is not recommended unless the seedlings can be given warm frame treatment.

(4) Plunge the potted seedlings in a frame which can be shaded if required.

(5) The seedlings may require stopping; if so, this should be carried out not later than early September and preferably by midsummer.

(6) Plant out as one-year-old plants or grow on for a further year in a larger container if required.

DAPHNES WHICH SET SEED REASONABLY FREELY IN CULTIVATION:

D. acutiloba	*D. laureola* ssp. *philippi*
D. alpina	*D. longilobata*
D. altaica	*D. mezereum*
D. caucasica	*D. mezereum* var. *alba*
D. euboica	*D. oleoides*
D. giraldii	*D. pontica*
D. gnidium	*D. retusa*
D. laureola	*D. tangutica*

Layering

The growth habit of a few species lends itself to propagation by this technique. The daphnes listed at the end of this section can be layered satisfactorily, particularly those having long, whippy, straggling branches which are easily pegged.

The method is simple provided one has established plants. In March or April (some authorities advocate autumn) shoots of the previous year's growths are pegged down around the parent plant using forked sticks or wire to hold the layer in place. Sometimes a large stone over the layer is advocated—one gentleman is known to have thrown bricks at his *D. blagayana* to encourage it to layer "naturally"! Certainly, this would help to keep the developing layer cool as well as retaining it in the soil. At the same time the tip of the layered shoot should be gently bent to an upright position and "staked" with a small piece of split bamboo or thin stick. This technique (which can also usefully be used with dwarf rhododendrons) provides a much better plant eventually, preventing the rooted layer from being one-sided and difficult to pot when removed from the parent.

It is advisable first to scrape or notch shallowly a section of the bark on the underside of the shoot to be layered a few inches from the tip and, although not essential, it is helpful to treat the "wound" with a hormone rooting powder. I.B.A. is quite suitable at 0.3% strength.

The layers should be pegged into a prepared compost (2 parts peat, 1 part coarse sand by bulk is suitable) and covered to about $\frac{1}{2}$ in. in depth. It is important that the compost used is well aerated and drained yet capable of retaining adequate moisture to prevent the delicate, developing young roots from drying out. As an alternative to the peat-sand mixture pulverised pine bark might be used, if obtainable. When used as a plunging material it is surprising how quickly roots from plunged pots will permeate the surrounding bark, obviously appreciating the combination of good air drainage and adequate moisture. It is advisable *not* to use bark which has been ammoniated or enriched with other chemicals as this might retard the development of the fine daphne roots.

Layers of daphnes put down in spring may occasionally be well rooted by August or September, but more frequently will not be sufficiently developed until the following March-April. If on examination the layer seems well-rooted, it should be severed from the parent plant, *but* left in position for a few weeks (3-4 weeks is normally enough) so that it has a chance to become fully established on its own roots before being moved. In due course the layer can be potted up into J.I. No. 1 (or the acid equivalent if you are a calciphobe!). Should bark have been used in the layering process, the potting compost can include $\frac{1}{4}$—$\frac{1}{3}$ by bulk of bark to help the young roots become accustomed to the new medium. Plunge the potted

27

layers in a cold frame, and during the summer "stop" the growths to encourage the plants to develop a bushy habit and a sturdy root system. We feel that stopping, particularly for stragglers like *D. cneorum*, cannot be emphasized too much. Unless it is done reasonably early after extension growth begins, all one has is an ugly "walking-stick" which seldom develops into a good, well-furnished plant. Overwinter plunged in a cold frame, giving protection in very severe weather, and plant out the following spring.

Mound layering is an extension of layering individual branches by covering the whole of the centre of a plant with a mound of compost or bark as mentioned above. By this method it is possible to obtain a larger number of rooted layers from one plant and is a very profitable way of dealing with old, straggling, semi-moribund plants of *D. cneorum* which one may be reluctant to dig up. Each branch is treated as an individual layer—scraped, hormone-treated, pegged down and staked in March or April, and the process as described above is carried out *en masse*. By this means it is sometimes possible to rejuvenate the parent plant, encouraging fresh growth from the centre of the "mound".

DAPHNES SUITABLE FOR LAYERING

(If grafted, the habit of some species may be more upright and layering is then less easy)

D. altaica
D. arbuscula
D. blagayana
D. cneorum and its forms
D. glomerata
D. jasminea (prostrate forms)

D. juliae
D. laureola ssp. *philippi*
D. odora
D. petraea (some forms if on their own roots)
D. pontica
D. x rossetii
D. striata

Layering is recommended in one work on propagation for *D. genkwa* but the habit of this species does not normally lend itself to this method of increase and we have traced no authentic record of successful layering with this species.

It would, of course, be possible to layer branches of any *Daphne* which has branches conveniently placed near ground level if so required, using the techniques outlined above.

Grafting

The thought of grafting often deters gardeners who are not sure of the technique and worried about the possibility of "suckering" which bedevils roses and some other shrubs and trees. Grafting simply involves taking a portion (or cutting) of the plant you wish to propagate—the SCION—and inducing it to unite its tissues with those of a suitable well-rooted seedling, young plant or even root—the STOCK—so that one complete plant is formed.

In fact grafting daphnes for a neat-handed, careful person is not a particularly difficult job, although slightly fiddly, and provided one has a simple propagating case and the forethought to have suitable seedlings to use as stocks, it is a most effective way of propagating daphnes which are difficult to obtain in other ways. Suckering is seldom a problem if grafting has been carried out correctly, although records of *D. mezereum* stock appearing from grafted *D. petraea* are known.

WHY GRAFT?

(a) Some daphnes produce little or no seed in cultivation, are difficult to root and may grow only slowly when raised from cuttings, and are of the wrong habit to layer simply. The only practical alternative method of propagation is to graft. *D. striata*, for instance, is often difficult to please on its own roots but reasonable to grow if grafted.

(b) Certain species (for example *D. arbuscula* and *D. petraea*) are slow growing when raised from cuttings but when grafted will form specimens of a reasonable size in a relatively short time, mainly due to the presence of the established, vigorous root system of the stock plant.

(c) In a few cases grafted daphnes will flower at an earlier stage and more freely than the same plant raised from cuttings. A notable example is *D. petraea* 'Grandiflora' which roots readily from stem cuttings but normally takes some years to reach flowering condition when propagated in this way. Yet there is a record of a nursery near Pontresina rooting several hundred cuttings of *D. petraea* from near Lake Garda, the resulting plants flowering well at an early stage.

(d) When one wishes to propagate a particularly good clone of a *Daphne* which does not root readily from cuttings or layer easily, grafting may be necessary to perpetuate and increase it. The double forms of *D. mezereum* comes into this category.

FACTORS INVOLVED IN GRAFTING DAPHNES

Once again a multitude of conflicting advice lies in wait for the inquisitive gardener. Authorities differ in their opinions as to the best time of year to graft, the most suitable stock for particular species, and the type of graft to use. No carefully conducted experiments have apparently been carried out to determine these points accurately and it may well be that there are several equally effective methods.

1. GRAFTING STOCKS

(a) *D. mezereum* is frequently recommended as the stock to use for both evergreen and deciduous species. Certainly it has the merits of hardiness and vigour (unless debilitated by virus) and is readily raised from seed; there are recorded examples of both evergreen and deciduous species growing well when grafted with *D. mezereum* as the stock.

The experience of some growers, however, is that such desirable species as *D. arbuscula* and forms of *D. petraea*, which are both evergreen and slow-growing, tend to try to become partly deciduous in the early stages when grafted on *D. mezereum* and are slow to grow away. A check early in their life may cause them to sit in their pots and sulk. Evergreen forms of *D. bholua* grafted on *D. mezereum* are also stated to become partly deciduous.

On the other hand, there is no doubt that there are many excellent plants of *D. petraea* 'Grandiflora' and *D. arbuscula* which have *D. mezereum* as an under-stock. In the *Bulletin* (Vol. 20, p. 72) Will Ingwersen mentions a series of experiments which he carried out using various evergreen species and hybrids in comparison with *D. mezereum* as stocks for *D. petraea* 'Grandiflora'. His findings were not conclusive but the most successful stock proved to be *D. mezereum*, although the white-flowered form was much less satisfactory. Good examples of *D. odora* forms grafted on *D. mezereum* are also known, although *D. odora* is usually better raised from stem cuttings as, in Britain certainly, they root readily and grow away without difficulty.

(b) *D. acutiloba* and *D. longilobata* are also easily raised from seed and are sometimes recommended as a stock for evergreen daphnes as they are themselves evergreen.

D. acutiloba is often stated to be a good stock on which to graft *D. arbuscula*, *D. petraea*, *D. retusa* and several other species, and apparently in California it is used to graft a wide range of daphnes. Although it appears quite satisfactory in terms of compatibility, we do not recommend its use if the plants are to be grown in areas subject to severe spells of cold weather, as in our experience, it is somewhat tender. A fine specimen of *D. caucasica* growing in a garden at Normandy near Guildford collapsed in a bad winter when the *D. acutiloba* stock was killed outright and it is quite possible that some of the "sudden deaths" recorded for grafted daphnes can be attributed to the tenderness of this species.

The closely related *D. longilobata* has been confused with it and undoubtedly is used as a stock by some nurseries. It appears to be rather hardier than *D. acutiloba* (at least the Ludlow, Sherriff & Elliott introduction of 1947—see p. 48) and as plants of *D. longilobata* survived the 1962-3 winter in Britain it can be assumed that the use of this species as a stock would be satisfactory.

(c) *D. laureola* and *D. pontica*. Both are evergreen species, easily raised from seed or cuttings and of reasonable vigour. They have been used successfully as understocks for a number of daphnes and are particularly good alternatives to *D. acutiloba* for stocks on which to graft the evergreen species. It is as well to remember that, although tolerant of a wide range of conditions, *D. laureola* and *D. pontica* are by nature woodland plants and should be used with caution as stocks for rock-dwelling *Daphne* species, for there is the

Daphne sericea (p. 173)　　　　　　　　　　　Photo: E. Hodgkin

Daphne bholua (p. 60)　　　　　　　　　　　Photo: B. Mathew

Daphne collina (p. 94)

Photos: E. Hodgkin

Daphne genkwa (p. 98)

The habitat of *Daphne arbuscula* (p. 54) Muran Hills, Slovakia. *Photo: J. Starek*

D. jasminea Sibth. et Sm.

D. arbuscula Čelak.

D. arbuscula Čelak. f. platyclada Halda

32

possibility that they might be unable to support the scion-growth in periods of drought.

(d) *D. giraldii.* We have not ourselves used *D. giraldii* as a stock but Halda states that it is better than *D. alpina, D. laureola* and *D. mezereum* when used as a stock for *D. arbuscula.* Certainly seed is quite freely produced and germinates readily, so it would be well worth carrying out comparative tests to establish this claim.

(e) Other *Daphne* species or hybrids to use as stocks. If one is fortunate enough to have surplus young plants of any *Daphne* species they can be used for stocks—there is nothing magical about the use of the species so far mentioned for this purpose—merely that they are reasonably available. It is probably better to graft only closely related species on to the stock concerned to avoid any possible incompatibility problems, but this is a counsel of perfection and there is no question that daphnes of differing botanical groups can successfully be united by grafting. Possibly the reputation of daphnes as short-lived plants may be due, in part, to the indiscriminate use of *D. mezereum* as a stock for almost any species, and in some cases the eventual breakdown of the stock-scion union may be responsible for the sudden demise which is associated with daphnes. It should be made clear that this suggestion is not based on factual knowledge, as no experimental work has been carried out on stock-scion compatibility with daphnes, and seed-raised daphnes are not always particularly long-lived. But it is a line of thought worth investigation.

(f) Use of the same species for both stock and scion. There is no reason why stock and scion should not be of the same species. If, for example, one has a particularly good clone of *D. cneorum,* which is difficult to increase from cuttings and will not come true from seed, it is perfectly feasible to graft scions of the good clone on to seedlings of *D. cneorum* or even on to plants raised from cuttings of a more tractable plant of that same species.

Similarly scions of *D. petraea* could be grafted on to plants of the same species raised from cuttings (which root readily but initially flower sparsely) with the possibility that plants grafted in this way would flower reasonably freely, a situation known to occur in other genera. We have not ourselves used this technique, but an obvious advantage over other stocks is that of grafting like with like and the probability that stock-scion incompatibility would be prevented. Only careful, long-term experimentation, however, will provide any reliable guidelines to follow.

As an extension of this suggestion it is worth using *D.* x *burkwoodii* or *D.* 'Somerset', which are easily raised from cuttings, as stocks for various daphnes. As *D. cneorum* is one parent, they could be particularly useful as stocks for the extremely slow *D. cneorum alba* and the variegated form of *D. cneorum.* Remember, however, the importance of ensuring that the plants used for cuttings are virus-free.

2. AGE AND CONDITION OF STOCK

The age of the stock used will depend on the growth of the *Daphne* to be grafted. Usually well-grown 2-year old seedlings of *D. mezereum* are suitable for most deciduous daphnes, but those with fairly thick growth such as the deciduous (or semi-deciduous) *D. bholua* var. *glacialis* will probably require a 3-year old stock. With evergreen species like *D. petraea*, with its thin branchlets, a 1-2 year old pot-grown seedling of *D. longilobata* (if preferred to *D. mezereum*) is often suitable but with daphnes of thicker-twigged habit like *D. collina* or *D. x hybrida*, a 2 or 3-year old stock may be required.

It should be emphasised that the stocks should NOT be pot-bound, but should be healthy and vigorous young plants. Quite frequently grafting failures with daphnes can be traced back to the poor condition of the stocks used. Remember that the grafted plant depends on the root system of the stock to survive and grow away vigorously—so do not use the odd, starved seedling that happens to be around, as the likelihood is that the resultant plant may not thrive.

3. SCIONS

The scions are basically cuttings made of the previous year's growth. As with all grafting it is most desirable to use firm, well-ripened healthy shoots and to avoid weak, straggly growths which are likely to pass on their bad qualities to the grafted plant.

The size of the scion and the age of the wood used will depend on the *Daphne* species involved. It will be found that with dwarf species, such as *D. jasminea* or *D. petraea*, one-year-old wood is often too thin to use and two-year-old shoots may be required. Vigorous one-year wood is preferable for stronger growing species such as *D. bholua* or *D. tangutica*. Shoots one or two inches in length are normally used as scions but one can quite successfully use slightly shorter or longer shoots depending on availability.

Single branches are usually used as scions, particularly when the plant to be grafted is rare and/or slow-growing, but small composite branches of 2-4 shoots can be grafted successfully and have the obvious advantage of providing a plant of reasonable size quickly. On the other hand if scion-wood is scarce and the graft fails, three or four potential plants may have been lost.

4. GRAFTING SEASON

Daphnes have been grafted successfully at most seasons of the year, but in our experience it is normally best carried out in late winter or in very early spring (December-February), just before growth is about to begin again in temperate climates. Others may prefer April-May; one nurseryman always grafts daphnes in September, whilst another large commercial firm does so in December. The stocks should be brought from the plunge frame into a cool greenhouse or propagating case about 2—3 weeks before grafting is to be done, so that the plants are dried out slightly and the roots are stimulated into active growth. If this is done in early December, grafting can take place from late December or early January onwards. Again some growers find that this is not essential, but in most cases it is desirable for the growth of the stock to be somewhat in advance of the scion to obtain a good percentage "take". Beggars cannot, however, be choosers, and sometimes grafting material of an unusual *Daphne* may be available out of the normal grafting season. As an example scions of *D. jasminea* collected in Greece in November, and also in May, have been grafted at Wisley with good results and there are other instances of equally out-of-season grafts succeeding perfectly well. If stocks are not available, and the chances of rooting the material as cuttings are small, root-grafting may also be attempted (see p. 38).

5. GRAFTING TECHNIQUE

Various grafting methods are available, and yet again opinions differ as to the best technique to use for daphnes. At least five methods have been used successfully and these are illustrated here, the illustrations serving to show how stock and scion are cut and matched in each case.

The sequence of events is as follows:

(i) Bring the pot-grown stocks into the greenhouse or propagating case from early December to dry them slightly and to stimulate root growth. The stocks (i.e. the medium in which they are growing) should be just moist before grafting takes place.

(ii) From late December to February cut or otherwise obtain the scion material and decapitate the stock to within an inch of the soil. (Some growers prefer to cut the stock almost to soil level).

(iii) Prepare stock and scion for grafting by the chosen method (see drawing overleaf (p. 36) for various methods of doing this). Use a very sharp knife or razor-knife as the wood is not easy to cut cleanly. It is helpful when preparing the stock to hold it firmly against one's chest to give it support.

(iv) Place stock and scion together and tie firmly using thin moistened raffia about $\frac{1}{8}$ in. wide (or grafting tape), leaving a thin gap between turns of the raffia. Sealing with grafting wax is sometimes recommended but is not essential. It is also useful to stake the grafted plant to minimise the chance of damage.

(v) Place the grafted plant in a closed propagating case at about 65—68°F, thoroughly moistened so that a humid atmosphere is provided. Gentle bottom heat in the propagating case is also beneficial.

(vi) No watering should be needed during the first 10—14 days after grafting unless drying out occurs. If so, water must of course be given, but with great care to avoid an upsurge of sap which could cause failure of the union.

(vii) Air can be given after this period for a few minutes a day and gradually increased. After about four weeks the union should

Grafting Techniques — Diagrammatic Representation

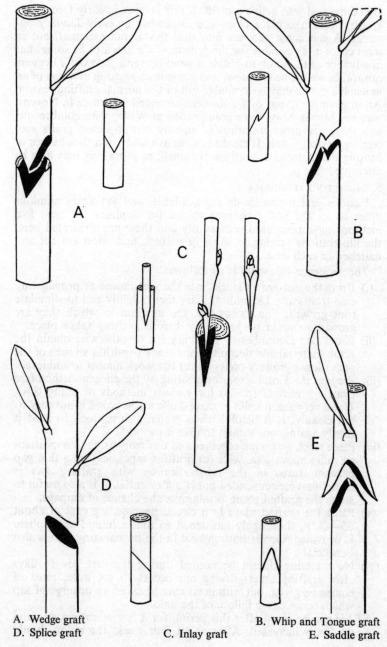

A. Wedge graft
D. Splice graft
C. Inlay graft
B. Whip and Tongue graft
E. Saddle graft

be complete and after a further two weeks the young grafted plant is ready to harden off and grow on in a shady plunge frame, protected during frosty weather but given ample air to prevent soft young growth. During this period care must be taken not to overwater, but still to maintain a humid atmosphere.

(viii) The raffia or grafting tape may be left on to strengthen the graft, but care should be taken not to let constriction occur if stem growth on the young plant is vigorous; once you are satisfied the union is strong the raffia or tape can be removed. By mid-April (if grafting in late January) the plants are ready to pot on into 4½ in. pots.

(ix) A foliar feed once or twice during late spring or early summer is beneficial, encouraging strong growth so that the plant is sufficiently robust to plant out the following spring.

(x) Some daphnes will produce vigorous long shoots after being grafted, and if so, the tips should be pinched out so that "breaks" occur and a well-furnished plant is the result.

(xi) If growth is vigorous it is usually necessary to pot on the young plant so that growth is maintained and a good-sized plant is formed by autumn.

The following points should be borne in mind:—

(a) Get plenty of practice with hazel or other twigs to try out the grafting method you choose, otherwise a lot of daphne seedlings can be wasted.

(b) The actively growing layer of cells between the bark and the woody centre of the stem is known as the cambium. It is essential if grafting is to be successful that the cut surfaces (and hence the cambiums) of stock and scion match as closely as possible with no gaps in between.

(c) When the stock is thicker than the scion the cambiums can only be matched on one side and care must be taken when tying the graft to make certain that the scion remains flush with one side of the stock to ensure adequate cambial contact.

An interesting method tried out successfully by Arthur Carter in 1975 could well simplify the normal grafting procedure. The technique is to graft seedling stocks very soon after germination whilst still at the cotyledon stage.

Seed of the stock species (*D. mezereum*) was sown in June, 1974, and germinated in April, 1975. The young seedlings, still at the cotyledon stage, were brought into an unheated glasshouse and cut off immediately *below* the cotyledons. A longitudinal cut was then made from the cut surface of the stock for a short distance downwards and the scion of one-year-old wood (*D. petraea*) cut with a wedge-shaped base and inserted gently into

37

the longitudinal cut. The join was sealed with "Blu-tac" and the grafted "plants" were placed in a propagating tray with a plastic cover in the unheated glasshouse and shaded. As union between stock and scion occurred and growth began the "Blu-tac" began to crack slightly. Only 3 grafts were made, all of which grew away successfully.

As Arthur Carter points out this method has been used for such a small number of grafts that it must still be regarded as in the experimental stage.

Nevertheless, the simplicity of the actual grafting method, particularly the ease of insertion of scion into the soft tissue of the stock, the lack of tying and the use of a standard plastic propagating case make it a technique suitable for any enthusiast to try.

GRAFTING ON ROOTS

Seedling stocks, or young plants raised from cuttings, are not always available. An alternative is to use small roots from an established specimen of one of the plants previously mentioned as suitable for stocks and graft directly on to the root pieces. Small pieces of root 2—3 inches long (and preferably with fibrous side roots) are cut from an established plant in January or early February. These should be approximately of the same diameter and length as the scions to be grafted, which are normally 1—3 inches long depending on the species or hybrid involved, but are shorter, of course, for *D. petraea* and other dwarf species.

The easiest graft to use is probably the saddle graft, the "saddle" being formed at the apex of the root and the graft tied with raffia or grafting tape. Sealing is usually unnecessary.

An equally good alternative is the wedge (cleft) graft but if the grafts are thin the splice graft or the whip and tongue grafts can be used although these are more difficult for the unskilled person to deal with successfully. See sketch on previous page.

The root-grafted plants can then be plunged in moist granulated, peat preferably in a propagating frame or case, with the grafting point just below the level of the medium used. The union is formed in about 7—10 weeks when the grafted plants can be potted up and grown on in frames for a year or more before planting out.

Records have been traced of the following daphnes successfully propagated by grafting on various stocks although this is not necessarily the best method for the species or hybrid concerned.

D. alpina	*caucasica*
altaica	*cneorum alba*
arbuscula	„ 'Eximia'
aurantiaca	„ *pygmaea*
bholua	„ 'Variegata'
blagayana	„ *verlotii*
x *burkwoodii* forms	*collina*

D. genkwa
  giraldii
  glomerata
  gnidium
  x *houtteana*
  x *hybrida*
  jasminea
  juliae
  longilobata
  mezereum f. *autumnalis*
     ,,   double forms
  x *mantensiana*
  mucronata
  x *napolitana*

D. odora and its forms
  oleoides
    ,,   *brachyloba*
  papyracea
  petraea
    ,,   'Grandiflora'
  pontica
  pseudomezereum
  retusa
  x *rossetii*
  sericea
  striata
  tangutica
  x *thauma*

Stem Cuttings (soft or half-ripe cuttings)

Many daphnes can be propagated without great difficulty from stem cuttings using only a simple propagating case or frame—or bell-jars if one is lucky enough to have them. That universal propagating panacea, the mist unit, is certainly effective, preferably with (but also without) bottom heat; some commercial growers however have found that it is not easy to prevent a proportion of the cuttings from damping off and have obtained better results with an ordinary propagating frame, using some bottom heat, although this does not appear to be essential. Commercially, some propagators prefer to use alternative methods of propagation, as many daphnes do not grow away readily after the cuttings have rooted. It is sometimes stated that deciduous daphnes, in particular, are less easy to root than evergreen species, but no experimental proof of this is known to us.

ROOTING MEDIUM

A variety of different cutting composts have been used successfully. Provided the rooting medium is well-aerated, yet capable of retaining sufficient moisture to prevent the cuttings drying out, it is doubtful whether one mixture is much more effective than another. A standard mix of 2 parts sharp sand to 1 part moss peat (by bulk) is perfectly satisfactory, but commercially a compost of 5 parts coarse sand to 1 part sifted peat is recommended. Results with rooting various shrub cuttings in pulverised pine bark suggest that it would be worth using as an alternative to the moss peat or on its own as a rooting medium.

STOCK PLANTS

Commercially, a nurseryman may use pot-grown daphnes as the source of cutting material, bringing the plants into a greenhouse early in the year and gently forcing them so that vigorous, sturdy young growths are produced for use as stem cuttings. There is some evidence that cuttings of daphnes taken from plants growing in good light conditions root more readily than from comparable plants growing in poorer light, perhaps due to the lower carbohydrate intake under the latter condition. The experimental work on this aspect of daphne propagation has been so limited, however, that it is unwise to attempt to draw any conclusions. Most amateurs will normally use cutting material from daphnes growing in the open garden unless the species and hybrids concerned are grown for alpine house or show use, but material for propagation should always be taken from healthy, vigorous and virus-free plants. Much further work remains to be done to discover the optimum conditions for the individual species and hybrids.

TYPE OF CUTTINGS

Much stress has been laid on the necessity for taking daphne cuttings when they have reached "the correct degree of maturity", but it is not easy to define this simply. As is the case with many horticultural operations, it is only with experience that one can get the "feel" of when cutting material is ready. Normally shoots of the current year's growth from $\frac{1}{2}$ to 3 ins. long are used, depending on the species or hybrid to be propagated. The young shoots chosen should be firm at the base although still soft at the tips. Heel cuttings, taken with a small sliver of the old wood at the base, or nodal (joint) cuttings prove satisfactory with most daphnes. If the cuttings are nodal a number of growers recommend slitting the base of the stem for about $\frac{1}{4}$ in. to assist in producing a good callus. No comprehensive results of tests to determine the comparative effectiveness of nodal and heel cuttings for daphnes have been published as far as we can trace but some growers have reported better success with heel cuttings taken from lateral rather than terminal shoots.

Some interesting work on the anatomy of the stems of *D.* x *burkwoodii* 'Somerset' carried out at East Malling Research Station suggests that the rooting potential of the tissues of the basal $\frac{1}{2}$ inch or so of a half-ripe cutting taken with a heel (i.e. the base of the current year's growth) is higher than that of the tissues an inch or more above the base. It is tempting but quite unsound to conclude that heel cuttings are likely to prove more satisfactory than nodal cuttings, and it requires a great deal of accurate experimental work with a wide range of daphnes to provide the answer.

It is sometimes suggested that with certain species it is better to insert young, soft cuttings, the percentage rooting decreasing later in the season with half-ripe material. Experimental work is needed to provide accurate information on this point but certainly there is some evidence that *D. cneorum*, *D. blagayana* and *D. mezereum* root more readily from very young cuttings than from older half-ripe shoots.

At the other extreme there are records of various daphnes being propagated from cuttings of mature shoots taken in the autumn,

40

placed in a cold frame until callused and then brought into gentle heat in a propagating case to assist root production.

TIMING OF CUTTINGS

It is obvious from what has already been said that it is not easy to provide an accurate timetable for taking cuttings, but in most cases the young shoots to be used will be ready between mid-June and the end of August, depending on the species involved and the growth of the individual plant in the climatic region concerned.

Eliot Hodgkin preferred "late spring" (June), and in his notes on the genus says that use of bottom heat produces roots more quickly but the likelihood of damage was increased when potting up the cuttings because more brittle roots appeared to be formed.

Commercially there are reports that cuttings of evergreen daphnes taken in late autumn, wounded at the base and dipped in 0.8 to 0.1% strength I.B.A. hormone root well under mist or in a closed frame with the temperature not more than 68°F.

As will be realised, advice is conflicting, but regrettably it is not possible at present to rationalise the various recommendations as adequate research has not been undertaken.

As a rough guide however the following table may be useful and further information is given under descriptions of the various species and hybrids, where available.

Group 1: Stem cuttings taken June—early August (soft or only just firming at the base)

D. alpina
D. aurantiaca
D. bholua
D. blagayana
D. x burkwoodii 'Albert Burkwood'
D. x burkwoodii 'Lavenirii'
D. x burkwoodii 'Somerset'
D. x burkwoodii (variegated clones)
D. caucasica
D. cneorum and forms
D. collina
D. genkwa
D. giraldii
D. jasminea
*D. jezoensis
*D. juliae
D. x mantensiana

Group 2: Stem cuttings taken mid-July—late August (half-ripe cuttings, firm at the base)

D. acutiloba
D. alpina
D. arbuscula and forms
D. blagayana
D. x burkwoodii and forms
D. cneorum and forms
D. collina
D. giraldii
*D. glomerata
D. x hybrida
D. jasminea
D. laureola
D. longilobata
D. x mantensiana
D. x napolitana
D. odora and forms
D. petraea
D. pontica
D. retusa

41

D. mezereum and forms	*D. sericea*
D. x *napolitana*	*D. tangutica*
D. odora and forms	
**D. oleoides*	
D. retusa	
D. sericea	
D. sophia	
**D. striata*	
D. tangutica	

These lists only include the more generally grown daphnes; those asterisked are daphnes which we suggest would probably come into the groups concerned although we have not necessarily ourselves propagated them in this way. It should also be made clear that some of the species or hybrids mentioned might well prove equally successful from cuttings of either type.

HORMONES

Opinions differ on the question of whether or not hormone dips assist the rooting of daphne cuttings. The experience of some research workers and growers is that a number of the daphnes listed in Group 2 (above) benefit from the use of hormones (I.B.A. at 0.1—0.8% strength in powder form is suitable); but that with softer cuttings (Group 1) the effectiveness is less certain.

USE OF FUNGICIDES

Some observations have been made using various fungicides, such as Thiram, to prevent rot occurring during rooting, but the results are so far inconclusive.

INSERTION OF CUTTINGS

Once the cuttings have been removed from the parent plant they should be carefully trimmed at the base (a sharp razor-knife is excellent for this purpose) and one or two basal leaves removed, leaving sufficient bare stem to insert the cutting. Work at Boskoop indicates that certain daphnes are apt to shed foliage during rooting under mist which apparently affects their establishment and subsequent overwintering. It seems sensible therefore to leave as much foliage as possible on the cuttings, perhaps removing only one or two leaves at the base to facilitate insertion. At no time should the cuttings be allowed to dry out or wilt. It is particularly important to prevent this with softer cuttings like those of *D. cneorum* or *D.* x *burkwoodii* as they seldom recover, or root satisfactorily, if drying out has occurred. If for some reason there is a delay between taking the cuttings and insertion, they may be sprinkled with water and kept in a polythene bag for a short time to prevent their wilting.

The cuttings may be inserted direct into the medium of the propagating case or frame, but sometimes, when small quantities are involved, it is more convenient to use individual containers filled with cutting compost and place these in the frame or case. Whichever method is used it is important to make certain that the cuttings are firmly, but not too deeply, inserted and thoroughly watered in. Some commercial growers apply a thin layer of silver sand or the equivalent to the surface of the compost so that, as the cuttings are being inserted, a little sand trickles down to the base of the cutting, helping to ensure that it is firmly in contact with the compost. It has also been suggested that callusing is encouraged by this procedure, but this requires experimental confirmation.

Once the cuttings are inserted and thoroughly watered-in they should remain in the closed propagating case, at about 50°—60°F if possible, and should be rooted and ready for potting 4—8 weeks after insertion, usually taking a shorter time to root if bottom heat is available. If the cuttings are maintained at a lower temperature (40°—50°F), rooting may take slightly longer. The propagating frame or case should be fairly heavily shaded and the humidity maintained by spraying or watering as required.

A mist unit is, of course, a suitable alternative to the propagating frame, if available, and it is worth remembering the maxim that a "warm bottom" and a "cool head" suit most cuttings in such a unit.

AFTERCARE

The rooted cuttings may be potted into 3 or 3½ in. pots using J.I. No. 1 Compost (or your preferred equivalent) as soon as they are well rooted, watered thoroughly, and kept in a closed frame for a few days until established when they can gradually be hardened off. In the case of *D. cneorum*, *D.* x *burkwoodii* and their allies, where single long growths often appear, it is advisable to pinch back the young growing shoots at an early stage to encourage side shoots to break and form a bushy well-furnished plant. It should be emphasized that stopping should be carried out very soon after the rooted cutting begins extension growth, particularly with *D. cneorum* as, later on, the side growths do not break so readily, and one is liable to end up with one of the "gawks" sometimes, sadly, offered commercially. With species such as *D. retusa* and *D. collina* which are naturally bushy, stopping is not usually necessary and appears, in some cases, to discourage growth. A foliar feed is beneficial as the side shoots develop, but should not be given late in the season as soft growth, which could be damaged in severe weather, may result.

The young plants can be overwintered plunged in a frame and protected in severe weather. Plants from cuttings rooted early the previous summer may be large enough to plant out the following spring, but usually will require growing on for a season before being planted in their permanent quarters.

SUMMARY
1. The cuttings should be from ½—3 ins. long depending on the species or hybrid concerned.

43

2. Soft cuttings (Group 1) (see p. 41) are taken from late June—early August, with or without a heel.
3. Semi-ripe cuttings (Group 2) (see p. 41) are taken from mid-July—late August, with or without a heel.
4. Rooting hormones may be used but are not essential.
5. A suitable cutting compost is 2 parts coarse sand to 1 part moss peat by bulk.
6. A propagating case or frame kept at 50°—60°F with bottom heat is preferable.
7. Rooting should occur within 4—8 weeks of the cuttings being inserted.
8. Pot on the rooted cuttings and gradually harden them off in a frame; stop and feed as required.
9. Overwinter the young plants in a frame. Plant out the following spring or grow on for a further year depending on their size.

Hardwood Cuttings

Halda states that various deciduous daphnes including *D. alpina*, *D.* x *burkwoodii* 'Somerset', *D. caucasica*, *D. giraldii* and *D. mezereum* can be propagated in winter by hardwood cuttings taken from the basal part of the plant. We have no personal experience of this method of propagating daphnes, but where ample material is available it would certainly be worth trying.

Root Cuttings

A few daphnes can be propagated from root cuttings. *D. genkwa*, *D. mezereum* 'Grandiflora' and *D. m.* 'Alba Plena' have been successfully increased in this way and probably several others are capable of regeneration from roots. It is easier to take root cuttings from pot-grown plants, although roots carefully removed from plants grown in the open may be used with equal success; but it is, of course, essential to ensure that the plant you wish to propagate is not grafted on to a stock of another species.

In the case of *D. genkwa*, every available root would probably be taken commercially but few amateurs would care to ravage their plant in this way. The method usually recommended is simple. The roots are removed from the parent plant in December and cut into ½—1 in. lengths. The thickness of the roots used does not appear to be particularly important, but one would expect thick coarse roots or very thin roots to give a lower percentage of success. Small pots (thumbs or the equivalent) are crocked and three quarters filled with J.I. Seed Compost covered by a thin layer of silver sand. Commercially, a mix of 2 parts moss peat, 1 part sand and 1 part loam by bulk has also been used with good results. The root cuttings are placed horizontally, one to a pot on the sand and covered by a further thin layer of silver sand, the pots then being filled with the same compost which is lightly firmed and watered. If preferred, the root cuttings may be placed upright in the compost—remember, however, to put them the *right* way up, that is with the cut end which

44

was nearest to the crown of the parent plant uppermost. The pots may then be plunged in a propagating frame on an open bench and covered with shaded glass until shoots appear, when the glass should be removed. When the young plants are growing actively they can be moved to a covered frame and gradually hardened off.

In some cases the resultant plants produce juvenile growths, slightly thinner and weaker than one would like. It is possible that these shoots, being juvenile, may have a fairly high rooting capacity and it would be interesting to use them as cuttings, particularly with *D. genkwa*, to see whether reasonable plants of this most attractive but fickle species could be produced.

No accurate figures are available to indicate the reliability of this method. The scarcity in cultivation of *D. genkwa* and the less usual clones of *D. mezereum* suggest that the percentage "take" is relatively small and this is the experience of the few growers we know who have tried this technique.

A possible alternative method suggested by Barry Starling involves growing the plant to be propagated in a pot and allowing it to root into prepared soil in another pot placed underneath. Once the roots have penetrated the soil of the lower pot they may be cleanly severed, covered with sharp sand and then treated as outlined in the previous paragraph.

We have not, as yet, attempted this method ourselves, but suggest to any who do that it would be advisable *not* to allow the parent plant to root too deeply into the lower pot but to sever the roots at an early stage. This should ensure that the loss of the roots will not affect the parent plant greatly, whereas if severance were left until later it is possible that the parent plant would wilt. Anyone who has let their pot plants root into the bench shingle will be only too aware of the effects once the plants are removed from the shingle.

Leaf-bud Cuttings

At least two evergreen daphnes can be grown from leaf-bud cuttings, that is thin slivers of the stems with axillary buds and leaves attached. The leaf-bud cuttings are removed from the current year's growth between July and September, are carefully trimmed and inserted in a cold sand frame. They will normally be rooted by the following spring and can be potted and grown on in the usual way. It takes two to three years to produce a reasonable plant, however, and unless the species or hybrid proves difficult to reproduce in other ways, propagation by this method is unnecessary.

D. retusa and *D. tangutica* (both easily raised from seed) can be grown from leaf-bud cuttings but no records of other species being propagated in this way are known to us.

DESCRIPTIONS OF SPECIES AND HYBRIDS

The following accounts cover all the species and hybrids we know to be in cultivation, with brief descriptions of some species which have been grown or may be available in the foreseeable future. The descriptions are listed alphabetically with the exception of a few species which are included under the account of the best-known member of a closely-related group in order to avoid repetition and to provide an easy comparison of the various entities concerned. A group of lesser-known species is briefly mentioned at the end of the chapter where a finding list of *Daphne* names and synonymy with cross-references to the appropriate text is given.

As will be seen the format of each account is more or less uniform. Where possible reference to illustrations in publications which are reasonably accessible has been given and where known chromosome numbers are provided and R.H.S. Awards listed.

Daphne acutiloba Rehder in Sargent, *Pl. Wilsonianae* 2: 539 (1916).

ILLUSTRATION. Colour plate (in fruit). Frontispiece, fig. 2.

This Chinese evergreen species is not one of the more attractive daphnes in flower, but a good specimen covered with its bright red fruits is an impressive sight in late summer.

It is easily raised from seed and has been stated to be suitable as a grafting stock for a wide range of species, being used for this purpose commercially in California and possibly also in Britain. Regrettably, in this country it appears to be slightly tender and in our experience in severe winters can be killed outright even in the south of England. In view of this its use as a rootstock in areas subject to prolonged spells of cold weather is, or should be, limited. Further comments on its use as a rootstock are given in the section on propagation (p. 21).

Apart from the hardiness factor referred to above, *D. acutiloba* is easy to grow in an open or slightly shaded position on both acid and alkaline soils, provided they are well-drained. As in nature it is a woodland plant, *D. acutiloba* might be expected to prefer a humus-rich soil, and, although succeeding well enough in relatively undernourished conditions, it certainly appreciates richer treatment. In good soils it rapidly forms a fairly open shrub 1.2-1.5 m. (4-5 ft.) high, flowering and fruiting generously from an early age. We have not found it particularly long-lived in cultivation, possibly due to its slight tenderness, but it is only fair to say that plants grown under this name (but possibly *D. longilobata*) survived the 1962-3 winter in the open at Winchester, and specimens up to ten years old have been recorded by the authors.

46

PROPAGATION

(a) Seed. Fruit is freely produced and self-pollination appears common as the pollen is often shed before the perianth-lobes expand. If the seeds are washed free of the soft pulp of the ripening fruit and sown immediately, germination will frequently occur after about 6—8 weeks. This usually means the young seedlings will appear just before the onset of winter, and in view of the possible tenderness of this species they should be over-wintered in a frame.

Storage until spring does not appear necessarily to affect viability of the seed, and from dry seed sown in March in pots in the open at Wisley germination occurred after 8 weeks. Plants flower in 3—5 years after germination occurs.

(b) Cuttings. Stem cuttings of half-ripe wood in July/August (Group 2, page 41) are quite successful, but usually unnecessary in view of the freedom with which seed is produced.

TYPE LOCALITY China: W. Szech'uan, Mupin, woods, June 1908. Wilson No. 2946.

DESCRIPTION Erect evergreen shrub to 1.5 (1.75) m. in height; young branches pubescent with short yellowish hairs; older branches glabrescent to glabrous and dark brownish-red or purplish in colour. Leaves, alternate, sessile or only shortly petiolate, bright green, glabrous, coriaceous (leathery), oblong-lanceolate to oblanceolate or lanceolate, the apex varying from acute to obtuse, sometimes mucronate or even emarginate; 4.0—9.5 cm. long and 1—2 cm. wide with short tufts of hair at the apex when young. Flowers white, sometimes purple-tinged, in heads of 5—7 on current season's growth; bracts of inflorescence quickly deciduous (caducous) and ciliate; flowers fragrant in some forms but lacking, or with only intermittent, fragrance in others; perianth tube about 11—14 mm. long, glabrous; lobes 4, ovate-oblong, acute, 5—7 mm. long; subsessile or with silky-hairy pedicels up to 1.5 mm. long. Dimorphism of the flowers (see p. 6) has been reported for *D. acutiloba*. Fruit fleshy, glabrous, red.

CHROMOSOME NO. Not recorded.

FLOWERING PERIOD (May) June-July (to September). Flowers and fruit frequently occur together on the plants.

DISTRIBUTION China: Szech'uan, Hupeh and Yunnan provinces.

HABITAT Woods and wooded cliffs, 1800—2500 m.

The form usually seen in cultivation apparently originates from Wilson's collections in 1907-8 in Hupeh and Szech'uan (possibly W. 2944, W. 2946 (the type) or W. 2949) and has narrow, lanceolate leaves. Herbarium material shows a considerable variation in the dimensions of the leaves, particularly in width and some specimens appear very similar to *D. odora* in foliage characters. Rehder in his original description refers to this relationship, stating that *D. odora* differs in having glabrous (not pubescent) young branches; distinctly stalked, broader leaves; sessile many-flowered inflorescences surrounded by persistent (not caducous) bracts, and comparatively shorter perianth lobes. As we know *D. odora* and *D. acutiloba* in gardens, they are very distinct, and of course flower at different times of the year.

More closely related is *D. longilobata*, which for garden purposes is very similar to *D. acutiloba* and quite frequently does duty for it. In view of this close relationship it is considered below.

47

Daphne longilobata (Lecomte) Turrill in *Bot. Mag., no.* 172, *n.s., t.* 344 (1959).

ILLUSTRATION Photo opposite; also *Bot. Mag. no.* 172, *n.s., t.* 344.

The similarity of this species, which is recorded from S.E. Tibet and N.W. Yunnan, and *D. acutiloba* is referred to above and the two have become confused in gardens. Somewhat surprisingly, *D. longilobata* was first described as a variety of the deciduous *D. altaica* (*D. altaica* Pall. var. *longilobata* Lecomte) from Central Asia and Siberia but, in our view, is much more closely related to *D. acutiloba* differing only in its pubescent (not glabrous) perianth tube and in the method of production of the young growth. The inflorescence in both species is terminal but in *D. longilobata* it is rapidly overtopped by a new shoot which develops just below the inflorescence, making it lateral. In *D. acutiloba* the inflorescence is terminal on young shoots and further growth does not occur until the following season. It is, however, difficult to be certain that this growth pattern is constant from the relatively small number of specimens seen.

In other respects it is scarcely possible to distinguish the two species and it is interesting to note that one collection cited by Rehder under the original description of *D. acutiloba* (A. Henry No. 11321) from Yunnan with white scented flowers has a pubescent base to the perianth, suggesting that this character may be less clearcut than it appears from our present knowledge.

The main stock of *D. longilobata* at present in cultivation in Britain is derived from seed collected by Ludlow, Sherriff and Elliot (No. 15803) at 9,500 feet in S.E. Tibet in 1947. A flowering specimen was shown to the R.H.S. Scientific Committee by the Hon. Lewis Palmer in July 1951 under this number but identified as *D. acutiloba*, which may account for the confusion between the two in gardens.

D. longilobata is also known to have been cultivated at Werrington Park, Launceston, Cornwall, before 1928, probably from Forrest's seeds, but no further specimens from this source have been traced.

As a garden plant *D. longilobata* (derived from L.S. & E. 15803) differs only slightly from *D. acutiloba*, in our experience, being somewhat hardier, flowering freely as a young plant and bearing quantities of its showy red fruits regularly. It is perhaps worth noting here that some plants have sweetly scented flowers, reminiscent of *Stephanotis*, but Turrill comments in the *Botanical Magazine* article referred to previously that "No odour has been

Daphne longilobata (opposite)

Photo: B. Mathew

Daphne arbuscula f. *platyclada* (p. 57)

Photo: J. Starek

D. alpina L.

D. laureola L.

50

Daphne arbuscula (p. 54), in the Muran Hills, Slovakia.   *Photo: J. Starek*

Daphne arbuscula (p. 54), R.B.G. Edinburgh.　　　　*Photo: R. Elliott*

Daphne blagayana (p. 65).　　　　*Photo: J. R. Jameson*

detected in the flowers . . . ". Eliot Hodgkin in his notes says "flowered this year (1951) and had greenish flowers throughout summer. No scent. It grows tall, rather fast and somewhat leggy. A dull plant." Propagation differs in no way from that of *D. acutiloba*. Thriving plants of *D. longilobata* are known on acid, peaty soils, on heavy but reasonably drained clay, and on soils with a high chalk content—a tribute to its tolerance of cultivation!

Daphne alpina L., *Sp. Pl.* 356 (1753).

SYNONYM *D. candida* Wittm.

ILLUSTRATIONS. See drawing on p. 50; also S.R.G.C. *Journal* Vol. 10 fig. 52 (Apr. 1967).

Although known in cultivation since 1759, *D. alpina* has never become a popular plant with gardeners. There are spasmodic references in the *Gardeners Chronicle* to its cultivation during the last century, but it is curious that it is not more frequently grown. It is by no means difficult, and is a neat, deciduous and hardy dwarf shrub of value for its fragrant vanilla-scented white flowers which appear during early summer.

In nature *D. alpina* occurs (apparently exclusively) on limestone formations over a wide area of the European Alps and varies slightly in the quality of the flowers, which are a clearer white in some forms.

The clusters of up to ten blooms are borne terminally and normally appear after the leaves expand, although the degree of development apparently varies to some extent depending on the situation. In foliage characters *D. alpina* is reminiscent of *D. oleoides*, having rather similar grey-green leaves.

In cultivation it grows happily, if slowly, in both alkaline and acid soils, and given an open, sunny, well-drained position on the rock garden is a pleasing, although not outstanding, species for general cultivation. It is also suitable as a trough plant, a specimen grown by one of the authors in this way having reached only six inches in height in over ten years from seed.

PROPAGATION

(a) Seed. Fruit is freely produced in cultivation and seed germinates well if cleaned and sown soon after it ripens. When stored until spring and then sown, seed is known to have germinated erratically over a 1—3 year period in one instance. *D. alpina* has been recorded as flowering after five years when raised from seed.
(b) Cuttings. Stem-cuttings of relatively soft or half-ripe growth taken from June to early August (Groups 1 and 2, p. 41) root satisfactorily and particularly fine forms should be propagated in this way as seed-raised plants will be slightly variable.

TYPE LOCALITY "Mountains in Switzerland (Geneva) and Italy."
DESCRIPTION Compact erect deciduous shrub up to 50 cm. in height with ascending or prostrate stems. Young branches grey or reddish-brown, very downy. Leaves alternate, grey-green, downy-pubescent on both sides, clustered towards the tips of the shoots, sessile (petiolate in one variety), oblanceolate or obovate, obtuse to emarginate at the apex, 0.8—4 cm. long, 0.4—1 cm. wide. Flowers white, fragrant, in terminal clusters of 5—10; tube greenish, silky-pubescent outside, 8—9 mm. long; lobes ovate, acute, 5—6 mm. long, 3.5—4 mm. wide. Fruit fleshy, pubescent, yellowish-orange or red.
CHROMOSOME NO. n=9
FLOWERING PERIOD (April) May—June.
DISTRIBUTION Mountains of southern and central Europe, from Spain to Yugoslavia. According to Halda the distribution of *D. alpina* extends eastwards through the Balkan peninsula to Asia Minor and southwards to N. Africa. No specimens seen by the authors from these areas match *D. alpina*, but we have seen material from Spain, France, Italy, Austria, Switzerland and Yugoslavia which is referable to this species.
HABITAT Subalpine areas in limestone crevices and screes, 300—1500 (2000) m.

The following variant has been described, but is not known to be in cultivation:—

> var. *petiolata* Keissler described in *Eng. Bot. Jahrb.* xxv, 46 (1898) differs from typical *D. alpina* in its distinctly petiolate, proportionately smaller, leaves, and in its looser, more erect habit and longer branches. It occurs south of Trieste, in Istria and the Velebit Mts. of Yugoslavia.

Daphne arbuscula Celak. in *Sitz-Ber. Bohm Ges.-Wiss.* 1880 (1): 215 (1890).
SYNONYM *D. cneorum L.* var. *abietina* Borb.
ILLUSTRATIONS. See drawings on p. 32. Illustrations p. 52 and (*forma platyclada*) p. 49. Habitat and environment illustrations on p. 31 and p. 51; *R.H.S. Journal*, 1953 (Jan.) fig. 3.
AWARDS. A.M. (1915); F.C.C. (1973).

Few alpine gardeners fail to be captivated when they first view the intensely fragrant, rose-pink blooms of this attractive dwarf shrub, set off by the dark polished evergreen foliage, and it is easy to understand why *D. arbuscula* has been grown for so long in British gardens and is one of the most sought-after and beautiful of *Daphne* species. It was originally discovered in 1855 by A. Richter in the Carpathian Mountains, at that time Hungarian territory but now in Czechoslovakia. The exact date of introduction to British gardens has not been traced but many, if not the majority, of the plants cultivated have probably been derived vegetatively from a single clone judging from the material seen, which varies little, if at all, in flower colour or habit.

In many gardens it grows extremely well in the open in spite of an undeserved reputation for fickleness, perhaps fostered by Farrer's statement that it "hardly deserves the fuss that attends it or the price demanded of it". There are records of *D. arbuscula* thriving in a variety of conditions and Dr. Amsler, writing in the *R.H.S. Journal* in 1953, stated that it was an easy species, growing well in ordinary loam. He was certainly very successful, "giving it away like lumps of privet" according to Clarence Elliott. Another equally successful cultivator of this species was Dr. Jenkin, who had a plant a yard across in his garden at Hindhead, whilst at Vrana, King Boris of Bulgaria grew it well planted in limestone cliffs. A further record is of a plant 3 feet across and 1½ feet wide in an iron-limestone soil in Northants and there are many other instances of *D. arbuscula* achieving large dimensions in Britain, particularly in Scotland, where it apparently enjoys the cooler more humid climate.

As may be judged from these examples, it is by no means as pernickety as some authors would suggest. In our experience a peaty-scree mixture providing sharp drainage but retentive of moisture is perfectly satisfactory both for plants growing outside on the rock garden or peat bank, and also for pot culture. It is useful periodically to pin down the branchlets as recommended in the section on layering to encourage the plant to spread, and incidentally to produce young plants to give away to deserving friends. This technique was used very successfully by Dr. Amsler and no doubt many others. Generally *D. arbuscula* seems to enjoy a sunny open position provided there is no lack of moisture at the roots, but is by no means averse to slight shade, although perhaps less floriferous in such conditions. Additionally, *D. arbuscula* makes a beautiful plant for the alpine house when grown in a large pot or deep pan.

PROPAGATION

(a) Seed. In Britain seed is rarely produced, and it has been suggested that this is due to the clonal reproduction of most plants in cultivation here and the consequent lack of effective cross-pollination. No proof of this has been forthcoming, but in the wild seed is evidently commonly produced, ripening according to J. Halda 2—3 weeks after flowering and being distributed by mice and birds. Regrettably, we have had no opportunity to raise *D. arbuscula* from seed, which could be horticulturally valuable as variation in flower colour from white to deep rose has been recorded in nature.

(b) Cuttings. Half-ripe cuttings of young shoots, with or without a heel, root with relative ease if taken from June—August (see Group 2, p. 41) and reach flowering size in 3—4 years under reasonable growing conditions. As an example cuttings received at Wisley in August 1971, sent by Josef Halda from Mt. Muran, rooted without difficulty under mist and the plants produced flower trusses in 1975.

Halda's experience suggests that summer cuttings taken with a portion of two-year-old wood and rooted outside in a partially shaded position are more successful than soft cuttings under glass or in a frame. It would be most useful to have this suggestion confirmed experimentally with *D. arbuscula*, and also other species which layer readily, to determine the relationship of age of wood and rooting potential.

(c) Layering. The semi-prostrate habit of *D. arbuscula* proves ideal for this method of propagation. Grafted plants may, however, be more upright in habit and difficult to layer.

(d) Grafting is often recommended but is by no means essential, although used commercially by a number of firms. Several methods of grafting have been used successfully but, as the shoots of *D. arbuscula* are relatively thin, splice (side) grafting is probably the most suitable. Rootstocks used include *D. mezereum, D. giraldii, D. laureola, D. acutiloba* (or *D. longilobata*), *D. pontica, D. retusa* and no doubt others; but only in cases where difficulty in rooting cuttings is experienced do we consider grafting to be necessary. It is interesting to note that Halda found *D. giraldii* to be more successful as a rootstock for *D. arbuscula* than either *D. mezereum* or *D. laureola*.

TYPE LOCALITY Czechoslovakia, in the Carpathian Mts.
DESCRIPTION Dwarf, much-branched, semi-prostrate evergreen shrub 10—20 (—50) cm. in height; young branches reddish or yellowish, glabrous or finely pubescent. Leaves alternate, deep shining green, thick and leathery, grooved and almost glabrous above, slightly hairy below; linear or linear-oblong with revolute margins, crowded towards the ends of the branches, 9—18 mm. long, 2—5 mm. wide. Flowers very fragrant, usually pink, but very variable from deep rose to white, in dense terminal clusters of 5 to 30 (up to 100 or more in f. *platyclada*); tube 1.2—2 cm. long, glabrous or finely pubescent; lobes ovate, subacute, 5—8 mm. long. Fruit more or less dry, not fleshy, greyish-white, often capped by the persistent perianth.
CHROMOSOME NO. Not recorded.
FLOWERING PERIOD April—June.
DISTRIBUTION Czechoslovakia: Muran region of the Carpathians, according to J. Halda, in an area only 15 km. x 6 km. Reports of its occurrence in Hungary refer to the time when the E. Carpathian region was part of Hungary. In the A.G.S. *Conference Report* (1961), Dr. Martin gives the Siebenbergen in Romania as the locality for *D. arbuscula*, but we have located no authentic specimens from this area.
HABITAT Ledges and crevices in dolomitic limestone and conglomerate rocks and cliff-faces; 700—1300 m. See photographs on pp. 31 and 51.

In his original account of the species published in 1890 Celakovsky described two varieties of *D. arbuscula*. In his var. *hirsuta* the stems, young leaves and flowers are finely pubescent, whilst in his var. *glabrata* all parts of the plant are glabrous.

More recently Josef Halda has published his studies of *D. arbuscula* in the wild and has described a number of variants. There are differences, however, between his account in the A.G.S. *Bulletin* (Vol. 39, pp. 129-134) and that in the Czechoslovakian publication *Skalnicky* (1972), where Latin descriptions are provided for the variants described. Unfortunately, there is some doubt as to the validity of some of these descriptions, which do not accord precisely with the rules of Botanical Nomenclature. Nevertheless Halda's accounts provide us with a most valuable study of this species and its variation, and we are very grateful to him for permission to include an account of the variants he has noted.

The following list of the variations has been compiled from Halda's accounts cited above. It must be pointed out that the classification shown is not yet acceptable botanically as certain of the variants require valid publication and it is difficult to relate these to the variants orginially described by Celakovsky.

A. *Daphne arbuscula* ssp. *arbuscula* (referred to by Halda as *D. arbuscula* typus). As accepted by Halda this occurs in the southern part of the ranges of *D. arbuscula* on the south facing cliffs of conglomerate rocks from Muran Castle to Tisovec. In comparison with ssp. *septentrionalis* it is characterised by the more compact habit, the reddish-brown or carmine-brown colouring of the older bark and the longer, less revolute leaves in laxer terminal rosettes.

As botanical forms of the "type" Halda distinguishes the following:—

1. forma *grandiflora* Halda. From Mt. Maretkina, 950 m. Flowers twice the size (12—15 mm. in diameter) of the "typical" form. He states "often cultivated", and it is possible that the clone or clones generally cultivated in Britain would be referable here. Halda, in the A.G.S. *Bulletin*, gives this taxon varietal rank but in *Skalnicky* prefers the lower rank of *forma*. In the A.G.S. article he also mentions " var. *grandiflora* f. *carminea*" with "flowers rich rose, carmine in bud" but this is not referred to in his 1972 account.

2. forma *albiflora* Halda. From Mt. Maretkina, 900 m. Flowers pure white. Difficult to propagate from cuttings and slow from layers.

3. forma *platyclada* Halda. From Mt. Maretkina, 900 m. A fasciated form with flattened stems 5—8 mm. wide and inflorescences with 100 or more flowers, larger than those of the type. Growth rate approx. 5 mm. per annum. This is apparently the form pictured on p. 49.
Halda recommends grafting these fasciated forms on to *D. giraldii*, and comments that when grafted on *D. mezereum* "degeneration" from the fasciated to the typical form occurs.

4. forma *platyclada* subforma *albiflora* Halda. From Mt. Sajba 1000 m. Differs from f. *platyclada* in the smaller, creamy-white flowers. This variant is described in Halda's article in *Skalnicky*, but it is not clear whether it is distinct from the plant he designates "*platyclada C*" in A.G.S. *Bulletin* account and considers to be a variant of ssp. *septentrionalis*.

B. *Daphne arbuscula* ssp. *septentrionalis*. Halda uses this name (as far as we can trace not validly published) in his *Bulletin* article to cover plants from the northern part of the distribution of *D. arbus-*

57

cula. He distinguishes ssp. *septentrionalis* from the "type" by its elongated rod-like branches with the older bark yellowish-brown and the leaves shorter, more revolute at the margins and more densely crowded at the ends of the branches. It occurs on the northern slopes of the Velka Stozka and Mala Stozka and Halda states that it approaches *D. petraea* in general appearance.

Curiously no mention by name of ssp. *septentrionalis* is made in the *Skalnicky* article. As far as can be ascertained it would appear that the following variants are referable to ssp. *septentrionalis* as defined by Halda.

1. forma *radicans* Halda. From Mt. Velka Stozka, 1100 m. A creeping form with slender stems and underground runners which root freely. Flowers smaller than those of the "typical form". Easily propagated by division.

2. "var. *albiflora*". Listed by Halda in his *Bulletin* article (p. 133)—flowers pure white, buds greenish.

3. "forma *platyclada* B". A fasciated form, two plants of which were found in 1967 on the slopes of Velka and Mala Stozka. The flowers are pale rose.

4. "var. *albiflora* forma *platyclada* C". A white-flowered fasciated form from the same area as "forma *platyclada* B".

The botanical status of these forms is uncertain and nomenclaturally unacceptable in some cases. We have not seen either the type specimens or cultivated material of the variants listed but whatever the botanical position our gardens will be very much the richer because of Josef Halda's diligence and enthusiasm in introducing these attractive forms of *D. arbuscula*.

Daphne aurantiaca Diels in *Notes Roy. Bot. Gard. Edinb.* 5: 285 (1912). SYNONYMS *D. calcicola* W. W. Smith; *Wikstroemia aurantiaca* (Diels) Domke; *W. aurantiaca* var. *pulvinata* Domke.

ILLUSTRATION *Bot. Mag.* t. 9313 (1933).

AWARD F.C.C. (1927).

Although still occasionally offered by specialist nurserymen *D. aurantiaca*, unusual in the genus in having opposite leaves, remains a rarity in cultivation in spite of receiving a First Class Certificate when shown at the Chelsea Show in 1927 by A. K. Bulley who obtained his plant from the Royal Botanic Garden, Edinburgh in 1915. Bulley's plant had been grown out of doors since that date attaining a height of about $2\frac{1}{2}$ ft. (75 cm.) in 12 years. It might have been expected that an evergreen daphne with bright yellow, intensely fragrant blooms would rapidly gain popularity, but sadly the form of *D. aurantiaca* in cultivation has proved slightly tender and undoubtedly, in most parts of Britain, cool greenhouse or alpine house cultivation is necessary.

George Forrest, who introduced this species from S.W. China in 1906 (Forrest 2115 from the Lichiang range), described it as "one of the most beautiful plants of W. Yunnan growing in loose, limestone rocks". From other comments he makes it is evident that in nature *D. aurantiaca* inhabits open stony situations on limestone cliffs, and to grow it to perfection the provision of perfect drainage and sufficient sun to ripen the growths thoroughly would seem essential. In the first edition of Bean's *Trees and Shrubs* (Vol. 3, 1933), he records this species growing successfully at Caerhays and Werrington Park in Cornwall, in both gardens being planted in small openings of a retaining wall where the roots had access to the soil behind.

In mild areas of the country *D. aurantiaca* might well be grown in this way, or in a tufa wall where the sharp drainage combined with sufficient moisture at the roots, should provide the conditions required to emulate the plant at Werrington, reported by Bean as over 6 ft. across in 1933.

The alternative for most of us is to grow this attractive species as a pot plant. *D. aurantiaca*, although growing on limestone formations in nature, is apparently quite tolerant of acid soils, and the provision of sharp drainage combined with moisture retention in the compost, together with some winter protection (particularly after sunless summers when the young growths may not have ripened properly), are the factors likely to lead to success in its cultivation.

As known to the authors, *D. aurantiaca* in cultivation (presumably derived from Forrest 2115) forms a rather straggly, semi-erect, loose shrub of somewhat untidy appearance but in nature it is known to vary from an open plant of 5—6 ft. in height to a rock-hugging, prostrate shrublet only a few inches high. Undoubtedly forms of more horticultural worth, possibly hardier, await introduction, but in view of Forrest's statement that it is "one of the most free-flowering of all shrubs of N.W. Yunnan", it is certainly worth persevering with the form we have—in spite of the unflattering habit description given above. This ungainly appearance may well be due to the less arduous growth conditions in cultivation, and a natural reluctance on the part of growers to stop the plants at an early stage to encourage a more compact habit. Hugo Money-Coutts, who at one time grew and studied a large number of *Daphne* species and hybrids, found that cuttings of *D. aurantiaca*, rooted under mist, could achieve two feet of growth in the first year. As is the case with *D. cneorum*, lack of stopping in the early stages is likely to encourage the production of a "walking-stick" instead of a well-furnished plant and may well account for the gawky appearance of *D. aurantiaca* in the few collections where it is still maintained.

PROPAGATION

(a) Seed. This has not been produced in cultivation as far as we can trace. It is possible that the stock at present cultivated is derived vegetatively from one plant and is self-sterile. Halda obtained no seed after self-pollinating three plants of this species.

(b) Cuttings. Soft cuttings taken in late spring or early summer root successfully under mist, as has already been noted (Group 1, p. 41). Halda comments that cuttings root well, but that the resultant plants on their own roots are less satisfactory than grafted specimens, being more tender and rotting easily in damp weather.

(c) Grafting. Grafting on to *D. mezereum*, *D. giraldii* and *D. longilobata* is known to be successful using various techniques, particularly splice (side) grafting. No doubt other species, particularly evergreens like *D. laureola*, *D. pontica* and *D. retusa*, could be used if available.

TYPE LOCALITY   China: N.W. Yunnan.
DESCRIPTION   Prostrate to more or less erect glabrous evergreen shrub up to 1.5 m. in height; young bark reddish-brown, later grey to brownish-black with persistent leaf bases. Leaves more or less sessile, opposite, distributed along the branches, not clustered towards the tip as in many species; shape extremely variable, oblong to ovate or obovate or more or less linear, rounded or cuneate at base, acute to obtuse at apex, 0.7—1.8 cm. long, 0.2—0.9 cm. wide, rather leathery, dull dark green above, paler almost glaucous below, with the midrib prominent, margins recurved. Flowers tubular, carried in pairs, axillary or terminal, bright yellow or orange-yellow, very fragrant; tube 7—10 mm. long; lobes 3—5 mm. long, ovate to more or less orbicular. Fruit not seen but stated by Halda to be yellow, densely hairy and up to 4 mm. across.
CHROMOSOME NO.   Not recorded.
FLOWERING PERIOD   April—May.
DISTRIBUTION   China: N.W. Yunnan, Szechuan.
HABITAT   Ledges and crevices of limestone cliffs and outcrops, sometimes tightly adpressed to rocks, 2,600—4,000 m.

Variation in habit has already been mentioned and the plant described as *D. calcicola* W. W. Smith (*Notes R.B.G. Edin.* VIII, 185, 1914), a dwarf, narrow-leaved variant of prostrate growth, appears referable to *D. aurantiaca*. Forms of this type occur with typical plants in the wild, and, although horticulturally distinct, botanically they are probably not separable. Regrettably they are not known to be in cultivation.

Daphne bholua Buch.-Ham. ex D. Don, *Prodr. Fl. Nepal.* 68 (1825).

SYNONYMS   *D. cannabina* Wall. partly, not of Lour.; *D. cannabina* Hook. fil. partly; *D. papyracea* Wall. ex Steud., partly; *D. cannabina* Wall. var. *bholua* (Buch.-Ham. ex D. Don) Keissler.

ILLUSTRATIONS.   Colour plate opposite p. 30; drawing on p. 69; also *Bot. Mag.* n.s., t. 681. (1974).

AWARD   A.M. (1946).

D. bholua is a member of a group of closely related Himalayan species known colloquially as "paper-daphnes" from the tenacious bark which is used for paper-making and also in the manufacture of rope in Nepal and Tibet. The method by which the Nepalese and Tibetans prepare paper from the bark is described by Hodgson in the *Journal of the Asiatic Society* 1: 8 (1832).

The specific epithet is derived from the vernacular name "Bholu Swa" which was used by the Newar tribe who inhabit the Khatmandu area. It is widespread in the Eastern Himalaya and occurs over a considerable altitude range, plants from lower altitudes normally being evergreen and considered somewhat tender in Britain, whereas plants from higher altitudes have proved hardier and are frequently deciduous.

Although described 150 years ago this fine winter-flowering daphne is still scarcely known to gardeners, and the first record of its blooming in Britain appears to be in January 1938 when Fred Stoker, one of the most discriminating horticulturists of the period, flowered it in his Essex garden. Later in 1946 it received an Award of Merit when shown by Mrs. Stoker, but has made little impact since in spite of at least five further introductions. The source of introduction of Dr. Stoker's plant is unknown, but Will Ingwersen, writing in the *Gardeners Chronicle* in 1953, reported flowering this species from plants sent to him from the nurseryman Ghose in India a few years previously. The plants proved tender and were killed in the 1962-3 winter. Later, in 1962, two further introductions were made separately by Dr. G. A. C. Herklots and Major Spring-Smyth.

A number of plants from Dr. Herklots' introduction, collected at about 2.600 m. (8,000 ft.) on Sheopuri, Nepal, grew and flowered well in the Savill Garden at Windsor with some wall protection. All the plants from this collection were apparently semi-evergreen or evergreen, but varied in flower colour from white, tinged purple at the base, to deep rosy-purple. Dr. Herklots tells us that *D. bholua* is common on mountains around the valley of Khatmandu, often between 2,300—2,600 metres (7,000—8,000 ft.), being abundant on Phulchoke mountain and particularly frequent on Sheopuri, where natural regeneration is common. It flowers in early March in this area of Nepal, producing quantities of the black fruits by April.

It is, perhaps, worth noting here that seeds of a red-fruited daphne of this group were also sent to Windsor by Dr. Herklots together with seeds of *D. bholua*. These were collected at a lower altitude but unfortunately it is not known whether plants were raised. It is possible that the red-fruited plant was the related *D. sureil* which occurs at lower altitudes in the eastern Himalaya and is tender. If so, no doubt, any plants raised from this sending would not have survived if planted out, even with wall protection.

Tony Schilling writing in the *Gardeners Chronicle* in 1967 mentions that he collected *D .bholua* in the warm temperate zone above Khatmandu (7,500—9,000 ft.) where it grew in shady, damp but

well-drained conditions with a dense canopy of *Quercus semi-carpifolia* and *Rhododendron arboreum*, flowering from January to March and scenting the forests with its very fragrant blooms.
The introduction by Major Spring-Smyth in 1962 (T.S.S. 132A-C) was made on the Milke Banjyang ridge in E. Nepal "growing amongst mixed scrub on a broad open ridge scattered with *Rhododendron barbatum*, alt. 10,500 ft." These plants proved perfectly hardy in his Hampshire garden. Further seedlings collected by Major Spring-Smyth (T.S.S. 50172) from Jarepain, west of Pokhara, Nepal, in February 1972 at 2250 m. (7,000 ft.) have not yet flowered (1974), but in February 1970 Sir Peter Smithers collected seedlings from the Daman Ridge, Nepal, which have proved evergreen in his garden in Switzerland, reaching almost 2 metres in 4 years, flowering freely and setting seed sparingly after hand-pollination. He reports that they have withstood temperatures of 12°F un-harmed, and, although susceptible to snow damage because of their rapid growth, appear quite hardy in his garden. This receives a heavy rainfall at 75 in. per annum (mainly in spring and summer), a sunny autumn and severe frosts, although not of long duration.

A recent account by Roy Lancaster (*Journ. Roy. Hort. Soc.* Sept. 1976 p. 455) provides further detail of *D. bholua* growing in eastern Nepal: also a colour photo. He mentions in particular the suckering habit (not always apparent on some cultivated plants) and refers to plants up to 3.6 m. (12ft.) in height in forest conditions.

As may be judged from the comments so far made, *D. bholua* varies very considerably in habit, hardiness and the retention or loss of its leaves during winter. Additionally there is variability in flower colour, basically white suffused rosy-purple or purplish-pink to varying degrees. In fact the only character with which everyone appears in agreement is the intense fragrance of the blooms which scent the air for yards around.

The number of true winter-flowering shrubs available to us is limited and this most attractive species is unquestionably worthy of much wider cultivation. The deciduous high altitude forms appear quite hardy in southern and central England and should be so elsewhere in Britain although we have, as yet, no definite reports on their performance in colder areas.

At Wisley an evergreen form of *D. bholua* has flourished against a south wall since 1961. A small plant was received from Ghose of Darjeeling then and is now (1976) about 3 m. high and 1 m. across. It flowers profusely each year and has shown no signs of being affected by severe weather. At the Savill Garden, however, many of the evergreen forms raised from Dr. Herklots' seed in 1962 have succumbed during severe winters and it is obviously advisable to grow plants from its lower altitude range as cool greenhouse plants in colder areas. A plant of this evergreen form collected by Dr. Herklots has, however, been growing for about 13 years against a warm wall at Findon in Sussex and is now about 3 m. in height

(1976), flowering very freely for several weeks around Christmas each year. In the very severe winter of 1963 it was cut by frost to within 60 cm. of ground level, but recovered and branched more freely as a result.

As a cultivated plant it thrives in both acid and alkaline conditions —even on very chalky soils—without special care or treatment in our experience. Eliot Hodgkin, writing in the *R.H.S. Journal* in 1961, found that a grafted plant (received in 1953 from the Ingwersen introduction via Ghose) took many years to bloom, but other growers have found that *D. bholua* flowers as a reasonably young plant. Similarly there are variable reports of the habit of growth from "a stick-like plant" to "well-proportioned with numerous side branches off the vertical stems".

PROPAGATION

(a) Seed. In the wild, seed is freely produced and natural regeneration is at a relatively high level. Seed from cultivated plants is apparently much less freely produced. The Wisley and Windsor plants have not produced seed, but in Switzerland Sir Peter Smithers obtained a limited amount of seed by hand-pollination of his wild-collected plants. Fresh seed sent to Wisley in late May 1974 and sown in pots plunged outside germinated within 6 weeks. Growth of the resultant seedlings was slow, and vigorous growth may not take place until the second season after germination—a phenomenon which is not uncommon with certain shrubby genera.

Dr. Herklots has also found that fresh seed germinates rapidly, whereas older, stored seed loses its viability quickly.
(b) Cuttings. Softwood cuttings (Group 1, p. 41), taken with a slight heel in late spring or early summer, have been rooted successfully but the resultant plants have, in our experience, been slow to grow away. Some growers report that callus forms readily but that initial root production is slow.
(c) Grafting. Using various techniques, this has proved very successful. Root-stocks known to have been used include *D. mezereum*, *D. longilobata*, *D. giraldii* and *D. laureola*, and if fresh seed is not available, grafting appears to be the most reliable method of propagation.

TYPE LOCALITY "Mountains of Nepal."
DESCRIPTION Erect or spreading, rather loosely branched to relatively compact, glabrous, evergreen or deciduous shrub from 2.5—4 m. in height. Young bark pale brown; older bark dark brown with a slightly purplish tinge. Young branches pubescent to almost glabrous. Leaves alternate, leathery and dark dull green, shortly petiolate, narrowly elliptic or oblanceolate, acute to short-acuminate, cuneate at the base, the margin rather undulate, prominently veined, 4—10 cm. long, 1—2.5 cm. wide. Floral bracts caducous. Flowers in terminal clusters of 7—15, white suffused purplish-rose or pink externally, very fragrant, the scent reminiscent of lemons; tube 6—10 mm. long, pubescent outside; lobes 7—8 mm. long, 5—6 mm. wide, ovate, subacute. Fruit black when mature, ellipsoid, about 7 mm. long.

CHROMOSOME NO. Not recorded.

FLOWERING PERIOD Dec.—March in the wild; Nov.—Feb. (March) in Britain.

DISTRIBUTION Eastern Himalaya: E. Nepal; N. Bengal; Sikkim; Bhutan; N.W. Assam.

HABITAT Light woodland and open hillsides, 1600—3500 m.

D. bholua var. *glacialis* (Smith & Cave) B. L. Burtt in *Kew Bull.* 437 (1936). Illustration: Stainton *Forests of Nepal* figs. 133 & 134. (1972).

As has been already pointed out *D. bholua* varies very considerably in the wild, and further study of the populations is necessary to determine the status of the one variety so far described, *D. bholua* var. *glacialis*. This occurs between 2,600 and 3,500 m. and is distinguished by its deciduous leaves and somewhat less pubescent young branches. It is likely, however, that it is connected by intermediates with typical *D. bholua* and although it is sometimes stated that the evergreen forms are tall and rangy in habit, whilst the deciduous forms are more compact and shorter, this is by no means always the case.

D. bholua 'Gurkha'. One of the clones collected by Major Spring-Smyth (T.S.S. 132B) has been named 'Gurkha'—see *Journ. Roy. Hort. Soc.* Sept. 1976 p. 457. The original seedling was collected in 1962 on the Milke Banjyang ridge in eastern Nepal at about 3,200 m. and is now (1976) about 2.1 m. tall by 1.5 m. through, suckering from the base and apparently quite hardy in the open garden in Hampshire. It blooms regularly and freely each winter from Christmas until March, the intensely fragrant flowers being white flushed with mauve-purple outside. Propagation by grafting on to *D. longilobata* has proved successful and this clone is now available in the trade. Botanically it appears referable to var. *glacialis*.

D. bholua 'Sheopuri' (a selected clone from the 1962 introduction by Dr. Herklots), which received an A.M. in 1973 when it was shown from Windsor Great Park, is of very compact habit, semi-evergreen to evergreen and with white flowers, slightly flushed purple at the base.

Variegated Forms.

In the same article in which 'Gurkha' is named Roy Lancaster mentions finding a specimen of *D. bholua* on the Milke Danda ridge with creamy-white striped leaves; and on the Barun Khola another individual with "leaves splashed pale green and yellow". Neither variant was brought into cultivation.

The taxonomic position and nomenclature of the Paper Daphnes, *D. bholua*, *D. papyracea* and *D. sureil* is complex,* and it is not surprising that the three species have been confused both botanically and horticulturally as they differ in only minor characters. Fuller

*See B. L. Burtt in *Kew Bull*, 1936: 437 (1936).

descriptions of *D. papyracea* and *D. sureil* appear on pages 157 and 178, but for convenience the features distinguishing the three are listed below:—

D. bholua Leaves acute to short-acuminate, dark rather dull green, leathery; floral bracts falling before the flowers open (caducous). Flowers white, fragrant, flushed purplish outside; tube 6—10 mm. long; lobes ovate, subacute, 7—8 mm. long, 5—6 mm. broad. Fruit black. Eastern Himalaya.

D. papyracea Leaves bluntly acute to retuse, dark rather dull green, leathery. Floral bracts persistent through flowering stage and often retained until young shoots appear. Flowers white or greenish-white, not fragrant; tube 10—13 mm.; lobes ovate, acute, 5—7 mm. long, 3—4 mm. broad. Fruit red. Western Himalaya.

D. sureil Leaves acute to acuminate, pale very shiny green, rather soft in texture; floral bracts falling before the flowers open. Flowers white, or greenish-white, fragrant; tube 13—14 mm.; lobes narrowly ovate, acute to acuminate, 6—8 mm. long, 3—4 mm. broad. Fruit reddish-orange. Eastern Himalaya.

Less well-known is a fourth member of the group, *D. shillong*, which comes from the Shillong and Khasia hills and is most closely related to *D. sureil* from which it is stated to differ in the slightly longer perianth tube and longer perianth lobes. The fruit colour is unknown but if it proves to be red or reddish-orange its distinctness from *D. sureil* may well be questionable. (See p. 179).

Daphne blagayana Freyer in *Flora* 21: 176 (1838).

SYNONYMS *D. lerchenfeldiana* Schur.; *D. alpina* Baumg.; *D. "man-zellii"* or *"mazellii"* Hort. not *D. mazeli* Carr.

ILLUSTRATIONS See drawing on p. 70 and illustration p. 52; also *Bot. Mag.* t. 7579 (1897).

AWARD F.C.C. (1880).

Throwing bricks at *D. blagayana* as one passes is a frequently recommended horticultural pastime and a rough and ready way of implementing the practice of layering, so what better introduction can we give than to quote Farrer who becomes quite lyrical (a not unusual occurrence!) about this species. He suggests that "each passer-by, to be popular in the garden, should cast a limestone boulder upon the daphne, until its pile becomes a sort of Absalom's grave, perpetually getting higher and wider, and the *Daphne* therewith, until in the end you have a cairn of stones as at Glasnevin, half a dozen yards across, filled everywhere with the flower heads of *D. blagayana*".

This beautiful evergreen species, with its creamy-white, intensely fragrant blooms, is found wild over a fairly wide area of S.E. Europe and generally occurs on limestone formations in alpine or sub-alpine regions often, although by no means invariably, in light woodland or scrub. Farrer's recommendations given above are based on the prostrate, almost straggling, natural habit of the plant in conditions where the long trailing stems ramble through stony soil and root down in the thin layers of leafmould formed from the surrounding vegetation. There are also records of colonies growing amongst bracken in open areas in the Pindus Mountains of N. Greece and on grassy, rocky slopes in the Carpathians where it is known as the *Königsblume* or King's Flower, as the King of Saxony once made a special journey to Transylvania to search for it.

D. blagayana was originally discovered in 1837 by Count Blagay on part of his estate on Mt. Lorenziberg, nr. Bilichratz in Carniola (now Slovenia), and was described the following year by Freyer. One of its companions in this area, and on Mt. Goestingerberg near Graz in Styria where it also grows, is *Erica carnea* (now regrettably to be known as *E. herbacea*), one of the few heathers to tolerate calcareous soils, and this natural association is one which works well in the garden, particularly if, as suggested by Stuart Boothman, the clone 'Vivellii' is used. The daphne and erica flower together in February and March creating a pleasing contrast of creamy-white and deep carmine with the additional benefit of the daphne's sweet scent and the "clothing" potential of the winter heather over the bare stems of *D. blagayana*.

Apparently this species reached Britain about 1875, being introduced by Messrs. Veitch who exhibited it in 1880 when it achieved the distinction of a First Class Certificate, an award few would disagree with today. It was certainly being cultivated in European gardens before 1877, being exhibited by Van Houtte in Ghent in April 1878, whilst in the *Gardeners Chronicle* for 1879 *D. blagayana* was described as a novelty "hardier than, and as fragrant as, *D. indica*" (now known as *D. odora*).

In cultivation *D. blagayana* has proved to be quite tractable and is by no means difficult to grow under either alkaline or acid soil conditions, particularly if there is adequate leaf mould available to provide the cool porous surface layer through which it loves to ramble. At Brockhurst, Sir Thomas Hanbury grew it very successfully on a semi-shaded ledge of the rock garden in leafy soil into which peat and sand were incorporated, giving top dressings of old orchid compost and layering the branches with lumps of porous sandstone. An even finer example of a colony over 17 feet across was was grown prior to the 1939-45 war by Sir George (then Dr.) Taylor in his garden at Rickmansworth—a remarkable achievement by any standards. The famous colony at Glasnevin (referred to in the quotation by Farrer) grew (but, alas, no longer thrives) amongst low stony mounds built up with loam and rocks from a granite area, but many of us are unwilling and certainly have no need to go to these lengths to make this attractive species happy in our gardens. Given leafy soil in a well-drained position in the slight shade it seems to prefer, there should be no difficulty maintaining it, particularly if, each season, last year's stems are pegged down in late spring close to the point from which the current year's growth is being produced. Young roots readily form at this point, and this seasonal layering appears to keep the plants in good condition, the same process often being achieved in nature by rock tumbles or the advances of the surrounding vegetation over the prostrate daphne stems. Dryness at the roots is often the main cause of reported difficulty in growing this species.

In spite of its relative ease of cultivation and propagation, *D. blagayana* is now seldom offered by nurserymen, which is a pity as it is one of the most attractive hardy, early-flowering shrubs available to gardeners and particularly valuable for the intense fragrance of its bunches of creamy-white, occasionally pink-flushed blooms.

PROPAGATION

(a) Seed. Rarely produced in cultivation in Britain, but if ever available it should be sown as soon as possible after ripening and treated as recommended under "Propagation". It is certainly desirable to establish different seed-raised clones, because in all probability *D. blagayana* in British gardens derives from only one or two vegetatively propagated individuals, perhaps one reason for the paucity of seed production in this country. It is probable, as Eliot Hodgkin suggested, that the stocks we grow have deteriorated in vigour, possibly due to virus infection and seed-raised stock would overcome this problem, at least for a time. Seed received at Wisley in August, 1975, from Jugoslavia germinated the following spring and it will be interesting to compare any resulting plants with the clones at present in cultivation.

(b) Cuttings. Stem cuttings of young shoots, taken early in summer when soft and an inch or two long, root without difficulty in about four weeks under mist or in a propagating case. See Group 1, p. 41. Some growers have found that half-ripe cuttings with a heel of old wood also root very satisfactorily, but there is also evidence that the percentage take decreases with the age of the cutting.

(c) Layering. The method of propagation most usually recommended. The technique is described on p. 27. It is sometimes stated that roots are most easily produced towards the tips of the old stems; other propagators have reported that the stems are capable of root production very easily along their length. No accurate observations to support either statement are known to us, but it is interesting to note that Will Ingwersen found *D. blagayana* in

Yugoslavia with shoots up to five yards long but very little root. A few of these were taken and being potted, coiled like watch springs, "grew like smoke".

(d) Grafting. Occasionally practised but generally unnecessary.

TYPE LOCALITY   Yugoslavia: Woods in the hills just west of Ljubljana.

DESCRIPTION   Trailing evergreen shrub less than 30 cm. in height with long bare stems; bark dark purplish-brown, becoming purplish-grey with age; leaves alternate, shortly stalked, dark green, galbrous, leathery, broadly ovate to obovate, rounded at the apex, often minutely apiculate, clustered towards the tips of the more or less upright young shoots, 2—5 cm. long, 1—1.5 cm. wide. Flowers creamy-white (rarely pinkish), in dense terminal heads of 20—30, very fragrant; floral bracts very conspicuous, pale greenish and silky-pubescent, about 1 cm. long, 0.6 cm. wide; perianth tube 10—13 mm. long, silky-pubescent outside; perianth lobes ovate, obtuse or subacute to acute, 4—6 mm. long, 2—3 mm. wide. Fruit whitish or pinkish, rarely produced in cultivation.

CHROMOSOME NO.   2n=18. (Nevling 1962).

FLOWERING PERIOD   March-April (in Britain); April-June (in the wild).

DISTRIBUTION   Yugoslavia, Roumania, Bulgaria, Albania, N. Greece.

HABITAT   In subalpine woods, light pinewoods, *Buxus* thickets; 800—2,300 m. on limestone, dolomitic and occasionally serpentine formations.

D. blagayana varies only to a limited degree in the wild, and no botanical variants have apparently yet been described. Undoubtedly if one were able to study the species throughout its natural habitat various clones could be selected for garden purposes. Dr. Giuseppi mentions a variant he found at the summit of Mt. Oloman in Albania which he stated to be peculiar to the mountain, being smaller than *D. blagayana* as he knew it and not spreading by the rooting down of the prostrate stems, and probably other slight variants may be reported in due course.

Eliot Hodgkin, writing in the *R.H.S. Journal* in 1961, mentions two forms in gardens, one more compact and flowering about a fortnight earlier than the other. This compact form grew in Lawrence Johnston's garden at Mentone and was put into commerce (date unknown but probably after the 1939-45 war) by Dr. A. Q. Wells of Shipton Manor as *Daphne "manzellii"*. This name has no standing and presumably was appropriated in some way from *D. mazeli* Carr., a synonym of *D. odora*. A large colony of *D. blagayana* over five feet across in the late Miss Raphael's garden at Kingston Bagpuize (1975) appears to be this form, and it is growing perfectly happily in front of a shrub border in slight shade—a fine example of what this beautiful species can achieve without being over-fussed.

It has not yet been possible to grow the two forms together so that a comparison of their flowering season and habit can be made, but plants obtained from Sissinghurst under the name "manzellii" are growing at Wisley so in future it may be possible to do so. If the two are considered sufficiently distinct to warrant clonal names being applied, it would be inappropriate to maintain "mazeli" or "manzellii" which are obvious sources of confusion.

It seems likely that this is the same clone referred to in Eliot Hodgkin's "Plant Book" (his list of plants received) as having been

D. bholua Buch. -Ham.

D. petraea Leybold

69

D. blagayana Frey.

D. odora Thunb.

obtained in 1951 from Wells as 'Wells' Variety'. At the moment no catalogue of Dr. Wells' nursery for 1951 has been traced so it has not been possible to check whether or not this name can be maintained or not.

Daphne x burkwoodii Turrill in *Bot. Mag.* 166: n.s., t. 55 (1949).

PARENTAGE *D. caucasica* Pall. x *D. cneorum* L.

ILLUSTRATIONS See under the comments on the individual clones.

AWARDS A.M. (1935) to 'Albert Burkwood', as *D. x burkwoodii;* A.M. (1937) to 'Somerset'; A.G.M. (1950) to 'Somerset'.

Few daphnes have attained the general popularity of *D.* x *burkwoodii* in the garden, and because of the ease with which it is propagated, allied with the undoubted attractions of the freely borne, fragrant, blush-pink flowers it seems likely that this fine hybrid raised by the Burkwood brothers will remain in the nursery trade for many years to come. In fact two clones are commonly grown in Britain and the story of their raising and introduction is an interesting one, gleaned from correspondence between Albert Burkwood and Eliot Hodgkin, together with information provided in *Baileya* II: 1—3 (1963) by Freek Vrugtman. There are, in fact, slight discrepancies between this latter account and Burkwood's letters which we have seen and information from which we use here.

In 1931 the two brothers decided to cross *D. cneorum* using pollen from *D. caucasica* and from the three seeds obtained were successful in raising three seedlings, not at their nursery but at the home of Albert Burkwood in Kingston.

Following the dissolution of their partnership with Geoffrey Skipwith, who owned the firm of Burkwood and Skipwith jointly with them, Albert moved to Poole in Dorset and took one of the seedlings. This is the clone now known as 'Albert Burkwood' (or quite frequently simply as *D.* x *burkwoodii*), and it was introduced by Longfleet Nurseries, Poole, with whom he was associated at that time.

The remaining two seedlings were taken by Arthur Burkwood, who joined Scotts of Merriott, Somerset, as propagator. One of the seedlings died; the other was named 'Somerset' and introduced in Britain by Scotts and later in the U.S.A. by Wayside Gardens.

The picture is somewhat clouded by the cultivation of a plant usually known as *D. lavenirii*, or less often as *D. laveniriensis*, which was introduced by Correvon's nursery. This occurred about 1919 or 1920 in the nursery of Morel & Lavenir at Lyon-Vaise, France, as a chance hybrid between *D. caucasica* and *D. cneorum* which were growing close to one another. It was seen in flower by Henri Correvon who named it after M. Lavenir and marketed it as *D. lavenirii* in 1930. The name was never validly published as far as can

71

be traced, but is available for use as a cultivar name as it was listed prior to the guillotine date for cultivar names in Latin form of Jan. 1, 1959. Correvon for some reason gives the parentage *alpina* x *cneorum*, but Money-Coutts located M. Lavenir who stated that it was raised from seed of *D. caucasica* apparently pollinated by *D. cneorum*, the reverse cross of the Burkwood introductions.

The forms of this hybrid are among the easiest of daphnes to grow, thriving in any reasonably fertile well-drained soil in an open position and flowering abundantly each season in May and June. They grow well in acid or alkaline conditions and their only drawback is the sudden dieback which sometimes occurs. In spite of this we know of plants which have lived for over fifteen years, and as is the case with so many daphnes, the demise of old specimens may often be attributed to drought, coupled with secondary fungal infection.

PROPAGATION

(a) Cuttings. The various clones all root readily from stem cuttings and, as has been mentioned in the sections on propagation, there is some evidence that short soft cuttings taken with a heel root more readily than firmer material. Experimental confirmation is required to provide accurate evidence as to the optimum time for taking cuttings, but from the amateur's viewpoint a good percentage of cuttings taken at any time from June—August, with or without a heel, should prove successful. Our own preference is for early-struck cuttings taken with a heel in June.

(b) Grafting. This is possible, but quite unnecessary. *D. mezereum* and *D. laureola* are known to have been used.

(c) Seed. No record of seed production by any form of *D.* x *burkwoodii* is known to us.

TYPE   A specimen preserved in the Kew Herbarium from material of *D.* x *burkwoodii* 'Albert Burkwood' grown at Kew.
DESCRIPTION   (Comparative details of the variants are tabulated prior to the comments on the individual clones).

A partly evergreen, densely-branched shrub, slightly spreading to upright in habit, up to 1.75 m. high and 2.0 m. across. Young branches green, sometimes purple-tinged, pubescent; older branches light to dark brown, becoming glabrous with age. Leaves alternate, fairly evenly spread along the branches, glabrous, sessile (sometimes subsessile); linear-oblanceolate to narrowly elliptic-oblanceolate, apiculate to obtuse or mucronulate at the apex, narrowed at the base up to 4.0 cm. long and 1.2 cm. wide. Flowers very fragrant, purplish-pink and white, in umbels of 6—16 clustered around the terminal branchlets and sometimes extending down the stems almost in spikes (like a flue-brush); tube 1.0 cm. long covered in short hairs, green or white, heavily flushed purplish-pink; lobes pink or white flushed (or ageing) pink, 5—8 mm. long, 3—4 mm. across, rounded (and sometimes emarginate) to apiculate at the apex, slightly hairy on the outer surface. Fruit unknown.
CHROMOSOME NO.   Not recorded.
FLOWERING PERIOD   May—June, occasionally with a further flush of bloom in autumn.
DISTRIBUTION   A garden hybrid, occurring both as a chance seedling (Lavenir, circa 1919) and as a deliberate cross (Burkwood Bros., 1931).

The cross between these two species, one evergreen, the other deciduous, is interesting as they are usually placed in different sections of the genus. *D.* x *burkwoodii*, as will be realised from the description, varies to a certain extent in the character of the individual clones, but may readily be seen to be intermediate between *D. cneorum* and *D. caucasica* in flower and leaf characters and in its semi-evergreen habit.

As there is still considerable confusion between the various clones, the following table is provided in an attempt to clarify the position. It must be emphasised that we have not yet been able to grow the three clones next to one another in the garden, and the "distinguishing" features may not therefore be as clearcut as they may appear from this table. This applies particularly to 'Lavenirii' of which we have had only limited material from an old plant to examine.

CHARACTER	'ALBERT BURKWOOD'	'SOMERSET'	'LAVENIRII'
HABIT	A fairly dense, rounded shrub, rarely more than 1 m. high and usually broader than high.	An upright- somewhat "vase-shaped" shrub to 1.5 (1.75) m. usually only about 1 m. across. Less compact in habit than 'Albert Burkwood' but in some positions may be more spreading in growth.	Apparently fairly spreading in growth and intermediate in height between 'Albert Burkwood' and 'Somerset'
YOUNG SHOOTS	Purple-tinged (? always)	Green	Green
OLDER SHOOTS	Dark brown	Mid-brown	Dark brown
FOLIAGE	Semi-evergreen	Semi-evergreen	Semi-evergreen to virtually deciduous
LEAF SHAPE AND SIZE	Linear-oblanceolate to 3 cm. long x 7.5 mm. wide	Narrowly oblanceolate to 4 cm. long x 1.2 cm. wide	Narrowly oblanceolate to 3 cm. long x 7—8 mm. wide
LEAF APEX	Apiculate	Mucronate to rounded	Apiculate
COLOUR OF PERIANTH TUBE	Green heavily suffused deep purplish-pink	Pale purplish-pink	Deep purplish-pink
COLOUR OF PERIANTH LOBES	White usually flushed pink and deepening with age	Pale pink	Pale pink
THROAT COLOUR	Slightly deeper pink than lobes	Pale pink, the same colour as the lobes	Dark pink, producing a red "eye"
DIAMETER OF FLOWERS	15—19 mm.	12—13 mm.	11—13 mm.

D. x *burkwoodii* 'Albert Burkwood'
Illustration. *Bot. Mag.* 166: t. 55 (1949) as *D.* x *burkwoodii*.

The clonal name was first adopted in Bean, *Trees and Shrubs*, 2: 9 (1973), and until that date it had been marketed simply as *D.* x *burkwoodii*. Raised by Albert and Arthur Burkwood from a deliberate cross and first distributed by R. Aireton, Longfleet Nurseries, Poole, Dorset, about 1935 for Albert Burkwood.

As an example of its ultimate size, plants about 10 years old should, in reasonable soil, reach 3 ft. in height by 4 ft. or more across.

D. x *burkwoodii* 'Somerset'
Illustrations. p. 92; also *Baileya* II: 2, t. 1 (1963).

The clonal name was apparently first used by the introducers when the plant was exhibited on May 25, 1937, at Chelsea Flower Show, and received an A.M. Raised by Albert and Arthur Burkwood from a deliberate cross and first distributed by Messrs. Scotts of Merriott, Somerset, in 1937 for Arthur Burkwood. Examples over 5 ft. high and 3 ft. across are known after about 10 years from a cutting.

D. x *burkwoodii* 'Lavenirii'
Illustration. None traced.

Originally described and marketed by Correvon Fils of Geneva in 1930, see *Floraire*, p. 96 (1931). Raised by M. Lavenir of Morel & Lavenir, Lyon-Vaise, France, in 1919 or 1920. A chance hybrid.

VARIEGATED CLONES. At least four variegated-leaved forms of *D.* x *burkwoodii* are known to have occurred. These are listed below with appropriate information but accurate comparison of the clones must await the opportunity to grow them all in close proximity.

(a)   A branch sport of 'Somerset' with pale yellow variegated margins to the leaves was noted at Wisley in the early 1960's and was propagated but never distributed. This stock is still grown by one of the authors.

(b)   Eliot Hodgkin received a clone with silvery leaf-margins from Linz Botanic Garden, Austria, in July, 1968, as "*D.* x *burkwoodii variegata*". This plant is still growing in Mrs. Hodgkin's garden (1976) and appears to be a variegated form of 'Somerset', judging by the growth and flower characters.

(c)   'Somerset Variegated' is a clone listed by Messrs. Scotts of Merriott. A variegated shoot occurred as a sport on a plant of 'Somerset' about 1956 and was first noticed by Albert Roskelly, a nursery worker at Scotts. It was propagated and subsequently lost but since that date several further variegated branch-sports have appeared on plants of 'Somerset' at the nursery.

The present clone derives from one of these and is a vigorous plant of upright habit with most attractive foliage irregularly banded with gold at the margins. It appears quite stable.

D. altaica Pallas

D. caucasica Pall.

D. mezereum L.

(d) 'Carol Mackie' is an American cultivar which occurred in 1962 as a branch sport of a ten-year-old plant of *D.* x *burkwoodii* at the home of Mrs. Carol Mackie of Far Hills, New Jersey. It was marketed by the Watnong Nursery (The Don Smiths), Morris Plains, New Jersey, U.S.A. and the name registered with the Arnold Arboretum in 1969. It has a clearly pronounced gold band around the edge of the leaf. It has now (1976) been introduced to Wisley and, although it has not yet flowered, it should be a most attractive variant as it is a vigorous clone which so far has shown no signs of reversion. The original plant moved to the Watnong Nursery in 1966 is now (1976) 3 ft. high by 4—5 ft. across. The habit would suggest that the original clone of *D.* x *burkwoodii* grown by Mrs. Mackie on which the sport occurred was 'Albert Burkwood', but this needs confirmation.

Daphne caucasica Pallas, *Fl. Rossica* 1: 53 (1784).

SYNONYMS   *D. salicifolia* Lam.; *D. euphorbioides* Muss.—Puschk. ex Steud.; *D. cneorum* Guld.; *D. caucasica* var. *cognata* C. Koch.

ILLUSTRATIONS   See drawing opposite: also *Bot. Mag.* 120: t. 7388 (1894).

Although a useful and attractive deciduous shrub in its own right, *D. caucasica* usually only finds mention in horticultural literature as one parent of the illustrious *D.* x *burkwoodii*. We have found it easy to grow, young plants rapidly forming rather willowy shrubs up to 2 metres in height, flowering abundantly during May and June and often obliging with further sprays of the fragrant, glistening white blooms during late summer and autumn. The flower clusters are distinctive, being produced at the tips of short lateral shoots near the end of the previous season's growth, a character in which it appears to differ from the closely related *D. altaica* (p. 79) at least as far as can be judged from cultivated plants of both species.

As the specific name indicates, it is native to the Caucasus, growing in subalpine and mountainous regions at the edge of woodland or in light shade amongst shrubs and scattered trees in rocky, relatively open situations. Bean, in the 1914 edition of his great work *Trees and Shrubs*, writes of *D. caucasica* "many times introduced and lost", but this is probably due to neglect rather than any lack of hardiness or other quirk of the species in cultivation. We know of plants which have thrived for many years in both acid and alkaline conditions where the soil is well drained and reasonably humus-retentive. *D. caucasica* should be perfectly happy given a slightly shaded position in the shrub border, or at the edge or back of the rock garden, so that it will not intrude on more delicate neighbours but where its fragrance can be appreciated.

The earliest record we have traced of *D. caucasica* being cultivated in Britain is "before 1893" when it was grown (as *D. salicifolia*) by T. Smith of Newry, an Irish nursery then famed for its selection of rare and unusual shrubs.

PROPAGATION

(a) Seed. Fruit is plentifully produced in cultivation and germinates readily if sown fresh. Under reasonable conditions plants reach flowering size 2—4 years after germination occurs.

(b) Cuttings. Stem cuttings of soft wood taken from June to July root well with or without a heel. See Group 1, p. 41.

TYPE LOCALITY U.S.S.R.: Achalgory, Caucasus.

DESCRIPTION Erect deciduous shrub up to 2 m. in height; young branches purplish-green, downy or glabrous. Leaves alternate, pale green, rather thin in texture, glabrous, sessile or very shortly stalked; linear-lanceolate or oblanceolate acute to obtuse, with a minute mucro, borne along the entire shoot not clustered near the apex; 2—7 cm. long, 0.5—1.5 cm. wide. Inflorescence with caducous bracts, flowers white in clusters of 2-20 borne terminally on short young lateral shoots produced from the previous season's growth (in var. *axilliflora* with additional flower clusters on sublateral spurs); fragrant; tube 9—10 mm. long, silky-pubescent outside; lobes ovate, more or less reflexed, 7—9 mm. long, 3—5 mm. wide. Fruit, fleshy, black (var. *caucasica*) or red (var. *axilliflora*); also reported as yellow, but possibly from incorrectly identified plants.

CHROMOSOME NO. Not recorded.

FLOWERING PERIOD May—June (July) in cultivation and in the wild.

DISTRIBUTION U.S.S.R.: Caucasus, E. & W. Transcaucasia, Dagestan, ? Asia Minor.

HABITAT In rocky places and fringes of woodland in mountains.

D. caucasica shows some variation in the wild and it is possible that both the "type" plant, *D. caucasica* var. *caucasica* and *D. caucasica* var. *axilliflora* Keissl. are still cultivated in Britain although no plants of the latter variety have been traced. The distinguishing features are as follows:—

D. caucasica var. *caucasica*. Fruit black. Inflorescence with terminal clusters of flowers on lateral growths. Widespread in the Caucasus.

D. causica var. *axilliflora* Keissler in *Engl. Bot. Jahrb.* 25: 39 (1898). Fruit red. Inflorescence with terminal clusters of flowers on short lateral shoots with additional axillary flowers on sublateral spurs. Apparently confined to the region around Tiflis and S. Transcaucasia. In the *Flora U.S.S.R.* it is treated as a species, *D. axilliflora* (Keissl.) Pobed.

In cultivation there may be some confusion between *D. caucasica* and either *D. acutiloba* or *D. longilobata*, as in Eliot Hodgkin's correspondence there is reference to *D. caucasica* growing in California and described as "evergreen, flowering from April until mid-November". A plant received as *D. caucasica* by one of the authors from California has the appearance of *D. acutiloba* (it has not yet flowered) and as *D. caucasica* is always deciduous in our experience it seems likely that some misidentification has occurred.

D. caucasica belongs to a group of closely related species including *D. altaica*, *D. sophia* and *D. taurica* which differ only in minor particulars and may well all be derived from the same ancestral stock. Separate botanical descriptions are not provided as they are so similar and in view of their close affinities they are discussed below.

Related Species

1. D. altaica Pallas in *Flora Rossica* t. 53 (1784).

SYNONYM   *D. indica* Schangin

ILLUSTRATIONS. Colour plate opposite p. 15, and drawings on p. 75; also *Bot. Mag.* t. 1875 (1817); *Lodd. Bot. Cab.* t. 399 (1823).

Native to the Altai region of Russia, *D. altaica* was originally collected by Monsieur Patrin, a friend of the botanist Pallas, and was apparently cultivated before 1817 as the *Botanical Magazine* plate of that date is a portrayal of a plant grown at the Cambridge Botanic Garden. In the *Botanical Magazine Index* this plate is referred to as *D. alpina*, but Sims' description refers definitely to the glabrous leaves of the plant depicted whereas those of *D. alpina* are downy on both sides. It seems probable that the plant grown at Cambridge was *D. altaica*, although no specimens have been traced to confirm this.

As a garden plant *D. altaica* has much the same value as *D. caucasica*, being useful in May and June for its very fragrant white flower-clusters. Some authorities dismiss it as "little-scented", but in our experience it has a refreshing scent and grows well in any well-drained, leafy soil in open or slightly shaded positions.

PROPAGATION
(a) Seed. Fruit is produced reasonably freely in cultivation and fresh-sown seed germinates without difficulty.
(b) Cuttings. As *D. caucasica*.
(c) Suckers/Layers. Sucker-shoots, or artificially layered shoots, may be used for propagation, see p. 27.

TYPE LOCALITY   Siberia, Altai region.
DESCRIPTION   *D. altaica* is scarcely distinguishable botanically from *D. caucasica*, and as known in gardens appears to differ only in its broader, more or less elliptical (not oblanceolate) leaves, and in the much less silky-pubescent perianth tube. In addition *D. caucasica* (at least in cultivation) does not apparently sucker, whereas *D. altaica*, according to Eliot Hodgkin, suckers "in an abandoned way". He records a colony 8 ft. across and up to 3 ft. in height at the Linz Botanic Garden, Austria (1961).

Bean (1973) suggests that it is a geographical form of *D. caucasica*, differing in its larger, more pointed leaves, in having fewer flowers per cluster, and in not producing a crowd of short flowering twigs from the previous year's shoots. In our view the form of the inflorescence of *D. altaica* and *D. caucasica* var. *caucasica* does not differ sufficiently for this character to be satisfactory in distinguishing the two plants. The fruit of *D. altaica*, however, is blackish-red to nearly black, not black as in *D. caucasica* var. *caucasica*.

CHROMOSOME NO.   Not recorded.

FLOWERING PERIOD   May—June in cultivation and in the wild. Martin (A.G.S. Bulletin, 1961) records it as flowering again in autumn.

DISTRIBUTION   U.S.S.R. Altai region, Sajan Mts.; Tsungaria.

HABITAT   As *D. caucasica*.

2. D. sophia Kaleniczenko in *Bull. de la Soc. Imp. des Nat. Moscow* 22: 311 (1849).

SYNONYMS   ? *D. altaica* Steven; *D. oleoides* Tschern. ex Meissn.

ILLUSTRATION.   Colour plate opposite p. 15.

Although little known in cultivation *D. sophia* has been introduced at least twice to British gardens and still thrives in Mrs. Hodgkin's garden in Berkshire where there are three plants growing perfectly happily without protection, the largest being about four feet tall (1976). These plants were obtained by Eliot Hodgkin in 1967 from the Moscow Botanic Garden and planted in an open well-drained site in slightly alkaline soil. They are growing well, suckering gently and forming rather upright shrubs, with a number of vertical stems as opposed to the (usually) single stemmed *D. caucasica* which is closely related.

Although grown by Correvon in Switzerland before 1914 the original introduction to Britain was by Tom Hay, who received a pot-grown plant from the Moscow Parks Dept. in 1939 which flowered in the spring of 1940 under glass at Hyde Park but was destroyed in an air raid during the war. He considered it to be an attractive plant, valuable for its early-produced, fragrant blooms. Although we have not ourselves grown *D. sophia*, it should prove a useful if not outstanding species for garden decoration when available commercially. It appears to be an undemanding plant as regards soil requirements but as (according to Hay) it occurs on very friable land on chalky mountain slopes in nature, a well-drained fairly fertile soil would seem advisable to produce the best results.

PROPAGATION   We have no experience of propagating *D. sophia*, but its suckering habit indicates a relatively easy method of increase, whilst soft or half-ripe stem-cuttings should not be difficult to root in view of its close relationship to *D. altaica* and *D. caucasica*. As far as we know seed has not yet been produced in Britain.

TYPE LOCALITY   European Russia, Volga Don region, Belgorod area.

DESCRIPTION   *D. sophia* resembles *D. altaica* in its suckering habit, but is of upright less spreading growth and has dark green, obovate leaves strongly attenuate at the base as opposed to the paler, more or less elliptical, weakly attenuate leaves of *D. altaica*. In comparison, *D. caucasica* has rather thinner, paler, narrower leaves which are oblanceolate or linear-lanceolate in shape. The inflorescence is similar in formation to that of *D. caucasica* var. *caucasica* and *D. altaica*, but the lobes of the flowers on the herbarium specimens seen are slightly narrower (2.5—3.75 mm.) than those of *D. altaica* (4.25—5 mm.) and *D. caucasica* var. *caucasica* (3.5 mm.). These differences are however very slight and might well be obscured on examining a wide range of material from Russian sources. The fruits of *D. sophia* are bright red.

CHROMOSOME NO.   Not recorded.

FLOWERING PERIOD   April—May in cultivation. Hay records that a second crop of flower appears in August whilst the fruits from the first flowers are ripening. A second flowering in autumn is also recorded in *Flora U.S.S.R.*

DISTRIBUTION   S.W. U.S.S.R. in the provinces of Voronezh, Kursk and Belgorod.

HABITAT   Calcareous mountain slopes in friable soil in open or shaded positions amongst thin stands of *Pinus cretacea* (a race of the Scots pine) and oak woodland.

It is perhaps worth noting that some Russian botanists consider *D. altaica* and *D. sophia* to be conspecific.

3.   **D. taurica** Kotov in *Bot. Journ. U.S.S.R.*, 55: 1336 (1970).

TYPE LOCALITY   U.S.S.R., Sympheropol in the Crimea.

Although we have no record of any introduction to cultivation of this species, it is mentioned in view of its close relationship to *D. altaica* and *D. sophia*. It is probable that in details of cultivation and propagation it will prove similar to these species should it be introduced, but from a botanical viewpoint it is stated to differ mainly in bark and leaf characters.

In *D. taurica* the bark is said to be darker than in other species of this group and the leaves to be tougher in texture with a revolute margin when compared with the flat rather papery leaves of *D. altaica*, *D. sophia* and *D. caucasica*. It is not stated to produce suckers. The flowers are said to be slightly larger than those of the other species in this group and cream rather than white in colour. The fruits are dark red.

DISTRIBUTION   Known only from the type locality.

HABITAT   "Calcareous hollows".

As may be realised "lumpers" might well regard *D. caucasica* as a variable species and perhaps reduce the other three species to sub-specific or varietal rank. They are certainly closely related, but until a detailed monographic study of the genus is undertaken it seems sensible to maintain them at species level particularly when one considers that *D. altaica* and *D. sophia* are separated geographically by about 2,000 miles of·steppe and desert.

Daphne cneorum L. *Sp. Pl.* 357 (1753).

SYNONYM   *D. odorata* Lam.

ILLUSTRATIONS.   See drawing on p. 86; also *Bot. Mag.* t. 313 (1795). Polunin, *Fl. Europe* pl. 74, t. 756, (1969). Colour plate, frontispiece fig. 4.

AWARD   Award of Garden Merit, 1927.

"Such a plant in a May morning with the beauty of the flowers and the fragrance they pour forth drives through the soul a stream of pleasure which is impossible to describe." Thus writes a correspondent in the *Gardeners Chronicle* of *D. cneorum* in June, 1843. Few will challenge the assertion that the Garland Flower is "the finest of all daphnes for the rock garden, since it is easy to grow, easy to propagate, prolific and beautiful in flower and deliciously scented into the bargain." Some may cavil at the statement "easy to grow", particularly if they have been the recipients of one of the peat-grown specimens which used to be imported from the Continent in quantity and are frequently difficult to establish. It is as well to be suspicious, too, of plants grown in modern peat-based composts, which suffer the same difficulty in transition from virtually pure peat to one's garden soil—even if the soil is very carefully prepared beforehand.

Good nursery stock of *D. cneorum*, however, grown in "proper" (i.e. John Innes type) composts, is by no means difficult to establish, rewarding the gardener annually with a fine mass of pink, fragrant flowers borne during April and May in large clusters on the lax, prostrate, evergreen mats of neat foliage. Frequently the whole plant can be virtually covered in bloom, almost obliterating the foliage beneath.

As is the case with so many daphnes, an open, sunny, well-drained but moisture-retentive site is the most suitable, and it appears relatively indifferent to the presence or absence of lime in the soil. We know of very fine specimens growing on the chalk of the South Downs which have reached 6 feet across without becoming bare in the centre, whilst at Wisley in a peaty, sandy acid soil there are old specimens on the rock garden which grow well and flower abundantly most seasons.

Bean (1914) also mentions very healthy plants grown on Plumstead Common, Kent, in plots under control of the London County Council. The area is on a limestone formation and *D. cneorum* apparently was in rude health in spite of "treatment similar to that meted out to privets and such-like . . . "!

The key to success appears to lie in maintaining a constant but not excessive supply of moisture at the roots by good initial preparation of the soil and an annual mulch of leafy material, particularly on dry soils whether chalky or acid. Curiously, in nature *D. cneorum* often occurs in dry, stony places.

Reference to the problem of die-back or sudden death is quite frequent in the literature. Comments are made in the section dealing with daphne troubles.

We have mentioned the matter of pruning *D. cneorum* in the section on layering, but it will do no harm to emphasize that in the early stages of growth it is most important to prune back the young shoots in order to encourage the formation of a well-shaped plant which is not a perpetual straggler. Unfortunately, plants received from nurseries have not always been pinched back early enough, and one may be faced with a tufted walking-stick with which to cope. One method of doing this is to ask the supplier for a properly grown plant! Failing this, the offending specimen can be planted in a slight depression on the chosen site and the shoots at the tops of the bare stem splayed out and gently pegged down as for layering. The resultant growths can be pinched back again at a fairly early stage to encourage the development of a bushy plant. The depression can gradually be filled with handfuls of gritty, leafy soil, but care should be taken not to do this until the plant and its layers are well established.

Although most references give the date of introduction to Britain as 1752, *D. cneorum* was probably in cultivation before 1740, when the second edition of Philip Miller's *Gardeners' Dictionary* was published. He refers to it as *Thymelaea Alpina linifolia humilior, flora purpureo odoratissimo* and in part of the Addendum *A Catalogue of Ever-green Shrubs which will thrive in the open Air in England* calls it "The Cneorum of Matthiolus".

Since that date it appears to have been grown fairly widely, although never so abundantly as to be a market flower, for which purpose it was used during the sixteenth century in Austria, where it was very common in the mountains.

In nature it is widespread through much of Central and Southern Europe from N.W. Spain to S.W. Russia and varies quite considerably in habit and to a lesser degree in flower colour and size. Some variants are mentioned later, but the majority of plants nowadays in Britain appear to be the clone 'Eximia' selected by that great gardener A. T. Johnson, and well justifying the epithet *eximia* (meaning beautiful).

The derivation of the name *cneorum* has been the subject of some debate. It comes from the Greek *kneoron* latinised to *cneorum*, but it is uncertain what plant the Greeks had in mind, although the leaves apparently left a burning taste in the mouth and looked like those of wild olives. The "burning taste" suggests a *Daphne* species, perhaps *D. oleoides* or *D. gnidium*, which are likely to have been known at that time. An alternative theory that the name derives from the Cneori, a Roman tribe, seems less likely.

Pronunciation of *cneorum* sometimes causes problems; the "c" is normally silent, i.e. "neorum" not "sneeorum" or "kuh-neorum".

PROPAGATION
(a) Seed. Seldom produced (or at least recorded) in cultivation. Seed from the wild, sown late winter 1974, germinated in spring

1975 at Wisley, but it had been dried and only a few seedlings appeared. It seems probable that sowing soon after ripening is desirable if seed can be obtained, as Halda reports rapid loss of viability after seed has been gathered.

(b) Cuttings. This is the normal method for producing the more robust forms of *D. cneorum*. There appear to be at least two schools of thought over the optimum period for taking cuttings. One favours soft-struck cuttings taken very soon after flowering (or commercially from stock plants cut back and brought into growth in a cool greenhouse); the other prefers autumn-taken material with a heel, overwintered in a cutting frame and brought into warmth in early spring. There is some evidence that a high percentage rooting is obtained with soft cuttings, but they may be less easy to establish when first rooted and can easily be lost through incorrect watering. One report in the *Proceedings of the International Plant Propagators Society* states that it was found that semi-hardwood cuttings taken from plants grown under dry conditions rooted better than cuttings from plants given more water, whilst other growers prefer material taken from late July onwards which is relatively firm! Our own preference is for fairly soft cuttings 1—2½ in. long (with or without a heel) taken in June-July from open ground plants, and these will normally root within 6—8 weeks in a propagating frame. A double glazed cold-frame (polythene will do for the second layer) is suitable and if necessary the young plants can be retained in the frame, pinched back and foliar fed to obtain bushy, firm growth by autumn, before being potted on in the spring. Slightly firmer cuttings under mist root well, but require more attention immediately after rooting when losses can be heavy.

A great deal of accurate experimental work remains to be done before any firm recommendations are possible, but any of the above methods should produce the few plants normally required by most gardeners.

(c) Grafting. Usually unnecessary but sometimes useful for the slower-growing variants such as var. *pygmaea*, var. *verlotii* and the white-flowered and variegated-leaved forms. These will also root from cuttings but are normally more vigorous if grafted. Stocks include *D. mezereum*, *D. cneorum* itself and probably others such as *D. giraldii* and *D. longilobata* could be used if available.

(d) Layering. A very useful method of increasing *D. cneorum*.

TYPE LOCALITY "Switzerland, Hungary, Pyrenees".

DESCRIPTION Trailing (rarely suberect) evergreen shrub, much branched, often less than 30 (40) cm. in height and usually prostrate, reaching 2 m. across; young shoots green, finely pubescent; older branches greyish. Leaves alternate, fairly rigid, oblanceolate, obtuse to apiculate at the apex, tapered to the base, sessile; glabrous, dark green above, greyish below, densely clothing the stems, not just at the apex of the branches, 10—18 (—25) mm. long, (2—) 3—5 (—6) mm. wide. Flowers in dense terminal clusters of 6—10 (—20), very fragrant, pale to deep rose pink, occasionally white; tube 6—10 (—12) mm. long, very downy outside; lobes ovate-oblong, 4—7 mm. long. Fruit fleshy, brownish-yellow.

Daphne cneorum 'Eximia' (p. 87)   *Photo: D. F. Merrett*

Daphne cneorum var. *verlotii* (p. 90).

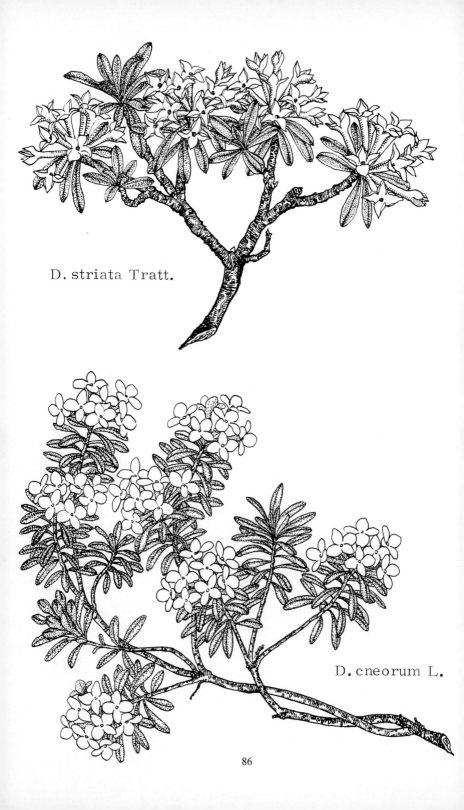

D. striata Tratt.

D. cneorum L.

CHROMOSOME NO. 2n=18.

FLOWERING PERIOD April—June, usually May in Britain. Occasionally again in autumn.

DISTRIBUTION Throughout C. Europe, from N.W. Spain east to Bulgaria and Ukraine.

HABITAT Very variable, on acid or alkaline soils, in sandy or rocky places, from sea level to 2,500 m.

As will be appreciated, considerable variation occurs throughout the range of the species which awaits thorough botanical investigation. A detailed and most useful ecological study of *D. cneorum* by G. Aymonin is to be found in *Revue Gén. Bot.* 66: 281-328 (1959).

ALBINOS

White forms both of typical *D. cneorum* and of var. *pygmaea* are known. There is some confusion over the use of the epithets *alba*, *flore-albo* (used by Loudon) and *albiflora*. Whichever is the earliest validly published epithet (as yet untraced by us) applied to albinos of *D. cneorum* it would seem suitable to apply the botanical rank *forma* to encompass these.

A white-flowered plant of *D. cneorum* received an A.M. in 1920 shown by Messrs. Tucker of Headingley, Oxford.

VARIEGATED-LEAVED FORMS

Probably clones, but at present it is impossible to determine their status or the accurate application of the names.

albo-variegata Hort. A variant with white-dotted leaves according to Halda. Not known to us.

argenteum Loddiges (Syn. *elegantissima* Hort.; *argenteo-marginata* Hort.) Leaves margined silvery-white.

variegata Knight (Syn. *aureo-marginata* Hort.; *luteum* Hort.; *foliis variegatis* Hort.; *foliis luteo* Hort.). Leaves margined yellow. Perfectly hardy. The clone in cultivation now has paler pink flowers than 'Eximia' but is fairly vigorous. There is a fine plant 3—4 ft. across in Mrs. Hodgkin's garden (1976).

NAMED CLONES

'Carminea'. A name used by Halda but possibly only loosely applied to slight colour variants.

'Eximia'.
ILLUSTRATIONS see p. 85; also *R.H.S. Journ.* 82: fig. 97 (1957) and 86: fig. 149 (1961).
AWARDS A.M. 1938; F.C.C. 1967.

As previously stated, the most widely grown and, in our view, the most satisfactory form for general garden cultivation.

A vigorous clone with leaves about 15 mm. long x 5 mm. wide and long trailing stems which should be pegged down and layered to maintain the plant in first class condition. The flowers are large, deep rose-pink in colour with tubes 7—12 mm. long and lobes 3— 4 mm. long. Seed is occasionally produced—see *R.H.S. Journal* 85: 396 (1960).

Similar forms occur in the Landes district of S.W. France, a lowland area close to sea-level where *D. cneorum* grows in damp, sandy soil with such companions as *Gentiana pneumonanthe*, pinguiculas and carex. It has been suggested that this area is possibly the source of 'Eximia', but we are never likely to solve this mystery. What we do know (from Eliot Hodgkin's correspondence) is that the late A. T. Johnson received a batch of plants of *D. cneorum* from Messrs. Stormonths of Carlisle in the 1930's and, when they flowered, picked out one with larger foliage and flowers he describes as ruby-crimson in his book *The Garden Today* (1938). His original plant reached six feet across without layering before it expired. He said that it was fully one third larger in all its parts than var. *major*, to which it is sometimes assigned.

Meadows, in the A.G.S. *Bulletin* (Vol. 36, p. 327), gives an interesting account of *D. cneorum* in the Spanish Pyrenees, with which he compares (in quality) 'Eximia'—to the latter's detriment. Comparison cannot be easy when there is only one of the contenders present, but these forms, as described, must be very much more compact in growth than 'Eximia' and more akin to var. *pygmaea* under which heading the matter is further discussed.

'Ruby Glow.'

A clone quite widely cultivated in U.S.A. We have no knowledge of its origin or any details of its garden performance.

BOTANICAL VARIANTS

In *Botanikai Kozlemenylek*, Vol. 10 (1911) Tuzson describes 9 forms of *D. cneorum* differing slightly from each other in leaf and flower dimensions. We refrain from including these names here, apart from forma *arbusculoides* which may be of interest.

forma *arbusculoides* Tuzson in *Bot. Koz.* 10: 51 (1911).

A variant of somewhat erect habit and leaves with a distinctly revolute margin. Occurs on acid soils in W. Hungary, S.E. Austria and N. Jugoslavia. Not known to be cultivated in Britain.

Other names which are applied to forms of *D. cneorum* in gardens include:—

var. *latifolia* Reichb.

This apparently differs only in the slightly wider leaves, and falls well within normal variation of the species.

forma *major* (Dippel) Schelle in *Beissn. et al. Handb. Laubh.-Ben* 356 (1903).

A name used to cover forms of more vigorous growth and larger flowers than "the type". 'Eximia' is sometimes referred here but it is not really possible to define the limits of f. *major* accurately.

var. *maximum* Jacques. (var. *grandiflorum* Lodd.; var. *pyramidale* Makoy; var. *stricta* Hort.).

A horticultural name applied to a hybrid of *D. collina* and *D. cneorum* raised by M. Jacques near Paris (date unknown; ? mid 19th century). As described by George Gordon in *The Garden* 9: 568 (1876) it appears distinct from *D.* x *napolitana* which is also thought to be of the same parentage. Further comments are made under *D.* x *napolitana*.

var. *pygmaea* Stoker in *New Flora and Sylva* 7: 275 (1935).
ILLUSTRATIONS *New Fl. and Sylva* 7: fig. 90 (1935); *R.H.S. Journ.* 85: fig. 124 (1960) as dwarf form.

The plant on which Fred Stoker based var. *pygmaea* was originally collected in the Venetian Alps at about 8,000 ft. and is basically smaller in all its parts than the type, as the name indicates. It differs also in its compact, prostrate habit and seldom attains more than 5—10 cm. in height. From the botanical viewpoint one would suspect that the dwarf forms from the Spanish Pyrenees and from the French and Swiss Jura might well fall within the aegis of var. *pygmaea*, judging from the descriptions given by Ruffier-Lanche, Meadows and others in the *A.G.S. Bulletin*.

Ruffier-Lanche, A.G.S. *Bull.* 26: 66 (1958), describes under his "third form" plants of low stature, (2—10 cm.) erect and slightly decumbent in habit (not sprawling), very slow growing, with leaves 6—8 mm. long and 3—4 mm. wide, and small, congested bright pink flowers. Apart from the length of leaf (11 mm., according to Stoker for var. *pygmaea*) there is no significant difference between them— and Meadows, A.G.S. *Bull.* 36: 328 (1968) describes plants from the Spanish Pyrenees which are scarcely separable. A good photograph of a plant from the Spanish Pyrenees appears on p. 332 of the same *Bulletin*.

It is worth noting here that there is an error in the localities given by Ruffier-Lanche for this form in his 1958 account (corrected in the 1959 *Bulletin*, Vol. 27, p. 156) but perpetuated by Meadows in 1968 (Vol. 36). The form from the "Préalpes" does *not* come from "Quéyras, Piedmont and possibly Bavaria" but from "Devoluy and Vercors to the French and Swiss Jura"—an important difference.

Obviously it is unwise to say at this stage that plants with this dwarf habit from these localities should be called var. *pygmaea*, as a very thorough study would be needed even to attempt to unravel the botanical status of the group. What does seem clear is that these dwarf Pyrenean forms are *not* referable to var. *verlotii*, although frequently confused with them. It seems possible that the confusion has arisen due to a belief that var. *verlotii* is a dwarf, compact plant—which is incorrect, although it is perhaps slow-growing compared with "typical" *D. cneorum.* Dr. Roger Smith refers plants growing in the Central Pyrenees near Gavarnie to var. *verlotii* and was taken to task for so doing by a correspondent—see A.G.S. *Bull.* 17: 155—156 (1949). Certainly most of the illustrations in the *Bulletin* attributed to *D. cneorum* var. *verlotii* appear much closer to var. *pygmaea* than to *verlotii*—see further under var. *verlotii* for the distinctive characters of this variety.

To add to the confusion there is a slow-growing, dwarf, white-flowered plant which is in gardens as "*D. cneorum alba*" or "*verlotii alba*" which is almost certainly an albino of var. *pygmaea.* Such albinos have been recorded from Switzerland and are distinct from other white-flowered forms of *D. cneorum* which occur occasionally in the wild and, although perhaps less vigorous in gardens than their pink-flowered brethren, are similar in growth and flower characters to the "type".

Whatever the botanical status of these dwarf variants, they make very fine plants for screes, raised beds, sinks and the alpine house, being quite hardy and not too difficult in a scree mixture with moisture-retentive, gritty compost beneath.

In the Alps Ruffier-Lanche says they are found in sub-alpine regions in cracks or humus-filled pockets of limestone rocks, whilst Meadows states that those in the Spanish Pyrenees grow in alpine pastures or with *Pinus uncinata* in what he believes to be decalcified soils.

The assertion in Meadows' account that some forms of *D. cneorum* dislike lime is debatable. Whilst some variants certainly are found mainly on non-calcareous soils in nature, it does not necessarily mean that they *dislike* lime and in cultivation may well tolerate alkalinity. Very probably it is more complicated than simply lime versus no lime, with other ecological factors coming into play. Again only study of *D. cneorum* throughout its range is likely to provide answers to the problems.

var. *verlotii* (Gren. et Godr.) Meissn. in *DC. Prodr.* 14; 533 (1857).

SYNONYMS   *D. verlotii* Gren. & Godr.; *D. farreri* Hort. (nomen nudum).

ILLUSTRATIONS Photo p. 85; also Bonnier, *Fl. Compl. Fr., Suisse, Belg.* 9: 104. (1927).

AWARD   A.M. (1916).

A sub-montane form of *D. cneorum* up to about 1,000 m. which is only definitely recorded to our knowledge from St. Eynard near Grenoble in the Dauphine with a dwarf variant (forma *humifusa*) from Rozans in the Hautes-Alpes. Records for Bavaria and elsewhere by Hegi and others are doubtful judging by the descriptions

Daphne juliae (p. 93) a species related to *D. cneorum*   *Photo: R. Elliott*

Daphne collina (p. 94).   *Photo: R. Elliott*

Daphne x *burkwoodii* 'Somerset' (p. 74)   *Daphne mezereum* (p. 129)
Photos: G. S. Thomas

given. So too are those from the French and Spanish Pyrenees which differ in habit, leaf shape and flower characters from var. *verlotii*.

It is similar to "typical" *D. cneorum*, having a rather open habit, spreading thin branches, and forming patches 2 ft. or so across. The basic differences are in the very much narrower leaves, which are linear-lanceolate in shape, acute and mucronate, 15—25 mm. long x 2—3 mm. wide; and in the narrower, linear-lanceolate (not ovate-oblong) perianth lobes 5—7 mm. long and the more slender perianth tube which is 8—12 mm. long. Eliot Hodgkin in a note on this variant (A.G.S. *Bull.* 25: 319 (1957)) says that the perianth ("calyx") is bright pink throughout whereas in *D. cneorum* the underpart (i.e. tube) is a deeper shade than the upper (i.e. lobes).

Ruffier-Lanche says "vivid pink, becoming paler with age" and flowering later: also that it withstands full sun and extreme dryness at the roots but is cut back in very severe cold weather. In Britain it is less vigorous than 'Eximia' but seems hardy enough in both acid and alkaline conditions. In nature it occurs on calcareous soils amongst scattered pines growing with box, genistas and coronillas.

var. *verlotii* (Gren. et Godr.) Meissn. forma *humifusa* (Verl. et Paz). Keissl. in *Engl. Bot. Jahrb.* xxv, 77 (1898).

Known only from Rozans in the Hautes-Alpes and distinguished by its creeping, thread-like stems and more compact growth. Not known to us from living material. It seems possible that confusion of the dwarf Pyrenean forms of *D. cneorum* with var. *verlotii* could be due to a belief that as they were similar in habit to forma *humifusa* they could be a variation on the same theme.

Related Species

D. juliae Kos.-Pol. in *Not. Syst. Herb. Petrop.* 2: 141 (1921).

ILLUSTRATION   See page 91.

This is a semi-erect plant from the Voronezh District of Russia, best treated as a variant of *D. cneorum*. There seem to be some marked differences of opinion about this plant, and it is possible that it is either very variable and several different forms have been introduced, or there have been mistakes in the identification of cultivated plants. J. Halda notes that the *D. juliae* which he grows is very like *D. cneorum* except for the flower colour which is wine-red.

Plants of *D. juliae* were received by Wisley and by Eliot Hodgkin from the Moscow Botanic Garden in 1960 and one of these grown by E. B. Anderson reached three feet across. A specimen obtained from Hugo Money-Coutts, who introduced this species in 1959 from seed collected at Voronezh, was planted in a chalky soil at Findon in Sussex, and in ten years grew into a dense pudding-bowl shape only 18 in. across and about the same in height, a most handsome small shrub. The flowers and leaves were like an average *D. cneorum* in colour and dimensions. Unfortunately this specimen suddenly collapsed in 1973 when in apparently perfect health, and the cuttings taken from the dying plant did not root.

In the author's original description he differentiates *D. juliae* from *D. cneorum* by the following characters.

D. JULIAE	D. CNEORUM	OUR COMMENTS
5—15 cm. high	30—40 cm. high	Over its range *D. cneorum* varies from 5—40 cm.
Leaves deciduous, narrower and clustered at the tips of the branches	Leaves evergreen, less elongated and spread along the branches	*D. juliae* in cultivation has proved evergreen. The leaves are wider than those of var. *verlotii*.
Inflorescence 15—25 flowered	Inflorescence 5—8 flowered	Inflorescence can be up to 20-flowered, perhaps more in some forms.
Bracts of inflorescence few	Bracts of inflorescence numerous forming a dense involucre	Some variation occurs over the range.
Ovary distinctly pedicellate	Ovary sessile	—

As will be seen, the distinctions are open to question, and it is arguable that *D. juliae* is only a geographical form of *D. cneorum*. *Flora Europaea* 2: 258 (1968) includes it under that species without comment.

It is, however, a most interesting plant found in a very restricted area near Voronezh on the mid-Russian plateau growing on open slopes in lime-rubble or lime-rich humus a few hundred feet above sea-level. As it is reasonably amenable to cultivation it is certainly worth growing in situations similar to those suggested for *D. cneorum* itself.

Daphne collina Dickson ex J. E. Smith, *Spicilegium Botanicum* 2: 16, t. 18 (1792).

SYNONYM   *D. australis* Cyr.

ILLUSTRATIONS   See colour plate opposite p. 31; drawing on p. 164; illustration p. 92; also *Bot. Mag.* t. 428 (1798).

AWARDS   A.M. 1938.

Although for botanical purposes *D. collina*, the Neapolitan Mezereon, is, in our view, best merged with *D. sericea*, it is described separately here as it is so well-known to horticulturists. Until a full-scale revision of the genus is carried out it seems wise to maintain the *status quo* rather than cause confusion amongst gardeners by sinking such a well-known name without very thorough research. It is perhaps worth pointing out that since confusion between *D. collina* and *D. sericea* has occurred ever since their introduction, it is inevitable that discrepancies are to be found in horticultural literature on details of cultivation.

D. collina is one of the finest of dwarf shrubs, and given full exposure to sun and a well-drained soil which does not dry out, it will thrive for many years in acid, neutral or alkaline soils. It is sometimes stated to prefer alkaline conditions but there are old plants on the rock garden at Wisley growing perfectly well in acid conditions, and it is our view that impeded drainage or drought are more probable causes of failure with *D. collina* (and many other daphnes) than soil pH. In nature *D. collina* apparently occurs in open rocky situations on limestone formations where there is sharp drainage and where the roots can penetrate deeply into cool, moist soil below. Similar positions in the garden should be provided if at all possible, and this may well minimise the dieback of odd branches which is one of the annoying habits attributed to *D. collina*. Doubts are also cast about the hardiness of *D. collina*, which we find has survived the coldest of British winters with little more than a browning of the foliage. Dr. Wacher records plants of this species withstanding temperatures down to 6°F during the 1947 winter in Kent, and the 1962-3 winter left plants of *D. collina* at Wisley quite unperturbed by its ferocity.

D. collina is represented in gardens by a single clone or possibly a few very similar clones. Its compact, broadly dome-shaped habit and closely-set branches densely clothed with neat, shining evergreen leaves make it attractive at any season but it is in April and May when the terminal clusters of intensely fragrant, deep purplish-rose blooms appear that its full value may be appreciated. It is usually to be seen as a small, rounded bush a foot or so in height and as much across, flowering freely from an early age when a mere stripling of a few inches, but occasionally reaching 5-6 ft. across.

As a guide to its normal dimensions a specimen of *D. collina*, purchased and planted by Eliot Hodgkin in 1949, is now some 3 feet across and 2 feet high and still (1976) in excellent condition.

It is said to have been in cultivation by 1752 and in the *Gardeners Chronicle* for 1880 is described as a "fine old-fashioned shrub". There appears, however, to be some confusion over its date of introduction. Aiton (*Hortus Kewensis* 2nd Ed. 1811) states that it was in cultivation by 1752 at the Chelsea Physic Garden, but Miller then curator, gives no description which matches *D. collina* accurately in the 1759 edition of his Gardeners Dictionary. Smith in his original description (1792) equates his *D. collina* with the *Chamelaea alpina incana* of Lobel and Bauhin's *Chamelaea alpina, folio inferne incana*, whilst Lobel's plant according to Parkinson (1629) is an evergreen with blush flowers.

95

Linnaeus, however, refers both to his *D. alpina* which is deciduous and the description of Miller's Daphne No. 5 (1759) is obviously derived directly from Linnaeus. It seems, therefore, that Aiton may have accepted Smith's *D. collina* and Miller's Daphne No. 5, as the same species in view of the references to Lobel and Bauhin quoted by both, but ignored Linnaeus' reference—hence his earlier introduction date. A tangled skein indeed! Smith states that his figure of *D. collina* was drawn from a specimen (provided by Aiton) grown at Kew where it had been sent from Italy by a Mr. D. Graeffer. According to the *Botanical Magazine* (1798) and *Botanical Cabinet* (1828) accounts, this same gentleman located *D. collina* with J. R. Smith in 1877 near Caserta and sent seeds to Messrs. Lewis & Mackie of Kingsland, Herefordshire who apparently first marketed it commercially.

References by Bean (1st Ed. 1914; 8th Ed. 1973) to the date of introduction as 1752 apply to plants growing at the Chelsea Physic Garden by that date and their origin is now lost in the mists of time. Whether or not they correspond to *D. collina* as we know it today is impossible to say, but in 1798 William Curtis (*Bot. Mag*. t. 428) states "it is usual to treat it as a greenhouse plant; in mild winters it will bear to stand abroad" which suggests that our garden plant is perhaps of different origin being considerably hardier than the plants known to Curtis.

As yet we have not been able to trace the origin of *D. collina* (as grown today) further, but this example shows very well the complex history of some of the plants we grow and perhaps helps to explain certain of the difficulties experienced by taxonomists attempting to deal with cultivated plants.

PROPAGATION

(a) Seed. In Britain records of *D. collina* producing seed are few. Will Ingwersen mentions that it occasionally produces seeds which germinate successfully; and Josef Halda has found that seeds germinated freely, but does not record the abundance or frequency of fruiting in Czechoslovakia.

(b) Cuttings. For the amateur, the most satisfactory method of increasing *D. collina*. Soft cuttings taken both with or without a heel (Group 1, p. 41) in July 1975 rooted within 4 weeks in a closed case at Wisley, and later-struck, half-ripe stem cuttings (Group 2) have been equally successful. The use of bottom heat is sometimes said to be advantageous but no comparative data are available to support this statement although one would expect more rapid rooting to occur.

(c) Grafting. Often used by nurserymen to produce a saleable plant more quickly, but unnecessary for amateurs. Stock of an evergreen species (*D. pontica, D. laureola*) is perhaps preferable but *D. mezereum*, and probably other species, have been used successfully. Splice (side) grafting proves quite satisfactory.

TYPE LOCALITY   Italy, hills near Naples.

DESCRIPTION   Densely branched, compact, erect evergreen shrub sometimes reaching 60 cm. in height and 180 cm. across, but usually much less; young branches brown, pubescent. Leaves alternate, shiny green, leathery, more or less glabrous above, paler green and silky-pubescent beneath; shortly stalked, obovate, rather rounded at the apex, tapered at the base, 2—4 cm. long, 0.6—1.3 cm. wide. Flowers deep purplish-rose, very fragrant, in terminal clusters of 5—15; tube 8 mm. long, densely silky outside; lobes broadly elliptic, obtuse, 4 mm. long, 3 mm. wide. Fruit fleshy, orange-red. (Description based on the plant in cultivation as *D. collina*.)

CHROMOSOME NO.   Not recorded.

FLOWERING PERIOD   April—May and occasionally autumn in cultivation; March—April in the type locality.

DISTRIBUTION   S. Italy, especially in the Naples area, "hills and fields by the banks of the Vulturnus". Records from Sicily, Crete and other areas of the Mediterranean apparently refer to *D. sericea*.
HABITAT   In rocky places and in maquis; 0—1500 m. altitude.

The taxonomic status of *D. collina* and the closely related *D. sericea* has been the subject of much debate. In *Flora Europaea* (Vol. 2, p. 258) *D. collina* is united with *D. sericea* under the latter, earlier published, name. Botanically this would appear a sensible conclusion as, although the extremes are easily separable, they are linked by a complete range of intermediates and it is not possible to distinguish the two satisfactorily as species.

As known in gardens, however, they appear distinct, *D. collina* usually being more compact in habit than *D. sericea*, with wider and less pointed leaves which are more densely hairy beneath, and up to 15 flowers in each inflorescence compared with up to 8 flowers for *D. sericea*.

These distinctions are found to be unreliable when one examines a wide range of material from Turkey, Crete and Italy and this view is supported by Money-Coutts who visited the type locality of *D. collina* in 1962. He found it growing on Monte Argentario (at 450 m. approx.); on high wooded ground (about 300 m.) north-east of Talamone as far as Albarese; and in one area by the mouth of the canal at Albarese at only 3 m. above sea level. Some of the plants at this latter site were over 5 ft. high. Money-Coutts considered the plants to be more like *D. sericea* as he knew it in cultivation than *D. collina*.

Present evidence suggests that *D. collina*, as grown in our gardens, is a form—possibly no more than a horticultural clone—of *D. sericea*. Even at the time the *Botanical Magazine* plate of 1797 was published there was apparently some confusion as Curtis, only five years after Smith described *D. collina*, points out that the cultivated plant did not "answer to the description of authors" who referred to the grey undersurface of the leaves, apparently lacking in the plant known to him. Small wonder that arguments still occur as to the status of *D. collina* taxonomically!

97

Daphne genkwa Sieb. and Zucc., *Fl. Jap.* 1: 137, t. 75 (1840).

SYNONYMS *D. fortuni* Lindl.; *Wikstroemia genkwa* (Sieb. and Zucc.) Domke.

ILLUSTRATIONS See colour plate opposite p. 31; drawing on p. 109; also *Bot. Mag.* 173, t. 360 (1957).

AWARD F.C.C. (1885).

There can be no more tantalising member of the genus than *D. genkwa*, unique among cultivated daphnes in its soft lilac flowers borne on bare, twiggy branches, usually during April and May. The literature is full of contradictory statements on how best to grow and propagate it, but in spite of the interest and enthusiasm it arouses, very few gardeners report continued success in its cultivation.

Its history in gardens is a long one. Robert Fortune is credited with its introduction from China in 1844, finding it first "in a nursery garden near Shanghae" but later seeing many plants wild in the province of Chekiang. This particular introduction first flowered in Britain in 1846 and was described as *D. fortuni* by Dr. Lindley in 1844, but does not in fact appear to be a distinct species, falling within the variation of *D. genkwa* which occurs over its range.

This species has been cultivated in Japan for a very long time and is often stated to be native to that country, although it has not been found wild outside China, Formosa and possibly S. Korea. The following extract from E. H. Wilson's *A Naturalist in Western China* Vol. I: 17-18 (1913) seems worth quoting here as it provides very useful information about *D. genkwa* in the wild.

"However, it is not to these low hills that we look for the floral wealth of Ichang, but to the limestone cliffs of the glens and gorges. Here the variety is astonishing, a striking feature being the quantity of well-known flowering shrubs.

"The two first shrubs to flower in the early spring are *Daphne genkwa* and *Coriaria nepalensis*. It is a thousand pities we cannot succeed with the Daphne in England, since it is such a lovely plant—by far the finest species of the genus. Here, at Ichang, it grows everywhere, on the bare exposed hills, amongst conglomerate rock and limestone boulders, on graves, and amongst the stones which are piled around the tiny cultivated plots in the gorge, sometimes in partial shade, but more usually fully exposed to the scorching sun. The plants are, on the average, about 2 feet in height, and are but seldom branched. Imagine the annual suckers from a Plum tree and you have the appearance of these Daphne plants. For two-thirds of their height they are so densely clad with flowers that they look like one large thyrse. The colour is lilac, often very dark; but a white form is not uncommon. Its outward resemblance to Lilac leads to its being so called by the foreign residents at Ichang."

The first introduction by Fortune apparently died out, but further introductions were made in 1866 (according to the *Gardeners Chronicle* from gardens in Russia) and by Charles Maries for Messrs. Veitch in 1878 from between Chin-Kiang and Kui-Kiang with the additional bonus of seed of a white-flowered form from the Lu-Shan Mts. Sadly it seems that both the lilac and white forms introduced gradually died out. Maries' account bears repeating here and is interesting in providing details of *D. genkwa* as it was cultivated in China at the time.

"My object in visiting Ningpo", he wrote, "was to find a "Lilac" I had heard about. It was said to be in a certain garden easily found; I knew the owner of the garden and obtained permission to take any plant I found there. I searched in vain, however, and therefore made up my mind to start at once for the Snowy Valley, some sixty miles up the Ningpo river . . . I found the natives here rather troublesome, so I determined to try another place in order to get up to the hills (i.e. Ning-cum-jow) . . . I did not find the "Lilac" or anything new to me here after searching the hills several days, so I returned to Ningpo and Shanghai.

"I now prepared to go to Japan, and as the steamer was leaving the following day, I went to get my ticket. As I came out of the office I was struck by seeing a bunch of lilac flowers in a native's hand on the opposite side of the road; it appeared to be a Persian Lilac. I asked him where it grew, and he said in his garden. I asked him for a flower, and he gave me the lot. Then I found to my inexpressible delight that it was the very "Lilac" for which I had been looking. I went with the man to his garden, or rather small nursery, in the midst of some rice fields, and there I saw about 160 large bushes of my "Lilac" in full flower—a perfect mass intermixed with young purplish leaves. I found it was not a Lilac but a Daphne. The flowers issue from every joint in bunches on shoots two-and-a-half feet long. I have seen flowers from the ground to the top bud, like a stick bound round with Lilac. It is in bloom from the latter end of March till May, and I think when properly understood and acclimatized in England it will prove a valuable plant for forcing. It thrives only in yellow loam and leaf-mould; the Japanese variety, I afterwards found, is not so particular as to soil, but the flower is inferior . . . I returned to the hotel at Shanghai with a lot of the "Lilac"—perfectly happy now I had found the very plant I came from England to discover."

Later Maries found it growing wild as outlined previously.

Most of the recent introductions have been from Japan, where it apparently is grown in some quantity, although unfortunately we have no information at present as to the methods of propagation and culture used. Strong young plants are occasionally imported

99

into Britain but few growers appear to be able to provide the conditions *D. genkwa* requires—perhaps due to the variety of advice available, much of it directly conflicting!

Dr. Amsler suggested a shady, sheltered lime-free position well supplied with peat or good leafmould; Sir Frederick Stern stated that it grew better in an alkaline soil in some shade; Professor Lyttel preferred a neutral loam; whilst at Glasnevin we are back to an acid soil once more!

Again some of the difficulties of cultivation are attributed to whether a plant is grafted or not, but there is no agreement on this and it seems quite probable that the explanation for the generally poor behaviour of *D. genkwa* in Britain is due to climatic rather than soil conditions. One has only to read the accounts by E. H. Wilson of *D. genkwa* in the wild to realise that the hot, bare exposed limestone and conglomerate hillsides are the lot of this lovely species in some areas of China. Like most daphnes it presumably pushes its roots well down into cool soil below and in summer must be subjected to intense heat resulting in very well-ripened wood. Bean (1973) provides information that *D. genkwa* often grows at the edge of rice fields in China which would suggest moister conditions than is recorded by Fortune, Maries or Wilson. There is also the suggestion that the reason for failure in this country is not tenderness, but lack of summer heat and sun. Certainly this explanation would agree with what is known of its natural conditions, and although our own experience of cultivating *D. genkwa* is limited, it would seem reasonable to provide a well-drained but moisture-retentive soil in an open position in full sun, with the addition of a few small pieces of limestone around the roots to slow down the soil moisture loss in very hot weather. Alternatively, a tufa wall or the top of a retaining wall with moisture-retentive soil behind, again in full sun, might well provide the formula for success.

It is perhaps worth noting that Halda states that *D. genkwa* grows in dry forests and forest steppes, but we can find no confirmation of this habitat.

Sometimes it is considered that there are at least two forms in cultivation, one hardier and easier to grow than the other. The famous plant in the New York Botanic Garden (now (1976) lost, we understand from the Director of that Garden) was reputedly of the hardier type and in 1962 had reached 10 feet in diameter with over 30 stems! It had then endured thirty or so winters with sub-zero temperatures unharmed, but although plants propagated from this source are in cultivation in Britain they appear to fare no better than other introductions. *D. genkwa* varies considerably in flower and leaf size as will be seen from the measurements given in the description; the New York plant represented the upper size limits of these measurements and matches well in this respect with material in the Kew Herbarium sent by Veitch in 1879, reputedly from Japan, and possibly from the Maries introduction of 1878.

It is also occasionally stated that one form (apparently Japanese), apart from being less hardy, is of more untidy growth with long, slender branches as opposed to the more compact, hardier entity. Comparison of plants of the two "forms" in similar conditions would seem the only way to confirm the claims, as both habit and hardiness are characters which could be affected by conditions of cultivation.

Not all is failure. Both E. B. Anderson and Eliot Hodgkin grew *D. genkwa* outside for a number of years. Apparently the plants were derived from that growing in the New York Botanic Garden and Eliot Hodgkin records growing his plant outside for 7 or 8 years, finding it hardy as part of that period included the severe 1962-3 winter.

Even in the positions suggested above, there is the possibility that the flower buds, which are well-formed very early in the year, may be frosted, particularly in a "stop—go" winter of alternating mild and severe spells.

Cool greenhouse treatment either planted out or grown as a pot plant may then be the answer, and certainly there are records of success with *D. genkwa* under glass.

Herbert Whitley in his famous collection near Paignton grew this species in a cold greenhouse whilst Roy Elliott succeeded with it protected by a scree frame for a number of years, in full sun and a slightly limy soil. In addition, it has been grown as an alpine house plant using "long tom" pots and providing that most difficult of all composts to prepare—the well drained and yet moisture-retentive medium. As will be appreciated from previous comments, it is essential that the plants are not allowed to dry out, and yet stagnant moisture at the roots could be death.

PROPAGATION

(a) Seed. Would that seed were available!

Only one record is known to us of seed being produced in this country on a plant grown by Albert Burkwood. He had two plants, one with much broader leaves than the other, growing in a border(!) and fruits (pearly white) were produced by one of the plants in 1912. He states (in correspondence with the R.H.S.) that the seeds germinated readily but seedlings were subsequently lost.

Burkwood suggested that a possible reason for lack of fruit-set on cultivated plants was that the majority of plants of *D. genkwa* grown tended to be "male" as he had made literally hundreds of crosses with no results, even having tried to self-set them! Curiously, Halda states that seeds germinate readily and begin to flower in the third year—but he also says that the fruits are red, which does not agree with either Burkwood's comments or *Plantae Wilsonianae*, (Wilson No. 19 from Ichang) where the specimens are described as white-fruited.

(b) Cuttings. Considerable success has been reported in rooting soft cuttings just beginning to firm at the base (see Group 1, p. 41), but it appears that they are by no means easy to grow on, hence the scarcity of plants in cultivation.

We have rooted soft heel cuttings 1—3 inches long under mist in a closed case (1975), and these have been potted (1976) and are growing well. Barry Starling has found that soft cuttings rooted readily under mist and in a propagating case, but that all died as soon as they were removed from the propagating environment. In view of the difficulties experienced in potting up the cuttings he suggests rooting individual cuttings in separate pots and careful weaning. On the other hand, Hugo Money-Coutts found that cuttings rooted very easily under mist at most periods of spring and summer and could put on up to $1\frac{1}{2}$ ft. in the first year!

At the New York Botanic Garden the most satisfactory results were obtained with cuttings rooted in double pots with a 75% rooting within 2—3 months of insertion. No comment on their subsequent treatment is made.

Arthur Carter has found that cuttings taken in early August rooted under mist (with bottom heat) quickly, roots appearing through the bottom of the cutting pots 4 weeks after insertion.

The rooted cuttings were potted off in spring when growth was just beginning.

Obviously considerable experimental work is required to perfect the methods so far tried.

(c) Root cuttings. The method of increase almost always recommended. (See p. 44).

(d) Grafting. *D. genkwa* can be increased successfully by grafting on to *D. mezereum*, *D. longilobata*, *D. giraldii* and possibly other stocks. Splice (side) grafting or saddle grafting techniques may be used, depending on the thickness of the stock and scion-wood available.

TYPE LOCALITY The type material was from plants cultivated in Japan.

DESCRIPTION Erect, slender, deciduous shrub up to 1.5 m. in height, young branches pubescent, at first green then chestnut brown; older bark glabrescent or glabrous, dark purplish-brown. Leaves with a distinct petiole, mostly opposite, but some alternate, 2.5—6.5 cm. long, 1.3—2.5 cm. wide, ovate to lanceolate, acute, rounded to cuneate at the base, pubescent on both sides, purplish when young, dark green above, paler below. Flowers carried on bare stems before the leaves are produced, in (usually) opposite, axillary, stalked clusters of 2—7, lilac (or white), fragrance variable, usually only slight; tube 8—10 mm. long, silky-hairy on the outside; lobes broadly ovate or obovate, rounded, wavy-margined, 3—9 mm. long, 3—5 mm. wide. Ovary silky-hairy to glabrous. Fruit rarely seen in cultivation, white (E. H. Wilson No. 19 from Ichang, W. Hupeh).

CHROMOSOME NO. n=9.

FLOWERING PERIOD (March) April—May. (February—April in a cool greenhouse).

DISTRIBUTION China: North and Central Provinces, Formosa (Taiwan). (Cultivated in, but apparently not native to, Japan; possibly native also to S. Korea according to Hamaya).

HABITAT Grassy hills and plains; often near ditches, below 1000 m.; and (*vide* E. H. Wilson) amongst conglomerate and limestone rocks exposed to full sun or in slight shade, 300—1000 m.

As will have been realised from previous comments, *D. genkwa* is somewhat variable in flower colour and size as well as other botanical characters.

Lindley's *D. fortuni* (not "*fortunei*"), first described in *Journ. Hort. Soc. London* Vol. 1; 147 (1846) cannot be differentiated even at varietal rank, as the variations in leaf-shape, ovary and other flower characters which have been suggested as distinctive cannot be correlated satisfactorily even geographically.

D. taitoensis Hayata from Formosa and Taitung, regarded by the author as distinct from *D. genkwa* in the shape of calyx-lobes and leaves, was reduced to *D. genkwa* forma *taitoensis* (Hayata) Hamaya in *Journ. Jap. Bot.* 30, 329 (1955). In view of the natural variation within the range of *D. genkwa*, it is doubtful whether even this rank is worth recognition.

Halda mentions a white form ("alba" Hort.) and a "coerulea" Hort. (presumably blue rather than lilac) but we have seen neither variant and can trace no valid publication of the names.

The specific epithet *genkwa* is derived from one of the Japanese names for the shrub and in that country the bark is, according to Fortune, used to "produce blisters on the skin particularly in cases of rheumatism". Exactly how this helps the sufferer is not recorded, but both bark and leaves of *D. genkwa* are poisonous taken internally—caution is therefore advised!

Some authorities consider *D. genkwa* to be anomalous within the genus in view of its (often) opposite leaves and other floral characters and it has been transferred to the related genus *Wikstroemia*. It is certainly an oddity compared to most other daphnes, but the grounds for this transference have not been generally accepted by botanists such as Rehder.

Related Species

Related, but not known to be in cultivation in Britain, is *D. championii* Benth. in *Fl. Hongkong* 296 (1861) (syn. *D. fortunei* Benth.). In overall appearance it is similar to *D. genkwa* but the leaves are usually alternate, rather than opposite, and the flowers white with smaller flowers (tube 5—7 mm. long; lobes 1—2 mm. long). If brought into cultivation it is likely to require cool greenhouse culture.

Daphne giraldii Nitsche in *Beitr. Kenntn. Gatt. Daphne* (*Diss.*) 7 (1907).

SYNONYM. *D. tangutica* Pritz. non Maxim.

ILLUSTRATIONS *Bot. Mag.* t. 8732 (1917); *R.H.S. Journal* 86, f. 148 (1961).

Curiously, the Chinese *D. giraldii*, one of the most attractive and one of the easiest of daphnes to grow, is thoroughly neglected in gardens. It is a first-rate small shrub and certainly the best of the yellow-flowered species available to us for general garden use, proving quite hardy in Britain (and also in central Europe) and showing no marked preference for any particular soil. Bean (1973) states that it is difficult to cultivate successfully, but in our own experience it has grown perfectly well in hot, sunny, chalky conditions on the South Downs; in heavy neutral soil in Surrey in fairly heavy shade; and in acid, sandy soil at Wisley—a plant of catholic tastes. Yet, in spite of the ease with which *D. giraldii* is raised from seed, it is rarely offered by nurseries and seldom seen in gardens. Fragrant yellow clusters of bloom are freely produced during May and June in cultivation, and are followed by small bunches of red, egg-shaped fruits in most seasons.

Its habit of growth is rather similar to that of *D. mezereum*, a mature plant having compact but fairly upright growth and being slightly taller than wide, eventually reaching three to four feet in height.

We owe the introduction to British gardens of *D. giraldii* to the great firm of Veitch & Sons, whose collector William Purdom sent back seed from Western Kansu, China in 1911, and the stock now in cultivation is probably descended from this collection. The *Botanical Magazine* plate of 1917 was drawn from a plant growing at Wakehurst Place in Sussex obtained from Veitch in 1913 and first flowered in 1916 having formed a bush "two and a half feet high with a crown four feet in circumference" in about five years from seed, a useful indication of its rate of growth.

Halda recommends the use of *D. giraldii* as a stock for grafting, as he has found that scions of several daphnes unite readily with stock of this species, possibly due to a more plentiful sap flow, even during the dormant season, than occurs with *D. mezereum* and other species commonly used as stocks. He has found that in terms of compatibility and the successful growth of the grafted species afterwards, it is superior to other stocks tried for grafting *D. arbuscula*.

PROPAGATION

(a) Seed. As has already been stated fruit is freely produced in cultivation and in our experience the seed must be sown as soon as possible after the fruit ripens to obtain maximum germination. Older seed has proved less satisfactory and germination appears to be considerably reduced if sowing is delayed unless the seed has been stored under cool conditions. Fresh seed sown in August-September will normally germinate the following spring and the resultant plants should flower in their fourth or fifth season given reasonable growing conditions.

(b) Cuttings. If seed is not available, soft or half-ripe cuttings (Groups 1 and 2, p. 41) are said to root satisfactorily, but we have not used this method ourselves.

(c) Grafting is a practical possibility, but unnecessary.

TYPE LOCALITY China: N. Shensi, Mt. Tue-lian-pu.
DESCRIPTION Erect, quite glabrous, deciduous shrub up to 1.2 m. in height, but usually about 60 cm. high in cultivation and rather less in breadth. Branches greyish-brown, younger growths reddish-brown. Leaves alternate, clustered towards the tips of the branches, pale, slightly glaucous green, sessile, narrowly oblanceolate, obtuse to subacute, sometimes apiculate, 3.5—6 cm. long, 0.6—1 cm. wide. Flowers ebracteate, yellow, occasionally purple-tinged in bud, in terminal clusters of 4—8, fragrant; tube 7—9 mm. long; lobes 4 mm. long, ovate. Fruit fleshy, ovoid, c. 6 mm. diameter, red.
CHROMOSOME NO. n=9
FLOWERING PERIOD May—July.
DISTRIBUTION China: W. Kansu and N. Shensi.
HABITAT Near streams in forests; 3000—3500 m.

Daphne giraldii has been collected on relatively few occasions and was first located in 1894 by Père Giraldi, after whom it is named, on Mt. Tue-lian-pu in Northern Shensi. A few years after it was described, Purdom collected it in 1911 at elevations of about 2,700 metres on mountains west of the Tow River in Western Kansu, and as far as is known our cultivated stock derives from his seed.

As we know it *D. giraldii* is remarkably uniform, showing little variation either in the herbarium or as living plants. Its closest relatives appear to be the species grouped round *D. alpina* which basically differ in having white, hairy flowers as opposed to the yellow, glabrous blooms of *D. giraldii*, and in their more northerly and westerly areas of distribution.

Daphne glomerata Lam. *Encyc.* 3:438 (1791)

SYNONYMS *D. imerica* C. Koch; *D. comosa* Adam.
ILLUSTRATION See drawing on p. 110; also R.H.S. *Journal* 91: fig. 202 (1966).
AWARD A.M. (1938).

D. glomerata is one of the finest species within the genus, but is still little known in gardens, which is a pity as it is one of the most exciting of all dwarf shrubs. Imagine an evergreen but slightly more compact *D. blagayana* (but even more beautiful—praise indeed!) forming clumps a yard or so across and no more than six or so inches high crammed during early summer with large, sweetly-scented, creamy-white flower heads! This is *D. glomerata* as it occurs in N.E. Turkey, rambling through leafy soil amongst thickets of the Pontic azalea.

Sadly its performance in cultivation in Britain has so far been relatively disappointing, and there are few good specimens to be seen in our gardens today. The original introduction must be credited to Dr. Jenkin who collected it in company with Dr. Giuseppi in 1935 in pine woodland close to the Baksan river near Adyl Su in the Caucasus. Jenkin grew it very successfully in his Hindhead garden, as did A. G. Weeks in his marvellous peat beds at Limpsfield, both providing slightly shaded conditions in loose, leafy acid soil akin to that of its natural habitat. Jenkin considered it an easy species to grow in cool, moist, peaty or leafy soil, although he found that grafted plants were miffy, the stock perhaps inhibiting the plants' natural habit of suckering.

Further material of *D. glomerata* (M. & T. 4356) was introduced in 1965 by the Mathew and Tomlinson expedition from the Zigana Pass in Turkey. The climate there is a cool damp one, the snow not leaving until May and the hills are often covered with low clouds, so it is likely that *D. glomerata* could grow well in some areas of Ireland or Scotland where parallel conditions occur. John Tomlinson grew plants from this introduction very well in his garden at Weybridge, planted in a cool peaty soil along with *Erythronium*, *Jeffersonia*, *Hacquetia* and *Ramonda* and after a year the daphne was sending out suckers quite freely and promised to make a good clump. It was probably one of "Tom's" most notable successes in cultivating difficult plants, and it is sad that he did not live to see the results of his efforts in collecting and growing this fine species.

Plants raised from seed of the Albury, Cheese and Watson expedition (A.C.W. 2390) from the Pontic Alps are in cultivation, and Eliot Hodgkin on two occasions obtained material of *D. glomerata* from the Moscow Botanic Garden. A fine plant raised from seed in 1962 is still (1976) growing in Mrs. Hodgkin's garden in partial shade in gritty, leafy soil which is slightly alkaline in reaction. It may therefore be tolerant of some lime in the soil, but is certainly more at home as may be deduced from the examples quoted above if given a cool, moist root run in slight shade—similar conditions to those in which many dwarf rhododendrons and such plants as *Sanguinaria* and *Uvularia* thrive.

PROPAGATION

(a) Seed. Halda states "easily raised from seed", and certainly the seed of the Mathew-Tomlinson and A.C.W. introductions cited above germinated readily. We have not ourselves raised *D. glomerata* from seed but in its natural habitat the seed undergoes a period of freezing and we would suggest the normal technique summarised on p. 22. We have traced no records of the period between germination and the advent of flowering.

(b) Cuttings. Propagation by cuttings of "young shoots" is stated by Halda to be relatively easy. Insufficient material has been available for us to make any useful comments as to the best type of cutting or optimum time for taking cuttings: probably Gp. 1, p. 41.

(c) Layering. With an established plant, this is the most satisfactory method.

TYPE LOCALITY "Levant".

DESCRIPTION More or less prostrate, suckering, glabrous, evergreen shrub up to
20 (—30) cm. in height; young branches yellowish-brown. Leaves alternate,
leathery, dark shiny green, clustered towards the tips of the branches, oblanceolate, obtuse or mucronate, margins revolute, 2.5—4 cm. long, 0.7—1.5 cm. wide.
Flowers creamy-white, sometimes with pinkish tubes, very fragrant, in terminal
heads of up to 30 (rarely more) in each head; tube 11—15 mm. long, lobes
narrowly ovate, acute, 5—7 mm. long. Fruit red, fleshy, ovoid, c. 5 mm. long.

CHROMOSOME NO. Not recorded.

FLOWERING PERIOD May—July.

DISTRIBUTION N.E. Turkey, Caucasus.

HABITAT In open alpine turf or in slight shade with *Rhododendron luteum*
(*Azalea pontica*) or among pines; 1400—3000 m.

D. glomerata is allied to *D. pontica*, which is somewhat more
widespread—although covering much the same geographical area.
Variation within the species appears to be slight, the following
varieties differing only in minor particulars:-

1. var. *nivalis* C. Koch in *Linnaea* 22: 613 (1849) is a high
altitude form usually less than 20 cm. high and often with many
flowers per head. M. & T. 4356 may possibly be referable to this
variety as in some specimens over 60 flowers per head were
recorded.

2. var. *pauciflora* Meissn. in *DC. Prod.* 539 (1857), is described
as a depauperate form with few flowers occurring at low
altitudes of up to 1500 m.

3. var. *puberula* Sosn. in *Mat. Fl. Kav.* 28: 271 (1910) is stated
to differ from the type by the external pubescence of the corolla
tube (*D. glomerata* is normally glabrous in all its parts).

Horticulturally these variations are probably of little value;
botanically a thorough study of the species throughout its range
would be required to comment on their significance.

Daphne gnidioides Jaub. & Spach, *Ill.. Pl. Or.* 414 (1850)

SYNONYMS *D. oleoides* d'Urville; *D. candolleana* Meissn.

ILLUSTRATION No useful illustration traced.

Even the most dedicated *Daphne* addict can find little to enthuse
about when faced with *D. gnidioides*, a tall lanky shrub of relatively
little garden value, and doubtful hardiness in most areas of Britain.
It has made spasmodic appearances in gardens but never seems to
have become established in cultivation. In nature it occurs in rocky,
dry situations at relatively low elevations often in association with
typical maquis plants such as *Phlomis fruticosa* and *Quercus coccifera*
and would undoubtedly require a similar sharply drained open
site in cultivation.

In April 1975 we found *D. gnidioides* in a number of localities in western Turkey growing among limestone rocks from sea level on the Marmaris peninsula to about 700 m. near the *locus classicus* for *Iris pamphylica*. The scraggy bearing of the plants with their rather spare, narrow greyish foliage did no more than confirm our previous opinion that *D. gnidioides* was best left in its natural habitat. Had we been able to see the white or occasionally pinkish, scented blooms later in the season our views might perhaps have been modified, but for general garden use it cannot compare with many other daphnes and is only likely to be of interest to collectors.

PROPAGATION   We have no experience of propagating *D. gnidioides*, but seed would probably prove the most satisfactory method if it can be obtained. In view of the low altitude range of the species it is unlikely to require a cold period to germinate satisfactorily and the young seedlings would almost certainly be very frost-tender.

TYPE LOCALITY   "Samos, Leros & W. Asia Minor (Caria & Lydia)".

DESCRIPTION   Erect evergreen shrub with long stout branches, up to 2 m. in height; young branches pubescent with brown hairs. Leaves alternate, glaucous, rather leathery, scattered along the branches, slightly pubescent when young, sessile, oblong-lanceolate with a sharply pointed tip, 2.5—4 cm. long, 0.4—0.7 cm. wide. Flowers fragrant, white or pinkish in terminal heads of 5—8, sometimes also with a few axillary flowers below; tube 5—6 mm. long, pubescent outside; lobes oblong, obtuse, 2—3 mm. long. Fruit brownish-red; not very fleshy.

CHROMOSOME NO.   Not recorded.

FLOWERING PERIOD   May.

DISTRIBUTION   ? Greece (possibly on Euboea); E. Aegean Islands, S. & W. Turkey.

HABITAT   In maquis, on limestone frequently in very rocky sites; 0—1000 m.

D. gnidioides is closely allied to *D. mucronata* (*D. angustifolia*) and may well represent a lowland west Turkish extreme of this species which occurs at higher altitudes in eastern Turkey across to Kashmir and Punjab. In general appearance *D. gnidioides* resembles *D. gnidium* but differs in its clustered, more or less terminal inflorescence (paniculate in *D. gnidium*) and in its much less fleshy fruits.

Daphne gnidium L., *Sp. Pl:* 357 (1753)
SYNONYMS   *D. paniculata* Lam.; *D. orthophylla* St. Lag.

ILLUSTRATION   *Lodd. Bot. Cab.* t. 150 (1821).

Like its eastern counterpart *D. gnidioides* this evergreen species is seldom cultivated, although it is a more attractive shrub with its larger panicles of sweetly scented, creamy-white blooms followed (in the wild at least) by clusters of red fleshy fruits. It grows in dry, sunny maquis conditions or in the light shade of pine woods, in nature forming an upright grey-foliaged shrub up to five or six feet in height.

D. genkwa Sieb. et Zucc.

D. pseudomezereum A. Gray

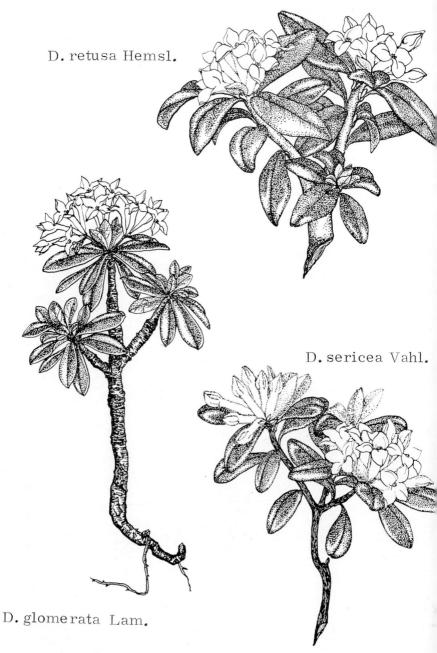

D. retusa Hemsl.

D. sericea Vahl.

D. glomerata Lam.

Theophrastus tells us the berries were used (in dough) to relieve constipation, and also of note is the reputed use of *D. gnidium* by Corsicans to catch trout by poisoning streams with an extract presumably derived from the fruits, which in many daphnes have some poisonous properties. In Britain it has not proved very hardy, although cultivated on and off since the sixteenth century. In warmer areas of the country it could be an attractive late-flowering, grey-foliaged plant to associate with tree heathers or to grow in company with cistus, lavenders and similar shrubs in sheltered but open, sunny sites or under the high cover of pines. In nature it occurs on limestone formations, but does not appear to be unduly fussy over soil pH in cultivation, although demanding sharp drainage if it is to thrive.

Halda reports that *D. gnidium* is hardier if grafted on to *D. mezereum* or *D. laureola* than if grown on its own roots, but we have not used this technique ourselves.

PROPAGATION

(a) Seed. Dry-stored seed originally collected wild in Portugal and sown in March 1974 germinated readily within eight weeks at Wisley, and it is probable that no stratification period is required for seed of this and some other low altitude daphnes from the Mediterranean region. It is also possible that the viability of seed of *D. gnidium* is not affected too greatly by storage, although our observations are at present based on a very limited amount of material. Young seedlings are unusual in producing thick, carrot-like yellowish roots soon after germination. Growth of the seedlings plunged in an open frame has so far proved to be slow, no more than three inches in two growing seasons.

(b) Grafting. Halda's comments, quoted previously, indicate that grafting could be a useful means of establishing *D. gnidium*, possibly by raising seedlings under glass and grafting shoots from the seedlings on to stocks raised at the same time.

TYPE LOCALITY "Spain, Italy, Narbonne".

DESCRIPTION Erect evergreen shrub with long slender branches, up to 2 m. in height; young branches brownish, covered in short, appressed hairs. Leaves heavily gland-dotted on the underside, glaucous, leathery, fairly evenly distributed below the apices of the branches, sessile, linear to obovate-oblong, acute, 2—5 cm. long, 0.3—1 cm. wide. Flowers cream, fragrant, in terminal panicles of 10 or more; tube 2.5—4 mm. long, pubescent outside; lobes 2—3 mm. long, ovate, acute. Fruit pear-shaped, fleshy, red (or blackish according to Halda and others).

CHROMOSOME NO. Not recorded.

FLOWERING PERIOD May—September. Flowers and fruits are sometimes borne together late in the season.

DISTRIBUTION Canary Islands, N. Africa and Mediterranean region as far east as Greece. Specimens recorded for Turkey in the Istanbul herbarium appear to be referable to *D. gnidioides*.

HABITAT Maquis and in open limestone areas and pine woods; 0—2000 m.

111

Although relatively widespread in nature *D. gnidium* does not vary greatly throughout its range. *D. gnidium* forma *latifolia* Keissler in *Engl. Bot. Jahrb.* xxv, 72 (1898) represents the upper range of leaf width whilst var. *lanata* Faure et Maire in R. Maire, *Contr. à l'étude de la Terre de l'Afrique du Nord* (1931), covers plants of more hairy character than the normal occurring in the Great Atlas mountains in Morocco.

Plants of *D. gnidium* noted at Cape Spartel, Morocco (A.G.S. *Bull.*, 14: 47 (1946) were stated to have chocolate-coloured flowers and black fruits, but we have not seen specimens which show this combination of characters.

Daphne x hendersonii Hodgkin ex. C. D. Brickell et B. Mathew in *Journ. Roy. Hort. Soc. Vol.* 101, 11: 550 (1976).

This hybrid of *Daphne petraea* Leybold x *D. cneorum* L. was first recorded by Mr. W. Scott Henderson and Mr. (later Sir) Arthur Hill, Director of Kew, in May 1930 in a valley on the west side of Lake Garda. A full account of this discovery is given in *Annals of Botany* 45:178, p. 229-231 (1931) by Hill, but no name is provided, although in correspondence with Eliot Hodgkin he indicates that he would like the hybrid called after his companion.

In Eliot Hodgkin's article on *Daphne* in the R.H.S. *Journal* for November, 1961, he mentions *D. x hendersonii* as being named after "Sir Arthur Henderson who found it" but this must be an oversight as the name of the discoverer is itself "hybrid" in origin (Arthur Hill x W. Scott Henderson!).

It is intermediate between the parents in both leaf and inflorescence and is most easily recognised by characters of the leaf-tip. The leaves of *D. x hendersonii* are acute whereas those of *D. petraea* are rounded and those of *D. cneorum* obtuse and apiculate. In addition the pubescence of the young branchlets is sparse in the hybrid whereas the branchlets of *D. petraea* are glabrous and those of *D. cneorum* densely pubescent. In general habit Hill states that it resembles *D. cneorum* although in flower colour it approached the soft pink colouring of *D. petraea*. The distinguishing characters of floral bracts and flower number per capitulum given by Hill do not appear to hold on examination of the type material and a fairly wide range of herbarium specimens of both parents.

As far as we know, this hybrid has not been re-located or introduced into cultivation, but as it was growing on limestone cliffs in nature, it would no doubt appreciate similar cultural conditions to *D. petraea* if ever re-collected.

Daphne x houtteana Lindley & Paxton in *Paxt. Fl. Garden* 1: 170 (1851)

SYNONYMS   *D. houttei* Low; *D. laureola purpurea* Hort; *D. mezereum* var. *atropurpurea* Dipp.; *D. mezereum foliis atropurpureis* Hort.

ILLUSTRATION   *Flore des Serres* 6:186-7, t. 592 (1850)

The origin of *D. x houtteana*, like that of so many horticultural hybrids, is obscure, but it is almost certainly the result of a cross between *D. mezereum* and *D. laureola*, an unusual combination which has produced a most attractive plant, unfortunately far less often available in the trade than its merits deserve.

There is a suggestion in *The Garden*, 9:570 (1876) by George Gordon that it "originated in one of the Belgian nurseries", but it was first brought to the general notice of the horticultural world by Louis Van Houtte in 1850, who provided an excellent coloured illustration in *Flores des Serres* for that year. He did not suggest a name at the time, and this was left until the following year when Lindley and Paxton named it in his honour.

In its evergreen or semi-evergreen foliage it takes after *D. laureola*, but the leaves are purple, although on occasion the purple colouration is only partially developed at first in the young leaves. The lilac-purple blooms are borne during March and April in short-stalked bunches spread out for two or three inches along the bare stem below the terminal leaf clusters, and also occasionally in the axils of the lower leaves of the clusters. Curiously, in the various descriptions we have consulted, no mention is made of any scent, and we have not been able to confirm whether or not the flowers are fragrant.

D. x houtteana is apparently quite amenable as a garden plant and Eliot Hodgkin grew it very successfully for almost 20 years in slightly alkaline conditions in a well-drained open site. It is also known to grow satisfactorily on acid soils and appears perfectly hardy, as might be expected in view of its parentage. It will also tolerate some shade.

Unfortunately it is subject to virus attack, and it is possible that its scarcity in cultivation is due to this factor. Certainly it is hard to find any nursery which can supply *D. x houtteana* at the present time, but both as a foliage and as a flowering plant it is valuable in the garden and well worth obtaining if offered.

PROPAGATION

(a) Seed.   *D. x houtteana* is probably sterile. No reports of fruit being formed are known.

(b) Cuttings.   Half-ripe cuttings (see Group 2 p. 41) have been rooted without difficulty, but care must be taken not to propagate from virus-ridden plants.

(c) Grafting on stocks of *D. mezereum*, *D. laureola* (and other species) proves successful. Saddle or side grafting methods may be used.

113

TYPE   The illustration in *Flores des Serres* t, 592 (1850).

DESCRIPTION   An erect, stiffly-branched, partially evergreen shrub to 1.3 m. high; young shoots purplish, glabrous, older shoots light brown. Foliage fairly evenly distributed along the young shoots, the lower ones deciduous, leaving a cluster of persistent leaves at the tips of the shoots at the end of the season. Leaves alternate, purple or sometimes green at first, quickly becoming purple, shortly stalked, glossy, leathery, glabrous; oblanceolate (sometimes narrowly ovate), acute, up to 9.0 cm. long and 3.0 cm. wide.

Flowers borne in short-stalked clusters of 2—4 (5), occasionally singly, below the terminal leaf cluster, the uppermost in the axils of the lower leaves and the inflorescence extending for up to 4—6 cm. along the bare growth of the previous year. Flowers lilac-purple (? also dark purple), or greenish-white tinged red outside. Fragrant (?), tube c. 5 mm. long, glabrous; lobes 3 mm. long x 2 mm. wide, lanceolate, recurved. Fruit unknown.

CHROMOSOME NO.   Not recorded.

FLOWERING PERIOD   March—April.

DISTRIBUTION   A hybrid of garden origin prior to 1850. Possibly originating in a Belgian nursery.

D. x *houtteana* varies slightly in flower colour (if the different descriptions consulted are accurate) from deep purple to pale lilac. Whether or not this is due to observation of the flower colour at different stages of their development is difficult to ascertain, but it seems likely as only one clone is thought to have been in circulation. It is, of course, possible that a batch of seedlings was raised and distributed originally differing somewhat in this character, but this seems improbable. Eliot Hodgkin mentions (1967) that this same hybrid "appeared spontaneously in a garden" but there is no trace of the source of this information in his notes. Certainly, as both parents are reasonably frequent in gardens, a repeat of the cross would be well worth attempting in order to obtain a virus-free stock, always assuming any resultant plants measured up to the original *D.* x *houtteana*. It is interesting that this hybrid has also been recorded occasionally as growing wild in Britain—see *Hybridisation and the Flora of the British Isles* ed. C. A. Stace (1975).

Daphne x hybrida Colv. ex Sweet in. *Brit. Fl. Gard.* ser. 1, 2, t. 200 (1827)

PARENTAGE   *D. odora* Thunb. x *D. collina* Sm.

SYNONYMS   *D. dauphinii* Loudon; *D. delphinium* Loudon; *D. delphinii* Meissn.; *D. fionina* K. Koch.; *D. fioniana* Dipp.

ILLUSTRATIONS   *Bot. Mag.*, n.s., t. 320 (1958); *Bot. Reg.* t. 1177 (1828)

This attractive long-flowering, evergreen hybrid is seldom seen in gardens but is certainly well worth cultivating, although it may be difficult to locate commercially. Its origin, like that of so many of our garden plants, is shrouded in mystery. The original cross is stated to have been made about 1820 by M. Fion, a gardener whose history—like that of his garden offspring—is ill-recorded.

Reports vary as to its hardiness. If the parents used by M. Fion were of the same degree of hardiness as the stocks of *D. collina* and *D. odora* 'Aureo-marginata' we grow today, one might expect *D.* x *hybrida* to be hardy in all but the coldest areas of Britain. It is possible, however, that the plants of both parents used were less hardy as various forms of *D. odora* some tender, were widely grown in the nineteenth century and *D. collina* as grown at that time might well have been derived from plants growing at low elevations.

One can only speculate on such matters in view of the lack of material or documentation available, but a specimen of *D.* x *hybrida* now 4 ft. high and 3 ft. across, obtained from Messrs. Reuthe in 1965, is still growing in Mrs. Hodgkin's Berkshire garden (1976) and appears quite happy in full exposure. On the other hand Bean (1973) considers it essentially a plant for a mild climate and the material used for the *Botanical Magazine* plate was taken from a plant growing in the Temperate House at Kew. It would seem wise therefore to choose a sheltered but open site for *D.* x *hybrida*, and in cold areas either to grow it as a cool greenhouse plant or to take the somewhat tiresome precaution of propagating it annually.

Apart from the question of hardiness it is undemanding as to soil, provided it is adequately drained, growing quite readily under both acid and alkaline conditions if not too extreme.

The basic garden value of *D.* x *hybrida* is in its welcome ability to provide sweet-scented clusters of its purplish-red blooms virtually throughout the year. In full summer it may have a moderate rest from flower production but at most other seasons it provides a modicum of bloom and even at Christmas there are usually a few flowers to be picked.

PROPAGATION

(a) Seed. As far as is known *D.* x *hybrida* is sterile and propagation by vegetative means is therefore essential.

(b) Cuttings. Half-ripe cuttings taken in mid-July to mid-August root without difficulty (see Group 2 p. 41).

(c) Grafting on stocks of *D. mezereum*, or an evergreen species such as *D. laureola*, *D. pontica* or *D. longilobata* proves successful but is usually unnecessary.

TYPE   Plate in *Bot. Reg.* t. 1177 (1828).

DESCRIPTION   (Based on a plant obtained from Messrs. Reuthe by Eliot Hodgkin in 1965.)

An erect, densely-branched evergreen shrub up to 1.5 m. (2m.) in height and 1 m. or more across; young branches green, pubescent; second year wood brown, pubescent. Leaves alternate, dark green, sessile or very short-petioled, glossy, leathery, scattered along first year stems and somewhat clustered towards tips of shoots; young leaves slightly pubescent on the lower surface, ciliate at the margins with a distinct tuft of hairs at the apex, quickly glabrous; older leaves glabrous; oblanceolate, obtuse to acute, sometimes mucronate; up to 5.5 (-7) cm. long and 1.7 (2.0) cm. wide.

Flowers in terminal clusters of 4—7 surrounded by groups of pale green recurving bracts with ciliate margins and appressed hairs on the outer surface; buds deep red-purple in colour (R.H.S. *Colour Chart* Red-purple 71A) opening with the four lobes curved at margins and pale purplish-red except for the white margins, intensely fragrant; tube to 1 cm. long covered with appressed silky white hairs which extend to the outside of the lobes; lobes 8-10 mm. long, 5—6 mm. wide, ovate to broadly ovate, with the tip obtuse and the margins slightly rolled inwards. Fruit unknown.

CHROMOSOME NO. Not recorded.

FLOWERING PERIOD Throughout the year, with the main flushes in spring and autumn and few or no blooms in July and August.

DISTRIBUTION A hybrid of garden origin *circa* 1820.

Although there are occasionally different statements as to the parentage of *D.* x *hybrida*, the structural features appear to be intermediate between *D. odora* and *D. collina*. As far as is known only the one clone of this hybrid is in cultivation and according to Lindley (*Bot. Reg.* t. 1177) it was grown and valued by French florists as far back as 1828 for its long-flowering habit.

Daphne jasminea Sibth. & Sm., *Fl. Graecae Prodr.* 1:260 (1809)

SYNONYMS *D. microphylla* Meissn.; *D. microphylla* var. *angustifolia* Meissn.

ILLUSTRATIONS See drawing on p. 32, and illustration p. 127.; also Sibthorp, *Fl. Gr.* 4: t. 358 (1823).

AWARDS A.M. (1968).

This delightful dwarf shrub has become very popular with alpine house enthusiasts in Britain during recent years and has proved reasonably tractable in a number of localities in spite of fears to the contrary.

As we have seen *D. jasminea* in nature, it grows as a crevice plant insinuating its roots deep into limestone rocks where it forms twisted networks of brittle branches which fan out from the gnarled woody rootstock and are fairly densely covered with neat, evergreen, blue-green leaves. During April and May, and often again in autumn, the plants are spangled with the purplish-red (occasionally yellowish-white) buds, borne singly or occasionally in pairs, which open to reveal the crystalline white interiors and emit their delicious fragrance.

Its requirements in cultivation appear to be similar to those in its natural habitat—full sun and very sharp drainage with a deep root run so that the neck is dry but the roots are cool and moist. For the alpine house a deep container (an old chimney-pot is ideal!) with ample humus at the base and a gritty, sharply drained limestone compost proves very successful.

Doubts have been expressed over the hardiness of *D. jasminea*, and certainly one might expect that plants derived from low altitude

116

sites such as those in the Isthmus of Corinth would be hard put to withstand our winters. The Delphi stock, however, appears somewhat tougher, and, provided protection from the damp of a British winter could be given, it is worth trying out of doors—perhaps in a nook under a slight overhang in a south-facing stone wall of a raised bed or tufa wall. Regrettably our own experience of growing *D. jasminea* is, as yet, confined to cultivating it in pots.

There are at least two forms of this plant in cultivation, one which corresponds with those growing at Delphi, and one very like plants from Megara and Cyrenaica. The first is the very dwarf semi-prostrate hummock-forming plant, usually with a reddish flush on the outside of the flowers, referred to above. The latter normally has no red colouration in the flowers and sends up vigorous erect stems to about 30 cm. Obviously the former variant is by far the more attractive to an alpine enthusiast and it is now regularly seen on the show benches. It is an incredibly brittle plant and much care has to be taken even when moving the pot for twigs will fall off even if it is put down carelessly on the bench. The upright form is much tougher in this respect. Only during the last twenty or so years has the true plant been available to us, and the first introduction traced is that by Eliot Hodgkin who collected a few twigs, some subsequently grafted successfully on to *D. mezereum*, during May 1954 at Kaki Scala in Greece. This plant flowered in 1955 and in subsequent years, but died in 1961 according to his records.

Further introductions from at least two different sites in Greece have been made separately by Hugo Money-Coutts, Brian Mathew, Ken Aslet and Ivor Barton, whilst in November 1973 on our first collecting expedition together, we brought back material from plants at Delphi (Brickell & Mathew 8150) which was grafted successfully on to *D. mezereum*. Since the plants located at Delphi are well-known, no doubt others have also introduced this saxatile rock-hugging form which is to be found near the site of the famous oracle. Happily many of the plants of *D. jasminea* grow on sheer rock faces, and so are safe from those marauders who over-collect, removing whole plants—which are most unlikely to survive.

PROPAGATION

(a) Seed. Unknown to us, but Halda records raising this species from seed.

(b) Cuttings. Stem cuttings of short growths root readily in a closed frame or under mist (see Groups 1 and 2 p. 41). Under reasonable conditions of growth the resulting young plants may begin to flower in their third (occasionally second) year. Halda states that *D. jasminea*, on its own roots, is less easy to grow (except in tufa) than when grafted. We have not, so far, found any great difference between the two methods. Someone who collected a

117

few cuttings at Delphi in April, 1964 (from which the superb plant which received an A.M. at Chelsea Show in 1968 was derived) says that soft cuttings taken in May and June root readily with bottom heat but emphasizes the extreme fragility of the young plants. He has found that young plants grow rapidly but as the plants become old and woody they appear to be prone to die-back.

(c) Layering. In theory quite possible, but in view of the brittleness of the shoots requires considerable care to carry out successfully.

(d) Grafting. We have found no difficulty in grafting *D. jasminea* on one-year seedlings of *D. mezereum* in both May and November—the timing dictated by the arrival of material at those times of year, not by choice. Normally we would advocate splice (side) grafting.

It is interesting to note that Halda has found that *D. jasminea* also grows well on stocks of *D. giraldii*, *D. oleoides* and *D. alpina;* whilst Ivor Barton has used *D. retusa* successfully; and *D. longilobata* is used commercially.

Plants of the prostrate form may also tend to be more upright in growth if grafted.

TYPE LOCALITY "Parnassus and Delphi".

DESCRIPTION Compact, prostrate or erect, intricately branched, usually glabrous evergreen shrub up to 30 cm. in height; branches brown, leaves grey or bluish-green, alternate, shortly-stalked, oblong-obovate, mucronate, scattered fairly thickly along the branches; 8—11 mm. long, 1.5—3 mm. wide. Flowers in terminal pairs (rarely 3) white or cream, sometimes reddish or purplish on the outside, fragrant; tube 10—12 mm. long, very slender, usually glabrous but occasionally slightly hairy; lobes narrowly lanceolate to triangular, acute, more or less reflexed, about 3—4 mm. long. Fruit unknown (red and 4—6 mm. across according to Halda).

CHROMOSOME NO. Not recorded.

FLOWERING PERIOD April—May and often again in autumn.

DISTRIBUTION Greece, Delphi, Parnassus, on the coast near Megara and on Euboea (also recorded from Elevsis in Attica and Nauplia on Peloponnese, but specimens not seen); Libya: Cyrenaica. (Also Albania and Turkey according to Halda; we have seen no specimens from these areas and the records may perhaps refer to *D. oleoides*.)

HABITAT Limestone cliffs, in crevices; 0—1000 m.

In literature, both botanical and horticultural, *D. jasminea* has long been confused with *D. oleoides* and is frequently stated, quite incorrectly, to be a variant of that species. It is immediately apparent to anyone who has seen and studied these species growing in the wild that the two are perfectly distinct even allowing for the very considerable variation of *D. oleoides* throughout its range. The confusion has arisen due to the use of *D. jasminea* by Grisebach to describe what is now regarded as no more than a form of *D. oleoides;* a further complication has occurred by the publication of *D. oleoides* var. *jasminea* Meissner, neither plant having anything to do with the species described by Sibthorp and Smith.

Variation within *D. jasminea* has been mentioned previously but insufficient evidence exists to decide whether the difference in habit and other characters are worthy of botanical recognition.

Related Species

D. malyana Blecic in *Bull. Mus. Hist. Nat. Pays Serbe*, ser. B.5-6: 23 (1953). This is described from one locality in Jugoslavia and is closely related. It is stated to differ from *D. jasminea* in the more spoon-shaped, obtuse (not mucronate) leaves which are sometimes hairy beneath, in the hairy ovary, white flowers and greenish fruits. We have not seen specimens and there is no record of it in cultivation in Britain. If brought into cultivation it would no doubt require similar conditions to *D. jasminea* inhabiting as it does in nature limestone rocks in the Piva Gorge in Jugoslavia.

Daphne jezoensis Maxim. ex Regel in *Gartenfl.* 15: 34, t. 496 (1866)

SYNONYMS   *D. kamtschatica* var. *jezoensis* (Maxim. ex Regel) Ohwi; *D. rebunensis* Tatew.; *D. pseudomezereum* Tanaka, not of A. Gray.
ILLUSTRATIONS   Colour plate opposite p. 14, illustration p. 127; also *Bot. Mag.* 187, n.s., t. 613 (1972)
AWARD   P.C. (1972).

D. jezoensis, at present rarely seen in gardens, is a most beautiful and valuable species, flowering as it does during the winter and early spring. A curious feature, both in cultivation in Britain and in the wild, is that the deciduous period occurs during the summer. Fresh green leaves appear during autumn at or shortly before flowering and fall in late spring. In spite of this peculiarity—which is somewhat alarming to those who are unaware of the growth habit of the species—the young leaves and flowers appear to be reasonably frost-hardy and plants grown unprotected outside have produced the scented, deep yellow blooms regularly for the last few years in both our gardens.

As far as is known, the first introduction to Britain of *D. jezoensis* was in the early 1960's when Hugo Money-Coutts obtained seed (as *D. pseudomezereum*) collected at Fukushima in N. Honshu, Japan, and distributed some of the resultant young seedlings. In 1971 Eliot Hodgkin received several young plants from Dr. Rokujo in Japan, one of which was exhibited in flower in February, 1972, and gained a Preliminary Commendation.

D. jezoensis has proved relatively slow-growing in gardens, forming a small, fairly sparsely branched shrub 30 cm. or so high after eight or nine years from seed. It appears to be happiest in an acid, well-drained soil, although it will tolerate slightly alkaline conditions as two plants growing in Mrs. Hodgkin's garden (1976), which has some lime in the soil, have grown steadily and shown no signs of chlorosis since being planted out 4-5 years previously. On the other hand, grown in highly alkaline soil on the South Downs, *D. jezoensis* did not flourish, and the foliage was severely chlorotic. In Japan it is found wild in woodland conditions and no doubt benefits from the annual mulch of leaf-mould from the deciduous trees with which it grows. It has certainly been found that it appreciates leafy, peaty conditions at Wisley, where it has also been grown as a pot plant for the alpine house, using a well-drained but humus-rich compost. In the open garden a slightly sheltered position in light woodland or on a peat bank should prove suitable, but it seems probable that *D. jezoensis* is reasonably tolerant of cultivation and, provided one follows our oft-quoted maxim of "a well-drained soil which does not dry out", it is likely to succeed in fairly open sunny sites, except possibly in dry areas where moderate shade would be preferable.

PROPAGATION

(a) Seed. Seed is occasionally produced in cultivation and if sown as soon as possible after, or even just prior to, ripening (before the fruit can be removed by birds!) germinates readily the spring following sowing.

(b) Cuttings. As yet untried (by us), but like the related *D. mezereum*, probably not easy to increase in this way. If tried, soft cuttings are likely to be more successful but might be difficult in view of the unusual period of leafing, which would mean cutting material would be available in very early spring.

Halda states that the related *D. kamtschatica* is easily propagated from cuttings in summer and winter, but does not specify the type of cutting or method used.

(c) Grafting. *D. mezereum*, as might be expected, has proved a satisfactory stock and it is likely that *D. giraldii* and *D. alpina* could also be used, as Halda has found these suitable for the closely related *D. kamtschatica*. In view of the unusual leafing period, August grafting is recommended; but as the stocks go dormant in autumn it may be necessary to keep the plants growing in warm conditions.

TYPE LOCALITY Japan: Hokkaido: Hakodate; Honshu: Senano.
DESCRIPTION Erect or suberect, summer-deciduous, glabrous shrub up to 0.5 m. in height; young branches brown; older bark greyish. Leaves alternate, often clustered towards the apex of the branches, more or less sessile, oblanceolate, mucronate to rounded or retuse at the apex, narrowly cuneate at the base, mid-green and slightly glossy above, paler beneath, 3—8.5 cm. long, 1—3 cm. wide. Flowers in terminal, rarely also lateral, clusters of 2—10, yellow, greenish on the outside of the tube, sometimes lemon-scented; tube 6—8 mm. long, glabrous; lobes ovate, acute, 6—7 mm. long, 3—4 mm. wide. (Ohwi, *Flora of Japan*, states fls. dioecious. The flowers examined have proved to be hermaphrodite.) Fruit 1.1—1.2 cm. long, reddish.
CHROMOSOME NO. 2n=18 (Kitamura).
FLOWERING PERIOD Nov.—Dec. (—March) (in Britain); Feb.—May (in Japan)
DISTRIBUTION N. Japan, in Honshu, Hokkaido, Rishiri & Rebun Islands; S. Sakhalin.
HABITAT Subalpine woodland.

There appears to be some variation in the presence or lack of scent, and in the depth of flower colour of the plants in cultivation. Those with deeper yellow blooms are usually scented and on occasion produce fruit, whilst the paler yellow-flowered plants are scentless and are not known to fruit. Whether or not these characters would have any significance if it were possible to examine larger numbers of plants is impossible to say.

There are also reports of forms with variegated leaves, but these are not known to be in cultivation in Britain and without seeing living material it is difficult to decide whether they should be referred to *D. jezoensis* or a related species. In view of the susceptibility of these relatives of *D. mezereum* to virus diseases, it is possible that this variegation may be due to virus infection rather than of genetic origin.

Related Species

There are several closely related species which have been in cultivation occasionally and there is undoubtedly some confusion between *D. jezoensis*, *D. kamtschatica* and *D. pseudomezereum* as grown in gardens.

Halda in his description of *D. kamtschatica* includes some characters which appear to refer to *D. jezoensis*, but there are certain discrepancies, notably in the flowering period given (April—June) and in leaf shape. Both *D. jezoensis* and *D. kamtschatica* are summer deciduous, and the flowers are produced with the leaves in late winter and early spring.

Halda mentions a var. *"citrina"* Hort. and a variegated-leaved form under *D. kamtschatica*, variations which are also recorded for *D. jezoensis*.

The various species in the complex have been studied by Hamaya (*Bull. Tokyo Univ. For.* 50:73, 1955) and in view of the confusion it may be helpful to provide details of the distinguishing features, based in part on the characters given by Hamaya.

> **D. jezoensis** Maxim. ex Regel
> Summer-deciduous. Flowers yellow; stamens $\frac{1}{2}$-exserted from the tube; plant about 0.5 m. tall, stiffly branched; ratio of tube to lobe length 1:1. Leaves strongly oblanceolate, with regular and well developed lateral veins.
> Distribution: N. Japan, in Honshu, Hokkaido, Rishiri & Rebun Islands; S. Sakhalin.
>
> **D. kamtschatica** Maxim. in *Prim. Fl. Amur.*: 237 (1859).
> Summer-deciduous. Flowers greenish; stamens included within the tube; plant 0.3—0.5 m. tall, stiffly branched; ratio of tube to lobe length 2:3. Leaves oblong or elliptic to oblanceolate with regular and well-developed lateral veins. Distribution: Korea; Russian Far East, Kamchatka Sakhalin Isles, Kuriles and Japan (Hokkaido).
>
> **D. koreana** Nakai in *Journ. Jap. Bot.* 13:880 (1937).
> Winter-deciduous. In other respects there appears to be no difference between this and *D. kamtschatica*, although Hamaya unites it with *D. pseudomezereum*. Distribution: confined to Korea.

D. pseudomezereum A. Gray in *Mem. Am. Acad.* n.s. II
404 (1959).
See drawing on p. 109.
Chromosome No; n=9.

Summer-deciduous. Flowers greenish (sometimes purple
outside); stamens half exserted from the tube; plant 1—
1.5 m. tall, slender branched; ratio of tube to lobe length
1:2. Leaves oblong or elliptic to oblanceolate with poorly
developed and irregular lateral veins. Distribution: Central
and South Japan (Honshu, Shikoku).

In other respects these species are very similar. The most distinct
is *D. pseudomezereum* which in growth, as the name suggests, very
much resembles the well-known *D. mezereum* but differs of course
in its greenish, lateral clusters of flowers which are borne with the
leaves. Halda refers to its "yellowish, more rarely rose flowers"
and states that in cultivation interesting colour forms (e.g. var.
"lutea" Hort. with good yellow flowers) occur. It would be interesting to see material of these variations to investigate their relationship
within the complex.

To the gardener *D. kamtschatica*, *D. koreana* and *D. pseudomezereum* with their greenish flowers, are far less attractive than *D.
jezoensis*, and are mainly of botanical interest for the collector of
unusual plants.

For the curious it is of note that the bark of these species has
occasionally been used for rope and paper-making; and there are
records of their use locally for medicinal purposes—not to be
recommended generally in view of the somewhat poisonous nature
attributed to daphnes!

Daphne laureola L., *Sp. Pl.:* 357 (1753)

SYNONYM   *D. arbuscula* Christ.

ILLUSTRATIONS   See drawing on p. 50 and photo on p. 128.

AWARDS   None.

Our native Spurge Laurel, *D. laureola*, has long been cultivated,
although it is seldom given much attention in gardens. William
Turner (*Names of Herbes*, 1548) knew it well as the seed was used
(or mis-used) in place of that of *D. gnidium*, which was employed in
medicine, while Gerard refers to it in his famous herbal of 1590 and
with his usual flair for medicinal detail states (of the leaves) "being
chewed, it draweth water out of the head"—a useful remedy should
one suffer from such a complaint! However, it is as well to remember
that daphnes contain strongly purgative chemicals ("it provoketh
vomit" in the words of Gerard) and the fruits and possibly other
parts of the plant are very poisonous.

Although *D. laureola* is not a showy plant, it can be a useful
evergreen both for a shady corner in the garden and for its early-

produced, yellowish-green flowers. In day-time these have a slightly unpleasant scent or may be virtually unscented, but towards evening the scent sometimes, although by no means always, can be pleasantly fragrant. No doubt variation in this character occurs throughout the range of the species, but whether or not it is linked to the dimorphic variation mentioned later or is an entirely chance occurrence is unknown.

It shows considerable variation in depth of flower colour, those individuals with light yellow-green blooms being the most attractive and contrasting well with the dark green, glossy foliage.

In Britain *D. laureola* is a very easy plant to grow in most soils, and is particularly successful in alkaline conditions. Essentially a shade-loving plant in nature, it also grows and seeds itself freely in full sun in one chalk garden we know on the South Downs, so may be considered sufficiently tolerant to be grown in any but the driest soils. For the best results provide semi-shade and a moist, calcareous woodland soil.

Apart from its place in the garden in its own right, *D. laureola* has been used as a grafting stock for many different daphnes, and as long ago as 1843 it was recommended in the *Gardeners Chronicle* as "the best stock on which to graft the smaller kinds of daphne".

PROPAGATION

(a) Seed. The black fruits are often freely produced and seedlings are easily raised, the seed usually germinating freely and evenly if subjected to a period of cold after being sown as early as possible following gathering and cleaning. Older dry and stored seed will germinate, but does so erratically.

The various virus diseases to which *D. laureola* is unfortunately very susceptible, are apparently not seed-borne and if plants of *D. laureola* (or any other species) are found to be suffering from virus, seedlings should be raised and the adult plants burnt.

(b) Cuttings. Stem-cuttings of half-ripe wood can be rooted without difficulty (see Group 2, p. 41). It is essential to ensure that the plants from which cuttings are taken are not virused as this will only result in passing on the disease.

(c) Layering can also be used to increase *D. laureola*, particularly in the case of the low-growing ssp. *philippi*.

TYPE LOCALITY "England, Switzerland, France".
DESCRIPTION Much branched, glabrous, evergreen shrub up to 1.5 m. in height. Young shoots greenish, older shoots brown. Leaves deep glossy green, leathery, alternate, clustered at the apex of the stems, sessile, obovate-oblanceolate, sub-acute to obtuse, 3—5 (—8) cm. long, 1—1.5 cm. wide. Flowers usually little or unpleasantly scented during the day, occasionally somewhat fragrant towards evening, green, yellow-green (or sometimes purplish in some forms of ssp. *philippi*), produced in congested, axillary clusters of 2—10, just below the apex of the shoots on the previous season's growth; tube 3—8 mm. long; lobes ovate, obtuse, 2.5—4 mm. long. Fruit ovoid, fleshy, black.
CHROMOSOME NO. 2n=18.

FLOWERING PERIOD   Feb.—March.

DISTRIBUTION   Widespread in Europe from Portugal to the Balkans; Britain, N. Africa and Azores.

HABITAT   In deciduous or (more rarely) semi-coniferous woods; up to 2,000 m. altitude.

Some variations in habit, leaf-shape and inflorescence characters occur throughout the range of the species and the following variants have been described.

ssp. *philippi* (Gren.) Rouy in *Consp. Fl. Fr.* 225 (1927). A low growing, compact high altitude form from the Pyrenees, usually under 40 cm. in height, with more or less decumbent branches. Sometimes stated to be stoloniferous. The size of flower is at the lower end of the range for *D. laureola* (tube 3—5 mm. long; lobes 2.5 mm. long). In cultivation seed-raised plants appear to be true to type. A plant of *D. laureola* ssp. *philippi* has been growing on the rock garden at Wisley for over 15 years.

The spelling *philippi*, with a single "i" not a double "ii" at the ending, is correct.

var. *latifolia* (Cosson) Meissn. in *DC. Prod.* 539 (1857) was described from Granada in Southern Spain. It has broadly obovate leaves and is also reported from the Great Atlas, Morocco, flowering in June.

var. *cantabrica* (Willk.) Willk. in *Prod. Fl. Hisp. Supp.* 68 (1893), a compact form of the species, is stated to occur in rocky alpine districts of the Cantabrian Mts.

Whether or not the latter two variants are distinct entities is difficult to decide on present evidence.

A variegated form is mentioned in the *Gardeners' Chronicle* 162; 14 (1967), but we have not seen any variegated forms—except plants with foliage yellow-mottled with virus!

As has previously been mentioned, *D. laureola* is one of several species in which dimorphism of the flowers has been reported. Hugo Money-Coutts has noted, both in the Pyrenees and Madonie in Sicily, normal large-flowered plants with fertile anthers growing with plants looking very similar but with smaller whitish flowers and poorly developed anthers. It appears that these characters occur mainly in high altitude forms, but thorough field studies throughout the range of this species are required to evaluate their significance.

Daphne macrantha Ludlow in *Bull. Brit. Mus. Bot.* 2: 77 (1956)

ILLUSTRATION   *Bull. Brit. Mus. Bot.* 2, pl. 6 (1956) of type herbarium specimen.

Although this superb species has not been introduced into cultivation, it appears from its description that it could be a plant of extreme garden value. Sadly it is unlikely to reach our gardens for many years as it is only known from S.E. Tibet, but it has the general appearance of *D. blagayana*, with enormous individual blooms each up to 3.5 cm. in diameter. This makes it the largest-flowered *Daphne* known and it must be a splendid sight when covered with the 4-10 flowered, terminal clusters of cream-coloured, fragrant blooms.

TYPE LOCALITY   S.E. Tibet: Tsari Sama, Langong.
DESCRIPTION   Semi-prostrate evergreen shrub up to 30 cm. high. Leaves dull green with deeply indented veins, obovate, obtuse or retuse, revolute at the margins, 3—5.5 cm. long, 1.5—2.5 cm. wide. Flowers cream, slightly yellow in the centre, fragrant, very large, 2.5—3.5 cm. in diameter, in terminal clusters of 4—10; tube 1.2—1.7 cm. long; lobes 1.2—1.3 cm. long, 0.7—1 cm. wide, ovate or broadly ovate, obtuse. Fruit not known.
CHROMOSOME NO.   Not recorded.
FLOWERING PERIOD   June.
DISTRIBUTION   S.E. Tibet—known only from the type locality.
HABITAT   Among rocks on open hillsides, 4,260 m.

Daphne x mantensiana Manten ex. T. M. C. Taylor and F. Vrugtman in *Baileya* 12: 39 (1964). (*D.* x *burkwoodii* 'Somerset' x *D. retusa*)

ILLUSTRATION   *Baileya* 12: 40, t. 21 (1964) of the type herbarium specimen.

A full description and account of this unusual and attractive hybrid is given by Taylor and Vrugtman in the *Baileya* article cited above where the name is validly published. Briefly its history is as follows. In 1941 Jack Manten, a nurseryman from White Rock, British Columbia, Canada, crossed *D. retusa* (the pollen parent) with *D.* x *burkwoodii* 'Somerset' (the seed parent) obtaining a single viable seed. This germinated and material from the resultant plant was grafted (stock unstated), the grafted specimens flowering for the first time in 1946.

Plants of *D.* x *mantensiana* grown on the nursery consistently produced three crops of flowers annually, in spring, summer and autumn, and in 1953 it was offered to the trade for the first time.

Eliot Hodgkin writing on some lesser-known daphnes in the A.G.S. *Bulletin* (1972) gave a brief account of its cultivation, but in British gardens it is still scarcely known. It was first introduced in 1948 and again in 1953 to Wisley, when the raiser sent plants to the R.H.S. Garden from his nursery in British Columbia. These plants evidently did not survive for very long and it seems probable that the stock at present grown in Britain derives from an introduction in 1962 by Hugo Money-Coutts who sent a plant to Eliot Hodgkin that same year. This plant still survives (1976) and has formed a rounded, evergreen bush some two feet high and as much across. flowering freely in spring and producing lesser quantities of its rosy-purple, scented blooms for much of the rest of the year. The semi-perpetual flowering habit is one of the most useful attributes of *D.* x *mantensiana*, and even in winter occasional inflorescences appear to brave the elements.

It seems to have few foibles, appearing to be quite hardy at least in the South of England. We have grown plants successfully in open, well-drained positions on both acid and alkaline soils without difficulty.

Both the raiser and Eliot Hodgkin, however, mention that complete branches suddenly die back (a not uncommon feature of the genus), and the latter recommends cutting out any affected branches completely, stating that unless this is done immediately the whole plant is likely to die. Manten attributes the die-back to rich garden soil, but it seems probable that factors other than nutrition are involved.

PROPAGATION

(a) Seed is not known to have been produced on *D.* x *mantensiana*.

(b) Cuttings will normally strike without difficulty, flowering in the second year. Although we have as yet made no comparative tests, both relatively soft and half-ripe shoots (Groups 1 & 2, p. 41) have been rooted successfully at Wisley. Manten himself in his nursery ledger wrote:- "I raised cuttings (500 each year) by cutting when the wood is still herbaceous appr. end July, 15 Aug. at the latest . . . inserted in *moist* sand (not wet). Hormone dip 2% I.B.A. (indolebutyric acid). Temp. 60-65° at the most. Roots within a month. Shade during first half year".

(c) Grafting. Manten's initial stock was grafted from the original seedling as already stated. If required, no doubt stock of either parent, or any of the species conventionally used, would prove satisfactory.

TYPE From a plant in the garden of Mr. H. Eddie, Vancouver, British Columbia, August 7, 1963, F. Vrugtman 1964.

DESCRIPTION An evergreen shrub of fairly erect habit reaching 60—70 cm. in height and as much across; young wood brown, pubescent, Leaves alternate, dull dark green above, paler below, leathery, glabrous, distributed fairly evenly along the branchlets of the current year, the lower leaves sometimes falling by winter and leaving clusters of persistent foliage at the apex; sessile, oblong to narrowly obovate-oblong, 3.0—3.5 cm. long up to 1.3 (1.4) cm. wide, entire; apex emarginate. Flowers in terminal clusters of up to 12 (or occasionally more), very fragrant, purplish-rose ("orchid-purple") outside, slightly paler within; tube to 7 mm. long, finely silky-hairy, lobes to 6 mm. long, ovate-lanceolate, acute, margins slightly rolled inwards. Fruit unknown.

CHROMOSOME NO. Unknown. Taylor and Vrugtman report that Dr. Nevling had found an apparent increase in pollen fertility compared with *D.* x *burkwoodii*, but had been unable to obtain a satisfactory chromosome count for *D.* x *mantensiana*.

FLOWERING PERIOD May (—June) and again in summer and autumn, continuing sparsely into winter in mild weather.

DISTRIBUTION A hybrid of garden origin raised in 1941.

As far as we know only the one clone of *D.* x *mantensiana* is known, and has been given the cultivar name 'Manten' by Taylor and Vrugtman (1964).

Daphne jasminea (p. 116)   Photo: Downward

127

Daphne jezoensis (p. 119)   Photo: R. Elliott

Daphne laureola (p. 122).

Photos: *R. Elliott*

Daphne odora '*Aureo-marginata*' (p. 147)

Daphne mezereum L., *Sp. Pl.* 356 (1753)

ILLUSTRATIONS   See drawing on p. 76, and photos on pp. 92, 145; also *Bot. Mag.* (n.s.) 171: t. 272 (1956); *The Garden* 29: opp. p. 602 (1886), a beautiful composite plate of *D. mezereum* and var. *alba* in fl. and fr., together with the double white form in fl.

AWARD   A.G.M. 1929.

It is scarcely necessary to extol the virtues of this superb, early-flowering shrub which has been a favourite for many centuries and is generally considered native to Britain, although there is some dispute on this point. It was apparently cultivated as long ago as 1561, but curiously was not recorded in Britain by botanists until 1759, when Miller mentions "a Discovery made of its growing in some Woods near Andover, from whence a great number of plants have been taken in late Years". Evidently conservation problems were not confined to our century alone. As may be expected, there are numerous references to *D. mezereum* in the literature and inevitably Gerard had quite a lot to say about it. He called it the "Germane Olive Spurge" stating that it grew "naturally in moist and shadowy woods of most of the East countries, especially about Melvin in Poland, from whence I have had great plenty for my Garden . . . " It was known to apothecaries of the period as Mezereon, still its common name today, and Gerard informs us that "The leaves of Mezereon do purge downward, flegme, choler and waterish humours with great violence"—an uncomfortable thought! He goes on to say, "Also, if a drunkard doe eat one graine or berry of this plant, hee cannot be allured to drinke any drinke at that time, such will be the heate in his mouth and choking in the throat".

Its basic medical uses at that time (in spite of its known poisonous properties) were to deaden toothache (using the dried root), to raise blisters by applying an infusion of the bark externally, as a general pick-me-up to purge "flegme and choler" and to clean ulcers using an infusion of the leaves. Warning should be given that all parts of the plant are poisonous, and it would be *most* unwise to sample the fruit or chew the leaves out of curiosity. Linnaeus tells us that six berries are sufficient to kill a wolf (!) and records a girl's death from eating the fruits. Gwendolyn Cadney, in the A.G.S. *Bulletin* 21: 194 (1953) mentions sampling the seeds and finding "a texture and flavour of cotton wool and slight astringent burning in the throat for some hours". Even the flowers impart this acrid taste if chewed or eaten.

Birds, however, are most appreciative of the seeds, quickly robbing bushes of the fruits even when green, although one report states that berries of the white form are usually untouched. In *R.H.S. Journ.* Vol. 81, Aug. '59, Dr. Max Pettersson reports that in recent years greenfinches have eagerly sought out *D. mezereum*, despoiling the bushes in June, not for the fleshy covering of the fruits but for the kernels of the "stone", unlike blackbirds whose main concern is the flesh. At least the blackbirds leave the poor gardener with some chance of self-sown seedlings from the droppings! The greenfinch despoliation has gradually spread in Britain since about 1900 and now covers most of the country, although it was apparently unknown on the Continent at the time the article was written.

In England *D. mezereum* occurs occasionally in woodland on calcareous soils, and Clapham, Tutin and Warburg accept it as native in certain areas from Yorkshire and Westmorland southwards (not in Devon and Cornwall) but many of the localities may well be of naturalised stands in view of its long record of cultivation and ease of spread by bird-sown seeds.

It undoubtedly grows best on fairly heavy, alkaline soils, but is tolerant of a very wide range of conditions provided drainage is sharp and the soil does not dry out. Even on the acid soils of Wisley plants have been growing (somewhat slowly) in the wild garden for over twenty years, and at Tower Court, Ascot, where the soil is extremely acid, there used to be huge plants of the white form which seeded around freely. In the Cairngorms it thrives in the garden of Jack Drake and numerous other examples could be quoted of its tolerance in gardens. The *Gardeners Chronicle* of 1856 calls attention to a remarkably fine specimen at Bishopthorpe Palace, 13 feet in circumference and 2—3 feet in height, growing in a vine border and apparently revelling in the surface coatings of manure applied to the vine roots each season. As has been mentioned in our comments on general cultivation, many daphnes benefit greatly from feeding and one of the reasons they suddenly die could well be attributable to the starvation diet which seems to be their lot in many gardens.

This does not mean, of course, the application of large quantities of rich manure or artificial fertilisers, but a sensible dressing of very well-rotted manure, mushroom compost or the like. Foliar feeding can also be beneficial, particularly early in the season when the young foliage is capable of absorbing the available nutrients readily.

As a woodland species it generally appreciates a modicum of shade, but is adaptable in this respect and plants can often be seen growing in full exposure in gardens where the soil is not too dry.

Unfortunately, *D. mezereum* is very prone to infection with virus diseases which mottle and sometimes distort the foliage. Affected plants usually linger for a number of years, becoming progressively less vigorous and less floriferous before finally dying. There is no known cure and as soon as signs of the disease are seen the affected plants should be burnt. Take care also to sterilise any secateurs or tools used in disposing of the plants as this virus is highly infectious and even handling an infected plant and then touching another daphne might pass on the disease which is probably aphid-spread. An obvious precaution is to keep the local aphid population at as low a level as possible.

The specific epithet *mezereum* is latinised from a Persian name and although *Daphne* is a feminine genus and one might expect the ending to agree in gender, i.e. "*D. mezerea*", it does not. In instances where specific epithets are derived from old generic names (in this case from the genus *Mezereum*) the spelling of the epithet remains unchanged whatever the gender of the generic name to which it is attached, hence the apparent anomaly of a neuter ending followed by a feminine ending as with *D. mezereum alba*.

PROPAGATION

(a) Seed. Unquestionably the most satisfactory method of increase. We have already advocated collecting the fruit before it is fully ripe, cleaning and sowing the seed as soon as possible to obtain good germination the following spring. This is no new technique as we discovered on checking through *The Gardeners Dictionary* where Miller comments of *D. mezereum:*—"This is propagated by seeds, which should be sown on a border exposed to the east, soon after the berries are ripe; for if they are not sown until the following spring they miscarry and always remain a year in the ground before the plants appear; whereas those which are sown in August will grow the following spring, so that a year is saved, and these never fail." Whilst one might query the last few words, it is a salutary lesson in accurate observation.

Mr. Arthur Carter has very kindly allowed us to include the results of a preliminary experiment carried out in 1974-5 with seed of *D. mezereum*, all taken from one bush and collected and sown on 15.6.74.

Treatment	No. out of 24 germinated
1. Red fruits—entire seed	4
2. Red fruits—entire seed rubbed	19
3. Red fruits—entire seed washed 1 hr. in running water ..	6
4. Red fruits—entire seed soaked 1 hr. in water	7
5. Red fruits—naked seed	2
6. Green fruits—entire seed	10
7. Green fruits—naked seed	1

Four replications each of 6 seeds were used for each treatment.
Entire seed=seed after removal from the fruit,
Naked seed=seed after outer grey coat is removed leaving embryo and cotyledons unprotected.

A dark green, almost black, film is present on the seed which can be rubbed off on a piece of cloth. Germination results were best with this technique, suggesting the removal of an inhibitor in the film or possibly damage to the seed-coat similar to that which might occur after stratification.

As will be seen, green fruits (entire seed) germinated better than red fruits (entire seed), suggesting that the presence of inhibitors or hardening of the seed coat might be dependent on ripeness.

131

We must hope that this experiment will be followed up and extended to other species to provide accurate data in this much-neglected field.

(b) Cuttings. Soft cuttings of young shoots with a heel are said to have been rooted successfully (Group 1, p. 41) and Halda also advocates hardwood cuttings taken from the basal part of the plant in winter. We have no experience or data of either method.

(c) Root Cuttings. A report in *Gard. Chron.* (1949) records that roots (left in the ground after transplanting *D. mezereum*) sprouted to form a new plant.

(d) Grafting. Stocks of *D. mezereum* are, of course, much used for grafting other species, but in certain cases variants which do not come true from seed, such as *D. mezereum* f. *plena*, may be grafted on to seedling stock of the same species.

TYPE LOCALITY "Woods of Northern Europe".
DESCRIPTION Erect, much branched, deciduous shrub up to 2.5 m. in height, usually only 1—1.5 m. in cultivation. Branches often pubescent in the first year, gradually becoming glabrous; bark ageing from pale to dark brown. Leaves spirally arranged, normally appearing after flowering time, rather pale green, glabrous, rarely ciliate or pubescent when young, oblanceolate, apex obtuse, subacute or sometimes shortly apiculate, cuneate at the base, more or less sessile or short stalked; 5—12 cm. long, 1—3 cm. wide. Flowers in lateral clusters of 2—4, scattered along the previous season's growth and often so crowded as to form a dense cylindrical spike, normally reddish-purple to pinkish, (white in f. *alba*) very fragrant; tube 5—6 mm. long, finely pubescent outside; lobes broadly ovate, obtuse, 5—6 mm. long, 4—6 mm. wide. Fruit fleshy, red, (yellow in f. *alba*) ellipsoid or almost globose.
CHROMOSOME NO. 2n=18 (Maude, 1940).
FLOWERING PERIOD Feb.—March in Britain, but often much later at high altitudes in the wild; var. *autumnalis* flowers in British gardens from Oct.—Feb.
DISTRIBUTION Widespread in Europe (except the extreme west, south and north); Asia Minor; Caucasus; Central Asia; Siberia. A rare native of Britain.
HABITAT In woods at low altitudes or in open rocky or grassy places higher up; 50—2,600 m.

With the very wide range of *D. mezereum*, considerable variation might be expected, but apart from colour variants extending from the deepest purple to pure white there has only been limited botanical activity in attempts to subdivide the species, although a number of horticultural forms and clones have been selected. Exceptionally fine large-flowered or deep coloured forms can sometimes be found in the wild. High mountain plants are often much more dwarf than those from low altitudes and are more suitable for small rock gardens; they are sometimes referred to as "var. *alpina*." Mrs. K. Dryden has a 12-year-old plant under this name which has formed a rounded, compact bush 120 cm. across by 60 cm. high which flowers well, with dark reddish-pink blooms, but which does not set seed. We have traced no valid publication for the epithet "alpina". Some forms collected in the Balkans are, in contrast, very tall (up to 4 ft. or more) with long willowy growths which become densely clothed with flowers.

132

The following variants have been traced, and, where possible, publication dates and information are provided.

Forma *alba* (Weston) Schelle in Beissner et al. *Hand. Laubh.—Ben.* (1903)

Synonyms, *D. mezereum* var. *alba* Aiton; *D. albiflora* J. Wolf; *D. mezereum* var. *albida* Meissn.

White-flowered variants, apparently always with yellow or amber fruit, occur wild and have, by some authorities, been considered sufficiently distinct to represent a separate species. Seed from white-flowered forms is reported as coming true as regards flower colour, although some variation from creamy-white to snow-white occurs (Amsler, 1953). This certainly bears out our own observations, even when mixed populations of white and purple forms are growing in close proximity. Support also comes from Miller in his *Gardeners Dictionary* (1768):—

"There are two distinct sorts of this, one with a white flower which is succeeded by yellow berries, the other with Peach-coloured flowers and red fruits. These are by some supposed to be accidental varieties arising from the same seeds, but I have several times raised these plants from seed, and always found the plants come up the same, as those from which the seeds were taken, so they do not vary, therefore may be called different species. There is a variety of the Peach-coloured Mezereon, with flowers of a much deeper colour than the common, but these I have always found to vary in their colours when raised from seeds."

One report we have received suggests that there may be some difference in the method of germination, seed from purple-flowered plants germinating with the cotyledons appearing above ground (epigeal) whilst the cotyledons of the germinating seeds from white-flowered plants remain below soil level (hypogeal). An experimental investigation of the germination processes and the genetic structures of the two entities should prove interesting.

VARIANTS OF *f. alba*

'Bowles' Variety' received an A.M. in April 1947 (not as 'Bowles' White' under which name it is also known). The flowers are pure white and the plant very vigorous with long branches up to 6 ft. in height. Plants grown under this name today are not vegetatively propagated from the original clone, but seed is said to produce offspring very similar to Bowles' original plant. There is no doubt, however, that seedlings of this stock vary to a certain extent, although many maintain the rather strict, upright habit of the original.

There were some superb specimens derived from seed of Bowles' plant at Tower Court, Ascot, which Amsler considered even finer than 'Bowles' Variety' and one of the authors who once weeded around these plants and their offspring can vouch for their magnificence. Seedlings he was given, alas, did not achieve the quality of the parents! It would seem, therefore, that a certain amount of selection is needed to maintain this stock at a high level.

'Paul's White', named by Bowles in *The Garden* 74: 255 (1910), was no doubt the plant from which 'Bowles' Variety' was derived but curiously Bowles makes no mention of any white form of *D. mezereum* in his famous *My Garden* trilogy. His description in *The Garden* indicates that 'Paul's White' reproduced itself quite true from seed and had large blooms which were pure white compared with the creamy-white of the normal albino. The illustration accompanying the article shows that the habit of 'Paul's White' was upright and the plant appears very similar in character to the stock grown as 'Bowles' Variety' today.

'Alba Plena' is a variant with double white flowers referred to in horticultural literature, but which we have not seen. According to Halda it has relatively large, full blooms. It is most probably an old garden clone, although given botanical rank as *D. mezereum* f. *plena* (Hort. ex Rehd.) Schneider, *Ill. Handb. Laubh.* 2: 402 (1909).

Propagation (if one can trace a plant!) would be by grafting, less certainly by soft heel cuttings and just possibly by root cuttings.

Other variants

Var. *autumnalis* Hort. ex Rehd. in Bailey, *Cycl. Am. Hort.* 1: 456 (1900).

Synonyms. *D. mezereum* var. *maxima* Hort. ex Schneid. *D. mezereum sempervirens* Hort.

An uncommon but very desirable variant which begins flowering in October or November and continues until February or later, apparently with larger flowers than the type.

There appears to be some confusion with a form of *D. mezereum* named "var. *grandiflorum*" by Jacques in *Ann. Soc. Hort. Paris* 32: 254 (1843) which is said to be large-flowered but does not appear to have been credited with flowering in the autumn. Schelle in *Beissn.* et al., *Handb. Laubh.—Ben.* 355, (1903) and later Rehder in *Bibliog. Cult. Trees and Shrubs* 479, (1949) both accept Jacques' epithet for this autumn-flowering variant, but his article makes no mention of this character and we therefore use the more appropriate *autumnalis* here.

It is referred to in the *Gardeners Chronicle* of 1856 (as *D. mezereum autumnale*) as "rare and valuable and now almost lost to our collections" so even last century it was by no means a common plant, although it is still (just) available in the trade.

Although frequently stated to be sterile (or to produce seed very rarely) there is some evidence that seed is produced and comes true to type. Following Eliot Hodgkin's lecture on Daphnes at the R.H.S. Hall in July, 1961, a Mr. G. E. Stone of Morden wrote saying that he had a 20 year old plant (about 7 ft. high) which most years began flowering in October or November and continued until early April. He had raised many plants from seed taken from this bush and all showed the same characteristics. One season he picked over 2 lb. of berries from the plant but greenfinches had discovered its charm, visiting it regularly in May and stripping the crop. Unfortunately we have not been able to trace this plant or its offspring. Propagation as for *D. mezereum* 'Alba Plena' and possibly also from seed.

'ROSEA' A name used to cover variants with pink or rose-coloured rather than purple-red flowers. Selection from seed is required to maintain a fairly even stock.

var. *rubra* Aiton in *Hort. Kew.* 2: 25 (1789)

A name applied to forms with deep red-purple flowers but not easily circumscribed, although a convenient group name to use. In Holland, work at Boskoop in the 1950's produced a stock known as Rubra Select—a group of plants with deep purple-red blooms. It is interesting to note that the more vigorous plants raised from seed during this work had pale rose flowers and seedlings from these vigorous plants were predominantly pale flowered. Care in selection to maintain stocks with deep-coloured blooms is therefore needed and in particular to avoid choosing the seedlings on vigour alone.

'RUBRA PLENA'. A variant with double purple-red flowers. Halda mentions it, and there are several references to this clone (if such it be) in horticultural literature. Again we have not seen this form. Propagation as for 'Alba Plena'.

'ATROPURPUREA' or var. *atropurpurea*. See *D. x houtteana*.

'BYFORD'S VARIETY'. Exhibited at the R.H.S. Hall on April 1, 1947, by E. A. Bowles. It is believed to be a pale-flowered form.

'COPPERGATE' A plant was received under this name at Wisley in 1963 from Hugo Money-Coutts. It appears to have been lost without a description being recorded.

'VARIEGATA'. A clone found in 1856 in a batch of seedlings by a Mr. Joshua Major, landscape gardener of Knosthorpe, Leeds. A plate in Lowe & Howard's *Beautiful Leaved Plants* (1861) depicts an attractive yellow and grey-green variegation of the foliage, very different from the unsavoury mottling due to virus. Apparently some branches on the seedling were variegated and scions from these branches were propagated by grafting. Sadly we can find no trace of this clone in cultivation today.

Related Species

In addition to these variants it is worth mentioning here the following recently described species:—

> **Daphne rechingeri** Wendelbo in *Nytt. Mag. Bot. Oslo* 8: 207 (1960). This comes from the Haraz Valley in Mazanderan, Iran, and is very similar to *D. mezereum*. It

is said to have dull purplish-violet flowers which are green-ish inside. An introduction of this species would be interesting to compare with D. *mezereum*.

Daphne mucronata Royle *Illustr. Bot. Himal.* 322, t. 81 (1839)

SYNONYMS   *D. angustifolia* C. Koch; *D. acuminata* Boiss. & Hohen-ack. ex Stocks; *D. acuminata* var. *kochii* Meissn.; *D. cachemireana* Meissn; *D. mucronata* var. *affghanica* Meissn.

ILLUSTRATION   None known.

AWARD   None.

D. *mucronata*, like the closely related *D. gnidioides*, is not a species which inspires immediate devotion. A very common species in some parts of its range, it can form a dominant part of the vegeta-tion, since it is avoided by grazing animals as it is poisonous. The wood was at one time used to make charcoal for the manufacture of gunpowder; and in the Sutlej area of Pakistan a spirit is distilled from the berries.

Not a particularly attractive species, often being rather lanky in growth with greyish-green foliage and small creamy-white or yellowish flowers. At the eastern end of its distribution the flowers are said to be primrose-yellow, which could be more interesting than the usual creamy-white forms which occur over much of its range. In eastern Turkey it inhabits a bitterly cold area, often in crevices of limestone rocks, where it makes a fairly dense shrub only 2 feet high. Collections from sites such as these might well be hardy and would undoubtedly require very sharply drained positions in full sun to thrive. Halda suggests that it is useful in a sunny position amongst heathers and small rhododendrons, but requires fairly strict pruning to maintain a dense, compact habit.

Although introduced on several occasions, it is only rarely avail-able in Britain. Possibly Paul Furse's collections (P.F. 3423 and P.F. 3454) are still being maintained.

PROPAGATION

(a) *Seed.*   The most satisfactory method of increase if avail-able.

(b) *Cuttings.*   As D. *oleoides*.

(c) *Grafting.*   Commercially D. *longilobata* has been used success-fully; seedlings of D. *oleoides*, which is closely related, would be worth trying.

TYPE LOCALITY   "Persia, Kurdistan and Upper Baluchistan".

DESCRIPTION   An erect, evergreen shrub with very wiry stems up to 2 (3) m. in height; young branches pubescent, reddish- or purplish-brown, older branches glabrous, greyish. Leaves alternate, sessile, scattered along the branches, narrowly oblanceolate, acuminate or mucronate, grey, leathery, glabrous or very occa-sionally pubescent, 2—7 cm. long, 0.5—1.2 cm. wide. Flowers creamy-white or yellowish, fragrant, in dense terminal clusters; tube about 6 mm. long, woolly outside; lobes ovate, obtuse about 3 mm. long. Fruit ellipsoid, somewhat pubescent, reddish-orange, about 1 cm.

FLOWERING PERIOD   June—July.

CHROMOSOME NO. Not recorded.
DISTRIBUTION E. Turkey, N.E. Iraq, Iran, Afghanistan, Chitral, Kashmir and Punjab.
HABITAT Open rocky places, 1000—2700 m.

A wide-ranging species such as *D. mucronata* is liable to different botanical interpretations, as may be judged from the above synonymy. There seems insufficient evidence to maintain any of the variants described, as, although individual plants may appear very different, the characters separating them merge on examination of a wide range of material, some forms even approaching the related *D. oleoides* in certain of its localities.

D. oleoides is usually a fairly compact shrub with much shorter leaves, but upright, loose-growing forms with long leaves similar to *D. mucronata* in general aspect are known to occur in parts of its range.

D. gnidioides, although described separately in this book, is scarcely different in appearance from *D. mucronata*, although it may perhaps be distinguished by the less fleshy, almost dry fruit and in being a maquis plant of low altitudes in the east Aegean and Western Turkey.

Related Species

Daphne linearifolia Hart in *Some account of the flora and fauna of Sinai*, 95 (1891) is also very closely related to *D. mucronata*, but has stems densely clothed with extremely narrow leaves, 4—6 cm. long and about 2 mm. wide. It is a native of south and east Jordan, especially around Petra, where it inhabits hot dry cliffs.

Daphne x napolitana Loddiges, *Bot. Cab.* t. 719 (1823)

SYNONYMS *D. collina* var. *neapolitana* (Lodd.) Lindl.; ? *D. fioniana* Hort.; *D. delahayi* and *D. delahayana* Hort.; ? *D. elisae* Vis.; ? *D. cneorum* var. *maximum* Jacques.
ILLUSTRATIONS Lodd. *Bot. Cab.* t. 719 (1823); *Bot. Reg.* 10: t. 822 (1824).
AWARD A.G.M. (1969).

One of the best daphnes for general garden use, *D. x napolitana* is a mystery plant as far as its origin and status is concerned. It is relatively easy to grow, forming a dense, spreading, evergreen shrub occasionally to 3 ft. in height but more usually about 1½—2 ft. tall, covered during early spring with fragrant, rosy-purple blooms borne in dense terminal clusters. The flowers appear slightly "greyed" in bud due to the hairiness of the perianth tube, opening to a brighter rosy-purple before fading to a paler hue. It has no apparent preference for soil conditions, thriving in open positions in acid sand, heavy clay or hot dry chalk, provided the planting position has been suitably enriched with moisture-retentive materials and that the site is adequately drained. It appears perfectly hardy in Britain, occasionally suffering slightly in extreme weather conditions, but otherwise is a plant without fads.

It was first described by Loddiges in 1823 and was apparently introduced by this firm to Britain. Although no hint of its origin is given, it is presumed from Loddiges' epithet that it was received from the Naples area. Grown under a number of names including *D. oleoides* and those listed in the synonymy given above.

Sadly *neapolitana*, the more familiar spelling of the epithet was not that originally used by Loddiges when he described it in the *Botanical Cabinet*. Both as a heading to the text and on the plate the spelling *napolitana* is used, and although this is sometimes treated as an orthographic error there seem no grounds for so doing. Somewhat regretfully therefore we adopt Loddiges' original spelling.

PROPAGATION

(a)   Seed is not known to be produced, and on specimens we have examined the stigma appears to be aborted.

(b)   Cuttings.   Both relatively soft and reasonably firm cuttings root without difficulty (Groups 1 and 2, p. 41).

(c)   Grafting.   Sometimes used but unnecessary. Stocks known to have been used successfully include *D. mezereum*, *D. collina* and *D. longilobata*.

TYPE LOCALITY   Probably of hybrid origin; the type is the illustration in Lodd. *Bot. Cab*. t. 719 (1823).
DESCRIPTION   Densely branched, erect, compact evergreen shrub, up to 50 (75) cm. in height, rarely more; young stems finely pubescent with pale hairs; older stems dark brown with darker hairs. Leaves alternate, dark green above, paler and glaucous beneath, leathery, scattered along the stems, glabrous, except at the base beneath, oblanceolate or narrowly obovate, obtuse, 2—3.5 cm. long, 0.5—0.7 cm. wide. Flowers in terminal clusters of 6—8 (—16), also sometimes a few in the upper leaf axils, deep rosy-purple in bud opening deep pink, very fragrant; tube about 1 cm. long, finely white-pubescent outside; lobes broadly ovate, obtuse, 3—4 mm. long, 3—4 mm. wide. Fruit unknown (the plant may be sterile as the stigma appears to be aborted).
CHROMOSOME NO.   Not recorded.
FLOWERING PERIOD   March—May; sporadically through the summer and autumn.

Controversy over the origin of *D.* x *napolitana*, and even more as to its status as a species or hybrid, is considerable. By some it is stated only to be a variant of *D. collina* selected from the wild, but by others it is also said to have been raised in or near Naples from a cross between *D. australis* (*D. collina* or *D. sericea*) and *D. oleoides;* or alternatively from *D. collina* x *D. oleoides*, or *D. collina* x *D. cneorum*!

In terms of measurements alone it falls within the range of *D. sericea* but nowadays it is generally considered to be a hybrid of *D. collina* with either *D. oleoides* or *D. cneorum*. The glabrous leaves with turned down margins certainly have the look of *D. cneorum* and in habit and leaf-shape *D.* x *napolitana* suggests a narrower-leaved *D. collina*.

Loddiges in his original, very brief description, says "This is supposed to be a hybrid plant, produced by the collina, which is a native of the neighbourhood of Naples, and the Cneorum".

As will be seen, Loddiges himself was not entirely sure of its status and in view of the slight differences in descriptions and parentage which appear in various accounts, one can speculate that the several clones (?) raised in the early 1800's under such names as *D. fioniana*, *D. delahayana* and *D. elisae* have become confused in gardens. This might also account for the differing views on the parents of *D. x napolitana*.

The following rather scanty information has been traced on the plants given these names:—

D. cneorum maximum Jacques

Synonyms *D. cneorum grandiflorum* Loddiges; *D. cneorum pyramidale* Makoy; *D. cneorum strictum* Hort.

Although always included under *D. cneorum*, the female parent, it is stated to be a hybrid of that species with *D. collina* raised by M. Jacques near Paris according to George Gordon in *The Garden* 9: 568 (1876). He provides a fairly detailed description mentioning the hairy young leaves and pale rose flowers which would distinguish it from *D. x napolitana*.

D. delahayana Hort. ex Visiani in *Rev. Pl. Min. Cognit. Hort. Patow*. 4 (1855) also referred to as *D. delahayi* Hort.

Apparently raised in 1827 by M. Fion of Paris, its parents being *D. collina* fertilised with pollen of *D. cneorum*.

D. elisae Visiani in *Rev. Pl. Min. Cognit. Hort. Patow*. 4 (1855) is apparently referable to *D. x napolitana*. The descriptions and plate given by Visiani (as well as the purported parentage) match *D. x napolitana* well and although its habitat is given as Mexico (!) it is plain from the accompanying text that it came from "The Belgian garden of Signor Cabianca with the name of Daphne from Mexico" and not direct from the New World.

D. fioniana Hort.

A name apparently applied to *D. x hybrida* (*D. collina* x *D. odora*) and also to plants of *D. collina* x *D. oleoides*.

According to George Gordon in *The Garden* 9: 568 (1876) it was raised by M. Fion near Paris and forms a dense, twiggy evergreen shrub to 3 feet high flowering from March to May, and very similar in character to *D. x napolitana*. It was cultivated fairly widely in Britain proving "quite hardy near London" and could obviously have become confused with *D. x napolitana* from which it apparently differed in its pale lilac (not rosy-purple) flowers, and in the smooth (not hairy) old shoots.

No authentic material of any of these hybrids has been seen and it is therefore preferable to maintain the *status quo* and refer to plants in British gardens as *D. x napolitana*, although it is quite possible that there is more than one entity involved.

Daphne odora Thunb. in *Nova Acta Soc. Sc. Uppsala.* 4: 39 (1783).
SYNONYMS *D. indica* Hort. non L.; *D. japonica* Paxton; *D. japonica*
Thunb.; *D. sinensis* Lam.; *D. chinensis*: Spreng.; *D. speciosissima*
Carr.; ? *D. triflora* Lour. (Other specific epithets which apply to
infraspecific variants or cultivars are listed under the appropriate
entries).
ILLUSTRATIONS See drawing on p. 70. There are few available
illustrations of typical *D. odora*, so for easy reference illustrations
of variants are listed under the appropriate entry.

If legend is to be believed we owe the discovery of this superbly
scented shrub to a monk of Lu Shan who fell asleep by a cliff and
during his dreams was conscious of a delicious fragrance. On
awakening he found that the source of the perfume was in the
flowers of what we now call *Daphne odora* and which he named
Shui Hsiang, meaning "Sleeping Scent", later to be known as
"Good Augury Perfume" (Li, *The Garden Flowers of China*, 1959).

In China *D. odora* has been grown and valued in gardens since
the Sung Dynasty (A.D. 960—1279), and, as is the case with many
plants cultivated in the East, it is now hard to trace plants which
approximate to the wild form.

It has a long history of cultivation in our gardens and greenhouses
under a variety of names, but the original introduction appears to
have been from China (not Japan as stated in Bean, 1973) when a
consignment of plants including this species was sent to Kew in
1770 by Benjamin Torin, an employee of the East India Company.
The actual date of introduction is usually given as 1771 when the
plants presumably reached this country after their long voyage
from China. As with so many plants imported from the Far East,
it was presumed to require stove conditions, but was soon found to
tolerate considerably lower temperatures, becoming a much favoured
winter-flowering pot-plant both here and on the Continent. This
first introduction evidently lacked the yellowish margin to the leaf
of the form most commonly seen in Britain today, which is probably
derived from what Siebold called "*D. japonica*" introduced about
1840. It is difficult to pinpoint accurately the dates when the different
variants of *D. odora* reached British gardens, but, where known,
further information is provided under the individual descriptions of
these forms.

In the milder gardens of Britain, the evergreen *D. odora* and its
variants appear reasonably hardy, forming small mounded shrubs
some 3—4 ft. high and as much across, but apart from the clone
'Aureo-marginata' it is doubtful whether they will withstand severe
winters unprotected in the open garden elsewhere. At Wisley *D.
odora* 'Aureo-marginata' has grown unprotected on Battleston Hill
for over 18 years. Although occasionally the foliage is singed in
extreme winters, it has proved one of the most useful of early-
flowering shrubs, wafting the sweet fragrance of its purplish-red and
white blooms through the open woodland in which it thrives without

much more care and attention than an annual leafmould mulch. Normally it flowers during February and March out of doors, but in mild weather may open its blooms earlier: under glass *D. odora* forms may be flowered in coolhouse conditions from November onwards.

Of the other variants 'Mazelii' is probably the hardiest, but is much less commonly seen than 'Aureo-marginata'. According to Bean (1973) it "requires winter protection near London" but we have not been able to locate authentic plants of this clone to grow, stock obtained under this name proving (very acceptably!) to be a good form of *D. blagayana*.

A white-flowered form is commonly cultivated in California and is occasionally offered in Britain, but like the type (or what approximates to it in gardens) is not of the same degree of hardiness as 'Aureo-marginata'.

Although *D. odora* will tolerate a wide pH range, its performance on very chalky soils is not always satisfactory, growth being poor and the foliage pale and "sick", but, in spite of this, flowers are often produced in abundance. A plentiful supply of humus in the soil and occasional foliar feeds will benefit plants grown under such conditions, but it is best given a well-drained but humus-rich soil in an open sunny position where it is sheltered from cold winds. "A corner outside by the kitchen and chimney, the sort of place where the cat goes to bed and where blue-bottles sit on the wall in late autumn . . . " is Bowles' recipe, to which masterly prose may be added in more prosaic fashion the suggestion that *D. odora* 'Aureo-marginata' is worth trying in any position in the open border where a larger, evergreen neighbour takes the force of the prevailing winds. In cold gardens, however, the shelter of a wall might be advisable, particularly under a window where the delicious fragrance could be appreciated from within.

There are reports that in full sun it proves less floriferous than in slight shade, even in the same garden, but it would be unwise to generalise as we know of good specimens which flower freely in both these aspects and it is only in dense shade that flower production seems to be less free.

D. odora was much in demand as an early-flowering greenhouse or pot-plant in the 19th century, and it is interesting to read some of the cultural hints given which tend to be contradictory—a state of affairs not unfamiliar today! As will be mentioned later, several different forms were grown at that time and it seems probable that the variation in advice might well be due to the differing flowering habits and cultural requirements of these individual forms. Certainly those with entirely green leaves appear to be somewhat less tolerant than forms with variegated foliage, but the effect of virus and possibly leaf spot could be additional factors involved as both diseases can seriously debilitate or kill *D. odora*.

Under cool greenhouse conditions and using J.I. No. 2 compost or the equivalent, there should be little difficulty in growing *D. odora* as a pot plant for winter decoration, when its clusters of pink-flushed blooms are virtually unrivalled in their intense fragrance.

Pinching, in the early stages of growth, is desirable both for pot plants and those to be grown in the open so that a bushy plant is produced. Left to its own devices *D. odora* can become somewhat straggly in habit and it may be necessary occasionally to prune out wayward branches in early spring, making certain that the cut surface is sealed to minimise the chances of fungal attack and possible dieback.

In China the bark, like that of several other *Daphne* species, has been used for paper-making, whilst the roots are stated to be used for local medicines, no doubt for similar purposes as the roots of *D. mezereum*.

PROPAGATION

(a) Seed. Evidently very rarely produced. *D. odora* is stated by Hara to be dioecious, and female plants are apparently extremely uncommon in Japan where it is widely grown. No record of fruit production in Britain has been traced, but Halda says "ripened after about 5 weeks", stating that it is easily raised from seed, which is somewhat surprising. In spite of this lack of seed production, some degree of fertility (more probably of the anthers) must occur in some cases as *D.* x *hybrida* almost certainly has *D. odora* as one parent.

(b) Cuttings. The most satisfactory method of increase. Cuttings of ripened or firm wood of the current season will root without difficulty in a closed case or under mist, and soft tip cuttings may also be used successfully. Both Groups 1 and 2 (p. 41) therefore apply.

Records of cuttings being taken and rooted in almost every month of the year can be found in the literature, the two "favourite" periods being January—February and July. In the *Gardeners Chronicle* for 1849, gentle bottom heat, a close humid atmosphere and a sandy peat mix are recommended for February-struck cuttings "which root easily". It is stated that "the best plants are from cuttings of the tips of last year's shoots which have flowered in winter" using the portion of the stem where the flowers were borne as part of the cutting. The resulting plants were apparently well-furnished, as several shoots were produced from growth buds on the inflorescence, obviating the need for stopping which is usually required if normal cuttings of unflowered growths are used.

In New Zealand where *D. odora* is of some importance in the nursery trade, research into propagation from cuttings has been

142

carried out. B. Haggo (*International Plant Propagators' Journal*, 1973:372) reports that tip-cuttings in pits with a 3 to 1 sand-peat mix, bottom heat of 75°F. and mist, root in 10 weeks. Some trouble has been experienced with Pythium root rot, but cuttings still unrooted after 10 weeks and re-inserted in these conditions appeared more resistant to Pythium than fresh material. It was also found that below pH 6 growth was restricted but between pH 6.0—6.4 growth was good.

(c) Grafting. Used occasionally, but in view of the ease with which cuttings may be rooted, generally unnecessary. Stocks of *D. mezereum, D. longilobata, D. pontica* and *D. laureola* have been used successfully.

(d) Layering. Sometimes suggested (Bean, 1973) and quite possible using the lower branches of a mature plant, but only of real use if facilities for taking cuttings are not available.

TYPE   A cultivated plant from Nagasaki, Japan, of unknown origin.
DESCRIPTION   Glabrous, sub-erect, sometimes spreading, evergreen shrub 1.5—2.0 m. in height; branches fairly stout, young shoots green, older bark purplish-brown. Leaves alternate, sessile, clustered towards the tips of the shoots, dark glossy green (paler in some forms), leathery, oblanceolate, narrowly oval, acute or subacute, 4—8 cm. long, 1.5—2.5 cm. wide. Flowers in dense terminal heads, or occasionally with additional, axillary lateral inflorescences, reddish-purple in bud, white or reddish with a purple flush outside when open, or pure white, strongly and sweetly scented, sometimes with a sharp lemon fragrance; tube 8—10 mm. long, glabrous (? occasionally hairy); lobes 6—7 mm. long, 4—5 mm. wide, ovate, subacute. Stated to be dioecious but perhaps modified through long cultivation. Fruit fleshy, red, rarely produced in cultivation.
CHROMOSOME NO.   n=12, 13 or 14; 2n=27. Other *Daphne* species counted have a chromosome number n=9 but it is possible that long cultivation and mutation have led to abnormalities in the pollen grains and embryo sacs which might account for this difference.
FLOWERING PERIOD   (Jan.) Feb.—March (April) in Britain outside; Dec.— March under glass.
DISTRIBUTION   China; Formosa; also Cochinchina according to Hara. The exact distribution is uncertain due to the long time it has been cultivated. Hemsley, *Journ. Linn. Soc.* 26: 395 (1891) records collections by Henry and others from Chekiang (at 3,000 ft.), Hupeh and Szechuan provinces in China but Rehder in *Plantae Wilsonianae* 2: 545 (1916) says "Typical *D. odora* does not seem to occur wild in China" although obviously aware of Hemsley's article to which he also refers. Widely cultivated in Japan.

Long cultivation has led to the production and naming of a large number of forms, some of which were given specific rank as they gradually filtered into European gardens during the late 18th and the 19th centuries. This recognition of various entities as species is understandable if one considers how difficult it must have been to relate them to one another from the scanty material available and the additional complication that in all probability each introduction was a horticulturally distinct clone.

Apart from variations in flower colour and leaf variegation, the different "species" were basically separated on inflorescence

143

characters. In some plants the inflorescence consists only of terminal clusters of flowers whilst in others additional flowers are produced in short-stalked clusters in the axils of the uppermost leaves; the terminal clusters may also be much reduced or, more rarely, absent.

When a plant as attractive as *D. odora* is widely cultivated for centuries, as it was in Chinese and Japanese gardens, it is only natural that gardeners would pick out seedlings or sports which differed markedly from one another in inflorescence and leaf characters, propagating them clonally. It is not unreasonable to suggest that over the years the different inflorescence types were gradually segregated by cultivation, thus emphasising the characters used to distinguish the different "species" which today we regard as no more than variants of *D. odora.*

This combination of terminal and axillary inflorescences also occurs occasionally in *D. laureola* in much the same manner and the same result might be achieved in this species by similar constant cultivation and selection.

Uncertainty appears to have reigned since Benjamin Torin's introduction of *D. odora* in 1770-71, which was grown as *D. indica* due to confusion with the plant described by Linnaeus under that name. Torin's introduction was apparently a white-flowered form of *D. odora* which inevitably became known as "*D. indica alba*", the situation being further complicated by later introductions of variations on the theme of *D. odora* under the names "*D. sinensis*" and "*D. japonica*", the latter stated to be distinct in having laterally produced flowers.

How best to group these variations is a matter of opinion. Some prefer to use cultivar names (often inexactly applied) whilst others have given low botanical rank to circumscribe variations which consist of a number of clones sharing distinct characteristics. We provide here a guide (no more!) to this nomenclatural spider's web.

Forma *alba* (Hemsley) Hara in *Enum. Sperm. Jap.* 3: 232 (1954).
Synonyms: *D. odora* var. *alba* Hemsl.; *D. odora* var. *leucantha* Makino; *D. odora* var. *albiflora* Hort.
Illustrations *Hortus Schönbrunnensis* 3:351 (1798); *Exotic Botany*, pl. 47 (1804).

As defined by Hara this includes all those forms of *D. odora* which are green-leaved and have pure white or creamy-white flowers. The original introduction to Britain by Torin is referable here and was figured in Jacquin's *Hortus Schönbrunnensis*, and, less well, in Sir J. E. Smith's *Exotic Botany.*

Whether or not the plants grown today descend directly from the original introduction is unknown, but in the late 19th century it was still a familiar greenhouse plant and cultivated outside in mild gardens of Britain. A white-flowered form has been grown in California (and no doubt New Zealand and elsewhere) for a considerable

Daphne mezereum (p. 129)　　　　　　　　　　　Photo: *R. Elliott*

Daphne oleoides (p. 152) Photo: *D. F. Merrett*

146

Daphne petraea 'Grandiflora' (p. 162). Photo: *R. Elliott*

period, often producing fasciated shoots. It is now seldom seen in Britain, although still grown, but is certainly more tender than 'Aureo-marginata'.

Forma *marginata* (Miq.) Makino in *Bot. Mag. Tokyo* 23:69 (1909). Synonyms: *D. odora* var. *marginata* Miq.; *D. odora* var. *variegata* Hort.; *D. odora* var. *variegata* Donn; *D. japonica* Paxton; *D. japonica* var. *variegata* Hort.; *D. indica* var. *variegata* Hort.

A name used to cover forms in which the leaves are margined yellow, cream or white, but which may vary in other characters, particularly of the inflorescence. The correct application of the names in this group poses considerable problems. The normal practice would be to consider forms of this type as individual clones, possibly using Makino's epithet *marginata* to refer to them as a group. As we are at present unable to apply the various names with certainty, we have included all the forms of *D. odora* with leaves variegated in any way under this heading for convenience.

> var. *albo-marginata* Hort. A name stated by Halda to belong to a form, very possibly a clone, with white margins to the leaves. We have not traced this name elsewhere or seen material, but it might possibly be a later name for plants grown as *D. odora variegata* around 1840.

'Aureo-marginata'.
Illustrations. Photo p. 128; also *New Fl. & Sylva* 9:274 (1937); and 12:126 (1940).
Award. A.M. (1976).

As grown today, this is a clone with leaves faintly and somewhat irregularly margined yellow, and red-purple flowers which are paler and sometimes almost white within. It is certainly the hardiest of the forms we have come across in gardens and has withstood very severe winters at Wisley virtually unharmed. It seems that this is the plant figured as *D. japonica* in Paxton's *Magazine of Botany* 8:175 (1841) as this differs only very slightly in flower colour which may well be accounted for in the reproduction of the plate. If this is the same plant we owe its introduction to Siebold who sent plants to Europe from Japan sometime during the previous decade. Plants reached England fairly soon after this (1838) and were grown and distributed by the nurserymen Messrs. Young of Epsom as *D. japonica*, under which name it is still occasionally listed, sometimes with the epithet 'Variegata' tacked on. Paxton compared it with *D. odora*, distinguishing it from that species by "the yellow band around the leaves" and also by the "much richer fragrance", characters which are of no specific significance.

147

Unfortunately, the confused name *D. japonica* has also been used for another clone in this group, 'Mazelii', and even in the *New Flora & Sylva* as late as 1940 Comber describes as *D. japonica* what is undoubtedly the plant we call 'Aureo-marginata' today. In an earlier article in the same publication (*New Flora & Sylva* 9:274 (1937) he refers to "a large-leaved sturdier form" of *D. odora* "having leaves edged with creamy-white, an inferior plant which rarely flowers . . . ", which might be the plant referred to above as var. *albo-marginata* Hort.

var. *albo-variegata* Hort. A name given by Halda for forms with white-blotched leaves. We have seen no material and would conjecture that such markings may be virus-induced both in this variant and the next.

var. *luteo-variegata* Hort. A name given by Halda for forms with yellow-blotched leaves. See *albo-variegata*.
var. *elegantissima* Hort. An F.C.C. was awarded to a plant under this name when exhibited by Messrs. Veitch in 1870, and it is also referred to in the *Gardeners Chronicle* for 1878 as growing at Mr. Fraser's nursery at Lea Bridge. The leaves were white-margined, so possibly this and var. *albovariegata* Hort. are synonymous. In *The Garden* for 1892, however, there is a statement that the name *D. indica elegantissima* (and also *D. indica variegata*) has been applied to 'Mazelii' which has yellow-margined leaves!

var. *foliis variegatis* Hort. According to Gordon (*The Garden* 1876 p. 567) a variety of *D. odora* with the leaves more or less margined with a band of yellowish-white. As synonyms he gives *D. odora marginatis* Hort.; *D. indica foliis marginatis* Hort.; and *D. indica variegata* Hort. This is possibly what we now grow as 'Aureo-marginata'.

'Mazelii'
Synonyms ? *D. japonica* Siebold; *D. mazeli* Carr.; *D. odora* var. *mazeli* Hemsley.
Illustration. *The Garden* 12, plate 154 (1878).
Sadly it appears that this most attractive clone has virtually disappeared from cultivation in Britain. Although originally described as a species (Carrière in *Revue Horticole*, 1872, p. 392), it is no more than a clone of *D. odora* and Carrière himself questions its specific distinctness. It was introduced direct from Japan by M. Mazel of Montsauve in 1866; he found it to be very hardy and considered it to differ from *D. japonica* only by its yellow-margined leaves. At that time the name *D. japonica* was applied to a form

148

(? forms) of *D. odora* with both terminal and lateral flower clusters. 'Mazelii', as figured in *The Garden*, shows this character well and is obviously a most attractive plant with (according to Mazel) large, sweetly-scented flowers which were purplish-pink outside and white within. Bean gives the flowering period as "November lasting through the winter" but suggests that near London winter protection is required. On the other hand, Hemsley, in the text accompanying the figure in *The Garden* mentioned above, says it is extremely hardy although the flowers being produced in midwinter are often damaged by frost.

Its hardiness is confirmed by Messrs. Rodger, McClelland & Co. of Newry, N. Ireland, who supplied the material for the plate in *The Garden* in 1878. They state that it grew well against walls or in the open, preferring a partially shaded position, but also succeeded well "in a full south aspect" where it began flowering in November. Of note is their comment that on smaller branches the flower heads may be terminal, further evidence of the unreliability of the formation of the inflorescence as a character for specific separation.

var. *striata* Hort. (*D. japonica striata* Hort.). A name used in some catalogues for 'Aureo-marginata'.

var. *variegata* Donn in *Hort. Cantab.* Ed, 13. 262 (1845).
The earliest application of this epithet traced, but Donn provides no information except that the leaves were variegated and the flowers blush-coloured.
Bean (1914) uses this name for a variant with the leaves margined yellow, quite possibly 'Aureo-marginata'.

Var. *punctata* Hemsley in *The Garden* 14:442 (1878)
Illustration *Bot. Mag.* t. 1587 (1813).

How this particular variety reached Britain is unknown, but the *Botanical Magazine* figure of *D. odora* cited above was considered by Hemsley to represent var. *punctata*. The plate was made from material obtained from Loddiges and is not the original white-flowered introduction by Torin but a variant with the outside of the flower speckled and suffused red. Whether or not similar plants are cultivated today we cannot trace, but it is of interest to note that in the *Botanical Magazine* account reference is made both to the terminal inflorescence (as depicted) and to elongated inflorescences with lateral bunches of flower. The latter were said to occur when artificial heat was applied at the beginning of the growing season and Hemsley in his later account compares them (in habit) to those of *D. odora* 'Mazelii'—confirmation of the variability of this character.

Forma *rosacea* (Makino) Hara in *Enum. Sperm. Jap.* 3:233 (1951).
Synonym. *D. odora* var. *rosacea* Makino
A name used to cover variants differing in their light pink flowers, white within.

References to *D. odora rosea* occur in the *Gardeners' Chronicle* for 1852 and 1853, where it is stated that "several inferior varieties" are to be found under this name. Very probably such variations would come under the umbrella of forma *rosacea* although they no longer appear to be grown in Britain.

Var. *rubra* D. Don in Sweet, *Brit. Fl. Garden* (Second Series) 4: t. 320 (1836).

The illustration in Sweet's *British Flower Garden* cited above shows a form of *D. odora* with terminal bunches of flowers, deep purplish-red in bud, which when open reveal white-centred blooms with red-margined perianth segments. The accompanying description gives the colour of the perianth as rich pink and mentions that the outside of the tube is sparingly silky-hairy, a character associated more with the closely related *D. kiusiana* than *D. odora*.

Hemsley (*The Garden*, 1878) says there is a good specimen in the Kew Herbarium (from a garden in the Isle of Wight) and that the plant from which it was taken had survived unharmed out of doors for many years, being uninjured even by the severe winter of 1845. Nevertheless, this variety is scarcely known in Britain today but is cultivated in New Zealand, although we have seen no specimens.

How var. *rubra* differs from Thunberg's original type of *D. odora* is difficult to say, except in its downy (not glabrous) tube and perhaps in flower colour.

D. odora var. *rubra* is subject to bacterial spot according to a number of reports, a disease which may well affect other forms of *D. odora*.

It is perhaps as well to emphasize here that the grouping of variation within *D. odora* we provide is merely a distillation of references in the literature—not our own views on the taxonomic status of the botanical or horticultural taxa listed.

Related Species

The following species are closely related to *D. odora* and are briefly considered here.

D. grueningiana H. Winkler in *Feddes Repert. Beih.* 12:443 (1922). This species is compared in the original description with *D. odora*, but it is not possible to obtain a very clear impression of its characteristics. The colour of the flower is not noted, but the tube length is given as being 1.7—1.9 cm. long. This is very long, and if it is in the *D. odora* group of species, then it is nearer to the related *D. sureil* or *D. shillong* in this respect. The type locality is in Chekiang Province of China at Hangtschou, 400 m.

D. kiusiana Miq. in *Prod. Fl. Jap.* 298 (1867).

SYNONYM *D. odora* var. *kiusiana* (Miq.) Keissler.

CHROMOSOME NO: n=9.

This Japanese species is very similar to *D. odora*, but the flowers are pubescent on the outside and the young branches are usually pubescent. It is slightly smaller in all respects, but is very attractive and worthy of cultivation. Although it survived several winters outdoors at Claygate in Surrey, next to a warm fence, it is a tender species and best results have been obtained as a pot plant in a cool house. The only form we have grown has pure white flowers and brownish-yellow anthers which give the impression of a dark 'eye' to the flowers. This form sets seed freely, the fruits being red. It is a wide-spread species in Japan, Honshu, (Shikoku, Kyushu and the Ryukyus).

D. luzonica C. B. Robinson in *Bull. Torr. Bot. Club* 35:72 (1908).

SYNONYM *D. odora* var. *luzonica* (C. B. Robinson) H. L. Li.

As far as is known this plant has never been seen in Britain and it is difficult to obtain a clear picture of the species from its description. It is presumably similar in appearance to *D. odora* since it has quite recently (1963) been reduced to a variety of that species. The flowers are said to be pale yellow with a tube 1.3—1.4 cm. long. It occurs in the Philippines in mossy forests on the higher mountains at 2,000—2,500 m.

D. miyabeana Makino in *Bot. Mag. Tokyo* 28:35 (1914).

Also a Japanese species from Hokkaido and Honshu where it grows in rocky places in the mountains. It is very similar to *D. odora* and *D. kiusiana* but has the flowers produced terminally on the current season's growth. Those of the other two species are produced terminally on the previous season's growth. The flowers are glabrous. *D. miyabeana* is not known to be in cultivation.

D. taiwaniana (Masamune) Masamune in *Trans. Nat. Hist. Formosa* 29:237 (1939).

SYNONYMS *D. odora* var. *taiwaniana* Mas.; *D. odora* var. *atrocaulis* Rehder.

This is said to differ from *D. odora* in having white flowers which are slightly pubescent on the outside of the tube, and in the acute lobes. It therefore would appear to be very similar to *D. kiusiana* to which Rehder compared it in *Plantae Wilsonianae* 2:545-6 (1916). The distribution is given as W. China and Taiwan, in thickets and forests.

Daphne oleoides Schreb., *Ic. Desc. Pl.* 1: 13, t. 7 (1766).

SYNONYMS   *D. glandulosa* Spreng.; *D. lucida* Lois.; *D. cretica* Steud.; *D. oleoides* var. *jasminea* Meissn.

ILLUSTRATIONS   See colour plate opposite p. 14, drawing on p. 164, and illustration p. 146; also *Bot. Mag.* t. 1971 (1817); *Bot. Cab.* t. 299 (1818).

Although known to botanists for more than 250 years and having a wide distribution in southern Europe and Asia Minor, *D. oleoides* is remarkably seldom seen in our gardens. Its introduction is credited to Messrs. Loddiges & Sons, who provided flowering material for the *Botanical Magazine* plate in October 1815 (somewhat out of season!), although it was not depicted until 1817. Loddiges himself in the *Botanical Cabinet* for 1818 says "A native of the Levant . . . only of late introduced into this country from France" and it seems reasonable to assume that his own firm was responsible for so doing. Neither of the two plates referred to looks particularly like the forms grown today, the inflorescences being depicted as pinkish-purple and the foliage in the *Botanical Magazine* figure resembling that of *D. sericea* although with more pointed leaves than is usual for that species.

Variations in habit, leaf and flower characters are considerable but the plant which one sees most often in cultivation is a dense, grey-green shrublet about 1—2 ft. in height and as much across with creamy-white, pointed-lobed, scented blooms which give way to attractive orange berries.

There is some dispute in various accounts as to the hardiness of *D. oleoides*, and no doubt this is due in some degree to the origin of the plants concerned, those derived from populations at the lower end of its altitude range perhaps being slightly tender. Provided *D. oleoides* is grown in full sun in well-drained soil, it appears to be quite hardy in most areas of Britain, and we know of plants which have been out of doors unprotected for many years in such diverse garden conditions as a peat bank and chalk soil with a high pH. In Mrs. Hodgkin's garden (1976) there is a specimen 5 ft. across and 3 ft. high planted in 1956 originating from the Sierra Nevada in Spain.

Walter Ingwersen, writing in the A.G.S. *Bulletin* Vol. 12 p. 203, provides a vivid account of *D. oleoides* growing in south-eastern Europe and the Caucasus and also in cultivation. He describes it as a mountainside plant, constituting the main undergrowth at the edge of wooded regions on mountains in the Balkans and on the upper slopes of Mt. Kasbek in the Caucasus at well over 3,000 m. (10,000 feet), inhabiting steep gradients where little snow could lodge and where the winter climate was very severe. Under such conditions the plants were apparently never more than a foot high; neat rounded bushes freely set with heads of sweetly fragrant flowers.

In nature it almost always grows on alkaline soils where the roots are able to penetrate deeply into the cooler strata below. Such are the conditions favoured by many alpines, and *D. oleoides* is perfectly easy to grow on the open rock garden or raised bed where comparable conditions to those of its natural habitat can be provided. Mortar rubble and crushed limestone are sometimes recommended as ingredients of the soil mixture but are certainly not essential, although an excellent way of providing free drainage. Similarly peat and leafmould are prescribed by some authorities as indispensable, helping, of course, by retaining moisture in the growing medium.

As has been mentioned in the chapter on general cultivation a combination of good drainage and moisture retention in the growing medium are the main ingredients for success with this group of daphnes, the acidity or alkalinity of the soil (unless extreme) being much less important.

Full sun is preferable as, although it will tolerate a certain amount of shade, flowering is often less profuse and the compact, neat habit is sometimes lost.

Halda recommends rejuvenating old plants by pruning them back quite hard, stating that plants treated in this way bloom more freely. We have not found it necessary to prune *D. oleoides* ourselves, but Halda's method is interesting in view of the generally held (but not entirely accurate) belief that pruning old daphnes is likely to lead to their immediate demise. *D. oleoides* is also attractive as a pot plant for the alpine house, requiring the same type of compost as plants in the open.

PROPAGATION

(a) Seed. *D. oleoides* can be propagated very readily from seed, which is abundantly produced both in the wild and in cultivation. The fruits form within a month or so of the flowers fading, and if the seed is rubbed out of the fleshy berries and sown immediately, it germinates freely the following spring. Seed stored in cool conditions will remain viable for a year or so unless kept too dry.

(b) Cuttings. A method seldom recommended. From our limited experience, it seems that soft cuttings, firming at the base (Group 1, p. 41) will root satisfactorily, but more mature cuttings appear less easy to strike. This is worth trying in order to propagate a good clone, in view of the variability of *D. oleoides*.

(c) Grafting. Scarcely necessary, unless to increase a particular variant with exceptionally good flowers. Seedling *D. oleoides*, not unexpectedly, proves a good stock, whilst other species, including *D. mezereum* and *D. longilobata* have also been used satisfactorily.

TYPE LOCALITY "Mountains of Crete".
DESCRIPTION Much-branched, dwarf, evergreen shrub up to 50 cm. (occasionally more) in height; young branches warm brown, pubescent; older branches usually glabrous. Leaves scattered along the branches, alternate, tough and

leathery, greyish, hairy when young (occasionally permanently downy), obovate to elliptical, obtuse to acute, 1—4.5 cm. long, 0.3—1.2 cm. wide. Flowers creamy-white to white, occasionally tinged pink, fragrant (sometimes stated to be lacking scent), in terminal clusters of 2—8; tube 6—8 (— 15) mm. long, pubescent outside; lobes 5—7 mm. long, narrowly triangular, acuminate, sometimes recurved at tips. Fruit fleshy, pubescent, orange-red.

CHROMOSOME NO. Not recorded.

FLOWERING PERIOD April—June (occasionally a second crop later).

DISTRIBUTION Widespread in the Mediterranean region from Spain and N. Africa to the E. Aegean Islands and Turkey; Caucasus; ? Kashmir and Western Himalaya.

D. oleoides is a very variable species, particularly in the degree of hairiness and the density of the leaves on the stem, as well as in the shape and size of the perianth lobes and tube. To a lesser extent there is variation in flower colour, pink forms being recorded (var. *rosea* Hort. and var. *carminea* Hort. according to Halda, although these names do not appear generally in the literature), but the majority of populations in the wild have white or creamy-white blooms which are usually fragrant, although there are reports to the contrary. Plants of *D. oleoides* we have grown have produced fragrant flowers, but the production of scent is likely to be affected by a number of factors such as time of day and temperature, which could account for the differing reports. The scent is not always immediately apparent, and in some cases is increased when brought into room temperature, one report describing it as similar to "mois-turising cream"!

Some plants produce disappointing flowers which scarcely open and are virtually worthless in this respect in the garden. This character does not appear to be associated with any particular population, as far as we know, although Lyttel says that pink-flowered plants grown under the name *D. oleoides* var. *glandulosa* have this trait. Some plants raised at Wisley have also produced dusky-pink flowers which look promising in bud but fail to open. They appear to be referable to *D. oleoides* but are not happily placed in var. *glandulosa* as it is at present defined. Only one horticultural variant has been traced—a form with variegated leaves mentioned in *The Garden* (1876).

Various attempts to subdivide *D. oleoides* have been made, none entirely satisfactory. The following variants have been described and we provide some of the characters given by the authors to distinguish them. As will be seen, the dividing lines are tenuous!

Var. *brachyloba* Meissn. in *DC. Prodr.* 14: 2, 534 (1857).
Branches pubescent, densely leafy; young leaves downy on both sides, adult leaves more or less glabrous above, sparsely pubescent below; inflorescence 5—8 flowered, sepals ovate.

Var. *buxifolia* (Vahl) Keissl. in *Bot. Jahrb.* XXV, 50 (1898). (Syn. *D. buxifolia* Vahl). Branches densely tomentose, densely leafy. Young and adult leaves densely hairy on both sides. Inflorescence 5—8 flowered, sepals ovate.

Var. *glandulosa* (Bertol.) Keissl., loc. cit., 50 (1898). (Syn. *D. oleoides* Schreb. var. *jasminea* Meissn.). Branches subglabrous, laxly leafy; young leaves downy, adult leaves more or less glabrous above, finely pubescent below; inflorescence 3—5 flowered, sepals lanceolate. Sometimes stated to be pink-flowered.

Var. *glandulosa* forma *puberula* (Jaub. & Spach) Keissl., loc. cit., 50, (1898). Similar to the above, but with pubescent branchlets, leaves and flowers.

The distribution attributed to these variants is confusing in the extreme and we refrain from making confusion worse confused by quoting the localities given. At the present moment it seems that the names quoted above are best forgotten from a horticultural viewpoint, as it is very difficult to allocate any cultivated (or for that matter wild) forms to them with certainty.

Related Species

There are, however, several closely related species which from a garden point-of-view are reasonably distinct, but botanically may be only considered as variants within an aggregate species.

D. euboica Rech. fil. in *Österr. Bot. Zeitschr.* 104: 176 (1957) is like an extremely vigorous *D. oleoides*, making an erect shrub to about 1 m., with larger, acute, elliptic, somewhat greener leaves and rather small flowers. It is hardy in a garden on the South Downs where it has made a large bush since it was collected in 1966 (B. Mathew No. 5125). The orange fruits are produced in abundance and the seed germinates freely. Unfortunately it is not a particularly attractive species and will probably not be of very great garden value. Money-Coutts found that cuttings also rooted reasonably easily. As its name suggests, it is endemic to Euboea. Although it looks very different from *D. oleoides* as known in cultivation, the two seem to be connected by intermediates in the wild and it is possible that it is not a distinct species. Similar large-leaved plants occur in parts of Spain.

D. kosaninii (Stoj.) Stoj. in *Spis. Balg. Akad. Nauk* 37: 137 (1928) occurs wild in S.W. Bulgaria in mountainous areas and is said to differ from *D. oleoides* in its rather taller stature, its smaller foliage and shorter, blunter, pink perianth lobes. Goulimis found a very similar plant in 1955 on Mt. Meneikon (Boz-dagh) of Serrae in Macedonia which was considered by Kew to represent this species, noting in particular the "semi-closed" flowers. *Flora Europaea* comments that it is possibly a hybrid between *D. oleoides* and *D. cneorum*, and that plants intermediate between it and *D. oleoides* in all characters can be found. As far as we know *D. kosaninii* is not cultivated in Britain.

D. stapfii Bornm. & Keissl. in *Verh. der Zool.-Bot. Ges. Wien*, 36 (1897) was described from 100 km. west of Shiraz in Iran. It is a steppe plant forming a gnarled, much-branched dwarf shrub, to 1 m. with very thick, broadly obovate, virtually glabrous leaves about 2 cm. long and 1 cm. wide, with a rounded apex; flowers are yellowish-white. It is not apparently grown in Britain, but Halda states that the flowers are dull purple with rusty-red hairs on the perianth tube, the lobes being narrow and acute. He has found it very difficult to grow, particularly on its own roots, and although seed germinates well he finds the young plants are winter-tender. Grafting on stock of *D. giraldii* has been more successful and Halda suggests a warm sheltered position in the garden where the shoots can become thoroughly ripened before winter.

His description is somewhat at variance with that of the authors, who give the flower colour as yellowish-white but colour forms may perhaps occur in this species.

In addition to the three species discussed above, the Russian botanist Pobedimov has described two further species in *Not. Syst. Herb. Inst. Bot. Acad. Sci. U.R.S.S.* 12:135-136 (1950).

D. baksanica Pobed. This Russian species from the area of the rivers Tersk and Baksan near Ozrov in the northern Caucasus is considered to be related to *D. oleoides*, although it has never been seen in Britain. We must, therefore, follow the statements made by Pobedimov, who says that it is distinguishable from *D. oleoides* by its generally narrower leaves (2—5 mm. wide) which are covered with long white hairs; by its shorter perianth lobes which are $2\frac{1}{2}$ times shorter than the tube (roughly equal in length in *D. oleoides*) and by its shorter, broader anthers. The tube is 10—12 mm. long.

D. transcaucasica Pobed. Another Russian relative of *D. oleoides*. This was described from the area of Lake Sevan in the Southern Transcaucasus, although its whole distribution is much wider in N.E. Turkey and adjacent U.S.S.R. It is said to differ from *D. oleoides* in having leaves covered with long white hairs and in its wider, broadly ovate lobes (4—5 mm. long, 2—3 mm. wide).

156

From *D. baksanica* it differs in having broader leaves and also in the broadly ovate lobes. This is not known to be in cultivation in Britain.

As will be appreciated, *D. oleoides* is a very variable species and the variations and related species mentioned above cannot be evaluated unless a really thorough study of material from the entire range of distribution is obtained. Where new species or other taxa have been described, there is often no adequate statement as to how they differ from all the other known variants. One therefore remains highly sceptical about their authenticity, for measurements often overlap and characters such as pubescence, or lack of it, are quite clearly a matter of degree with no rigid dividing lines.

It seems likely that *D. oleoides* is a "primitive" species within the genus and apparently some populations are dimorphic. Until detailed field studies can be made it is impossible to arrive at any satisfactory classification for the group.

Daphne papyracea Wall. ex Steud. emend Smith & Cave in *Rec. Bot. Survey India* 6, 2: 54 (1912).

SYNONYM *D. cannabina* Wall., partly; *D. cannabina* Hook. f., partly.

ILLUSTRATION Stainton, J.D.A., Forests of Nepal (1972) fig. 132.

Although as attractive a plant as the related *D. bholua*, this tender species is seldom cultivated in Britain, but is an admirable winter-flowering shrub for the cool greenhouse. In very sheltered gardens it would no doubt prove easy to grow against a south or west wall in a well-drained but moist site, particularly if the base of the plant could be protected, possibly by a dwarf evergreen shrub, against drying conditions and the occasional severe spell of winter weather.

In nature it occurs in woodland conditions and it is possible that plants from upper limits of its altitude range 3,300 m. (10,600 ft.) might be reasonably hardy and would certainly be worth introducing to test in Britain. Records of *D. papyracea* in cultivation are scanty although it was evidently cultivated by 1881 as a report in the *Gardeners Chronicle* for that year records it flowering at Kew in December, mentioning the manufacture of paper from the bark in Nepal, one advantage being the comparative immunity of the paper to insect attack and its consequent value for use with genealogical records, deeds and other important documents.

The use of *D. papyracea* as a garden plant is limited by its hardiness, and certainly it is unlikely ever to rival *D. bholua* which also has the advantage of intensely fragrant blooms whereas those of *D. papyracea* are virtually scentless.

PROPAGATION

We have no personal experience of propagating this species but it seems probable that the methods used for *D. bholua* should prove equally successful for *D. papyracea*.

TYPE LOCALITY   N.W. India: Mountains of Kumaon.

DESCRIPTION   Much-branched erect evergreen shrub up to 1.25 m. in height; young branches downy. Leaves with short petioles, alternate, tending to be clustered towards the tips of branches, glabrous, dark, rather dull green, leathery, elliptic or oblanceolate, bluntly acute to retuse, 5—12 (16) cm. long, 1.5—3 cm. wide. Floral bracts persistent through flowering stage. Flowers in terminal clusters of 3—10 (12) (most side branches also have terminal flowers), white or greenish-white, possibly rarely pinkish, not fragrant; tube 10—13 mm. long, very downy outside; lobes 5—7 mm. long, 3—4 mm. broad, ovate, acute. Fruit red or orange-red, about 1 cm. long.

CHROMOSOME NO.   Uncertain. There is a record for *D. cannabina* as n=9 which may perhaps refer to this species.

FLOWERING PERIOD   Dec.—Jan. (in Britain); Oct.—March (in the wild).

DISTRIBUTION   West Himalaya: W. Nepal, Punjab, Simla, Kumaon, Uttar Pradesh, Pakistan.

HABITAT   Evergreen oak woods; 1700—3300 m.

For a comparison of the botanical characters separating *D. papyracea* from *D. bholua* and *D. sureil* see under *D. bholua*.

Daphne petraea Leybold in *Flora* 36: 81 (1853).

SYNONYM   *D. rupestris* Facchini.

ILLUSTRATIONS   See drawing on p. 69, habitat photo on p. 163, and colour plate, frontispiece fig. 3.

AWARDS   A.M. 1906; A.M. 1918 to clone 'Grandiflora'; F.C.C. 1924 to clone 'Grandiflora'.

There is no more evocative name in the daphne world than that of *D. petraea*, darling of the show benches, and subject of constant debate as to details of cultivation. And there is good reason for the furore it creates, as few would disagree with the high praises bestowed upon it in the horticultural literature. *D. arbuscula* may perhaps, on occasion, rival it, but there can be few more beautiful sights, either in nature or in gardens, than an old plant of *D. petraea* in full flower, particularly the clone 'Grandiflora' which is the form almost always grown nowadays.

In its natural habitat it is a most spectacular sight when in full bloom and we cannot do better in attempting to describe it to the uninitiated than to quote from those masters of horticultural prose, Clarence Elliott and Reginald Farrer.

First, Clarence Elliott in the A.G.S. *Bulletin* as he describes it on the Cima Tombea, "limestone cliffs towering up stark and impregnable for hundreds of feet above us, with every crevice painted with close-packed masses of waxy, rose-pink fragrant blossom".

Farrer is even more effervescent (and long-winded!) in *The English Rock Garden* and says:—

"*D. petraea* dwells high and far in the Southern Alps, confined to one small district, and there haunting hot and terrible cliff-faces of rose-grey limestone fronting the full radiance of the Italian sun.

158

In the tightest crevices of the rock it grows, in chinks so close that the point of a pin will hardly enter; yet there the Daphne roots deep down into nothing, sending its fat masses of yellow rootage browsing far in, with only the lime of the rock to feed them; but so the neck grows thick and stout, emitting a mass of tiny branches, clothed in tiny oval leaves, grooved and dark green and glossy. Thus the plant develops, and its twigs lie close and flat against the sheer cliff which, as far up as you can see, is plastered with those mats of lucent green darkness, until at last they turn to mats and splashes of even more lucent rose, when every one of those shoots is ablaze with a head of three or four big waxy pink tubes of the most crystalline pure texture, the most brilliant clear colour, and the most intoxicating fragrance. The flowers begin in June and continue through August; the sight of those sheer awful faces blotted with scabs of living pink flat to the cliff and unbroken by any touch of green is one that amply repays the distance, difficulties, dangers, and despairs that sometimes wait on the worshipper of *D. petraea*. For the Daphne grows only in the most adamantine faces, and only long sedulous search (by very superior persons) may produce here and there a tuft from milder places; while in the rock it is brittle at the neck, and snaps sharp off at an irreverent touch. Seedlings indeed do occur, but seem of the utmost rarity; I have never yet seen sign of berry on the plants. Yet seed they do and must, for reasons to be more fully stated below, but in the cliff their increase is chiefly by a thready runner breaking along the crevice and erupting out of the blank wall again into what soon proves another tight flat huddle of sweetness and light."

Surely no more need be said of its occurrence in nature.

In view of its exacting habitat, one might suspect that *D. petraea* would prove very difficult to grow in our gardens, but contrary to expectations it is much easier than is sometimes anticipated. Basically, its requirements may be summed up as excellent drainage, sun, air and unfailing moisture at the roots, particularly during summer when the flower buds for the following year are being initiated. Failure often seems traceable to overdrying of the roots, particularly of pot- or trough-grown specimens. It should be remembered that even on the sun-drenched cliffs of its natural home, the roots penetrate deeply into the cool, underlying strata, where sufficient moisture is available for its needs.

Success with *D. petraea* has been reported under varying conditions—scree with underlying moisture-retentive compost; in tufa on a raised bed and elsewhere; rammed between a split limestone rock with a peat-sand compost for the roots to delve into; and of course in pots or deep pans for alpine house culture using an open but leafy soil mixture.

Although a limestone plant in nature, *D. petraea* appears relatively indifferent to the pH of the soil, but it is often recommended that limestone chippings should be included in the soil mixture—a sort of "sop to Cerberus" presumably. It certainly does not require limestone to thrive but appreciates the sharp drainage and warmth retention provided by some forms of limestone and tufa. In acid mixtures, if not too extreme, it grows well and we have also experimented with growing it in a peat-block on an open corner of a small peat garden, where it has been unprotected now for four years. As yet (it is a grafted plant) it has not flowered, but remains quite healthy (if slow-growing) and promises to bloom this season (1976).

In the open garden an appropriate position in which to try *D. petraea* would be a raised bed amongst rock or tufa surrounds (or in the tufa) where a "deep mixture of lime-rubble, leafmould, good loam, sand and peat all mixed up with almost an equal part of limestone chips" (Farrer)—or your equivalent—is provided. In spite of a reputation for shy flowering in the open (even of grafted plants) there are plenty of examples which indicate that this is by no means always so, particularly if one looks back at references to *D. petraea* in *The Garden* last century.

Feeding is also controversial. Some are firmly of the opinion that it is a bad thing, producing soft, out-of-character growth subject to disease. Others say that *D. petraea* reacts favourably to feeding and Farrer, commenting on its likes and dislikes, says "It even seems to appreciate the administration of these fertilising pilules called Plantoids". Feeding by use of a modern slow-release fertiliser in the compost or soil mixture provides a sensible middle-of-the-road answer.

In spite of its reputation as "difficult", specimens of 20 or 30 years of age are by no means uncommon, and until 1965, when it died, there was, in the late R. B. Cooke's garden at Corbridge, a venerable 40-year old specimen, which illustrates that, with sensible treatment, not all daphnes are as "miffy" as some writers would have us believe.

It is often stated that *D. petraea* seldom blooms satisfactorily on its own roots and must be grafted to flower freely. This is certainly the usual experience of growers but there are occasional comments which suggest that it is not always the case. Normally one would expect grafted plants to flower at an earlier age than cutting-raised specimens due to the advantage of the established root system of the stock. The original plant of *D. petraea* 'Grandiflora' was the result of rooting cuttings brought back by Dr. Jenkin and Robert Tucker, and this took five years to bloom on its own roots. Halda establishes young rooted cuttings in tufa and, although he does not actually say so in his most helpful article, presumably the resultant plants flower in due course—if not he would no doubt have resorted to grafting, which he does not even mention under *D. petraea*.

It would be very useful to carry out comparative tests to find out whether cutting-raised plants are merely slower to reach flowering size or whether there really is some feature of grafted plants which induces regular, free flowering as we are so frequently assured. And if so, why? One can speculate that nutrition is the key—perhaps one should provide a mixture with slightly more potash (source of one of the main chemicals involved with flower production in plants) than is normal? And if one rooted cuttings of *D. petraea* and used them, when established, as stocks for this same species, would it result in the plants flowering freely at an early age? What is the effect of climatic factors? Do those fortunate enough to live in regions where hot summers are the rule rather than the exception find that *D. petraea* on its own roots blooms freely at a reasonable age? As already referred to in the section on grafting, there is a recorded case of young plants raised from cuttings at a nursery near Pontresina flowering freely. These are the sorts of explorations which might produce an answer.

The date of introduction of *D. petraea* is difficult to ascertain, as although fairly widely grown (as *D. rupestris*) in the late 19th century all the publications we have consulted gloss over the actual date when it was first received in Britain. Krussman (*Handbuch der Laubgeholze*, 1960) gives 1894, but there are references in *The Garden* in the 1870's to this species' being grown "in the York nurseries" (presumably of Messrs. Backhouse) although curiously George Gordon in his extremely useful article on daphnes in *The Garden* for 1875 omits it entirely.

By 1891, however, it was well established, as in the R.H.S. Journal of that year *D. petraea* is included in a list of "The twelve most useful perennial herbaceous border plants under nine inches high" following a survey amongst a "large number of our foremost 'hardy' gardeners, both amateurs and nurserymen . . . "!

PROPAGATION

(a) Seed. Not to our knowledge recorded as being produced in cultivation in Britain, although there is a reference in the A.G.S. *Bulletin* (1973) to "healthy seedlings of *D. petraea* growing along the edge of a flat path . . . " in the garden of Herr Hauser of Toscolano, on lake Garda, in the region of Monte Baldo. Farrer bemoans that he could find no fruit during his visits to its natural habitat—but fruit it must!

(b) Cuttings. By no means difficult to root when taken after flowering in June or July, with or without a heel. We have not attempted soft cuttings of young wood, but it would certainly be worth doing so, if adequate material is available, in view of the success reported for several other species using young growths.

(c) Grafting. Universally (almost) recommended to obtain a reasonably-sized flowering plant in a relatively short time. Will Ingwersen carried out a short series of experiments on the suitability of stocks for *D. petraea*—see A.G.S. *Bulletin* 20:71 (1952)—and found that in general *D. mezereum* (not, however, the white form) proved the most satisfactory. Others, however, report a tendency for *D. petraea* to become semi-deciduous on *D. mezereum.*

Although we have not as yet tried *D. giraldii* as a stock, Halda's experience with this species for *D. arbuscula* would suggest that it might well be suitable for *D. petraea.*

Normally the scions obtainable from *D. petraea* are relatively thin and splice (cleft) grafting proves the simplest method, although other techniques have been used successfully, particularly saddle grafting.

(d) Layering. Practical with some shoots from an established plant but either cuttings or grafting would normally be preferable.

D. petraea, both in nature and when growing on its own roots in gardens, will sometimes sucker, which provides an additional method of increase.

TYPE LOCALITY   Italy: S. Guidicarie, 1,650 m. (west of Lake Garda).
DESCRIPTION   Much branched, dwarf, evergreen shrub up to 15 cm. in height (often less in cultivation) and to 30 cm. (rarely 60 cm.) across, forming a dense, gnarled clump or mat, and occasionally suckering; young shoots greenish-brown, sparsely pubescent; older stems grey-brown, covered with raised leaf scars. Leaves dark, shiny green, leathery, glabrous, sessile, clustered at the tips of the branches, linear-oblanceolate, obtuse or occasionally slightly pointed, tapered towards the base, triangular in cross section, 8—12 (— 16) mm. long, 2—3 mm. wide. Flowers in terminal clusters of 3—5 (2—12 according to Halda), bright pink, varying little but sometimes paler, fragrant; tube 9—15 mm. long, finely downy outside; lobes 3—5 mm. long, broadly ovate, obtuse. Fruit dry, sparsely pubescent, greenish-brown.
CHROMOSOME NO.   Not recorded.
FLOWERING PERIOD   (April) May—July (August).
DISTRIBUTION   N. Italy: N.E. of Brescia, around Lake Garda, Lago di Idro (Monte Baldo, Cima Tombea).
HABITAT   Crevices of calcareous rocks, 700—2,000 m.

Variation within *D. petraea* appears to be slight. Most of the plants in cultivation in British gardens now apparently derive from a collection made in 1914, from which the clone 'Grandiflora' was selected.

'GRANDIFLORA'. The selected clone most commonly grown. One of a batch of plants collected in July 1914 by Dr. Jenkin and Robert Tucker. These were grown on by Tucker at Brookside Nursery, Headington, Oxford, and established on their own roots. Some of the plants flowered five years later and one, subsequently named 'Grandiflora', was found to be outstanding, with larger flowers of an intensely rich glowing pink. Illustration p. 146.

"Var. *radicans* Hort." is a name applied to a prostrate form producing underground runners. 'Grandiflora' will also sucker on its own roots and this character is one of doubtful botanical significance in this instance.

In the A.G.S. *Bulletin* there are reports of plants with near white or white flowers, but we have seen no material. The report of the 1951

162

Daphne petraea on the Cima Tombea (p. 158).   *Photo: D. Holford*

D. oleoides Schreb.

D. pontica L.

D. collina Sr

164

Conference, A.G.S. *Bull*. 19: 225 (1951) provides a brief description of a plant of *D. petraea* with white, pink-shaded flowers which was growing at Kew and had been received from the Cima Tombea. Doubt is cast on its identity, but such colour variation is not unreasonable to expect, particularly in view of a report in the *Bulletin* by Molly F. Popper (1973) that she was shown a double-flowered form and a white-flowered plant in the mountains around Lake Garda.

Daphne pontica L., *Sp. Pl.* 357 (1753).

SYNONYM   *D. pontica* var. *szovitsii* C. Koch.

ILLUSTRATIONS   See drawing opposite; also *Bot. Mag.* t. 1282 (1810); Bean, *Trees and Shrubs* Ed. 8, 2:20 (1973).

As a garden plant the Pontic Daphne is perhaps under-estimated, as, although not particularly colourful, it is a pleasant woodlander of value for its fragrant yellow-green flowers in early spring and its dark polished foliage throughout the year.

D. pontica was apparently unknown to Gerard, but is referred to in the second edition of Miller's *Gardeners Dictionary* (1740) as *Thymelaea Pontica* with credit given to Tournefort as the discoverer. It is always difficult to be sure that some plants mentioned by Miller were actually in cultivation in Britain at the time, although he mentions that "some of these plants have been obtained and are preserved in curious Botanic Gardens for variety". In some of the later editions no mention is made, however, of the Pontic Daphne, although the date of introduction is given as 1752 by Aiton (*Hortus Kewensis*) and it was certainly grown by Messrs. Loddiges before 1810 as they provided the material for the *Botanical Magazine* plate of that date.

Like *D. laureola* it is usually a woodland plant, thriving in light deciduous or pine woods and thrusting its trailing growths through the leafmould layers to form small thickets, often in company with *Rhododendron ponticum*, epimediums, Solomon's Seal and the like.

In cultivation it prefers similar conditions, slight shade and humus-rich, acid, woodland soil, although it will also grow happily in comparable, light, alkaline habitats. As a guide to its ultimate dimensions, a specimen in Mrs. Hodgkin's garden planted more than twenty-five years ago is now some 3 feet high by 7 feet across (1976).

In Russia, the oil-rich seeds are used as a source of tanning material and also for various medical purposes.

PROPAGATION

(a) Seed.   Easily raised from seed, which is produced freely in cultivation. As is the case with *D. laureola*, the seed should be sown as soon as possible after gathering to obtain the best results. Seed stored over winter and spring sown will sometimes germinate reasonably well, but autumn sowing is, in our view, to be preferred.

Seedlings of *D. pontica* are suitable for use as grafting stocks.

(b) Cuttings. Stem-cuttings of half-ripe wood root without difficulty (see Group 2, p. 41).

(c) Layering. The trailing habit of some forms of *D. pontica* lends itself readily to propagation by layering.

TYPE LOCALITY "Habitat in Pontus".

DESCRIPTION Glabrous, spreading, evergreen shrub up to 1.5 m. high but often much less. Young shoots green. Leaves alternate, clustered towards the apex of the branches, sessile, leathery, deep shiny green, obovate, apex acute, 4.5—10 cm. long, 2—3.5 cm. wide. Flowers in many pairs (rarely in 3's or 4's) produced in the axils of leafy bracts at the base of the developing young shoots to form a dense mass of bloom; yellowish-green, fragrant (occasionally scentless); tube slender, 6—12 mm. long, glabrous; lobes 6—11 mm. long, 1.5—2mm. wide, narrowly lanceolate, acute, distinctly recurved. Fruit ovoid, fleshy, black.

CHROMOSOME NO. Not recorded.

FLOWERING PERIOD March—May (in Britain), February—August (in the wild).

DISTRIBUTION N. Turkey from Istanbul through Pontic Mts. to Georgian Caucasus; S.E. Bulgaria.

HABITAT In Pine or Hazel woods with Rhododendron or in the open at higher altitudes; 50—2,200 m.

Variation in the flower colour from green to pale yellow occurs and the degree of fragrance of the blooms of individual plants is also variable.

A form with variegated leaves has been mentioned in garden literature but we have not seen this and it is possible that such variegation could be virus induced.

In gardens *D. pontica* and *D. laureola* may occasionally be confused, but differ in leaf-shape and, in particular, in the form of the inflorescence and shape of the flowers. In *D. pontica* the flowers making up the inflorescence are normally borne in pairs, each pair being on a common stalk and arising from the axil of a bract-like leaf at the base of the *current* year's growth whilst the flowers are more starry in shape with long, recurving lobes. The inflorescence of *D. laureola*, on the other hand, is a congested, axillary raceme borne on the *previous* year's growth and the flower-lobes are much shorter.

> **D. albowiana** Woron. ex Pobed, in *Spisok.Rast. Herb. Fl.* URSS 11:134 (1949). (*D. pontica* ssp. *haematocarpa* G. Woron.) is closely related but is not known to be in cultivation in Britain. It is native to sub-alpine regions of the southern Caucasus and is stated to differ in the smaller leaves and in particular in the smaller, sub-spherical bright red fruits.

Daphne retusa Hemsl. in *Journ. Linn. Soc.* 29: 318 (1892).

SYNONYMS   *D. nana* Tagawa; *D. szetschuanica* K. Winkler

ILLUSTRATIONS   See drawing on p. 110, and illustration p. 181; also *Bot. Mag.* t. 8430 (1912);

AWARDS   Award of Garden Merit, (1946); A.M. (1927).

The Chinese *D. retusa*, originally discovered (although not apparently introduced) by A. E. Pratt in 1889 from Tachien-lu (Tatsien-lu) in Western Szechuan, is one of the most amenable and attractive members of the genus. There are many old examples to be seen in gardens which have withstood all that the British climate can throw at them and still remain healthy and floriferous after twenty-five or more years. It is certainly one of the finest shrubs we have available for the rock garden or the front of the shrub border, forming a dense, compact, 2—3 ft. mound with shiny dark green foliage which offsets the intensely fragrant, purplish-rose and white flowers admirably during April and May.

Henri Correvon says that neither *D. retusa*, nor the closely related (if not conspecific) *D. tangutica*, are hardy at Lautaret (2,100 m.) or Autrano (1,200 m.), which is curious as its hardiness in Britain is unquestioned and in the wild it occurs at altitudes up to 4,500 m.

To maintain its compact habit and flower freely, an open sunny position and a humus-rich soil should be provided but it appears far less pernickety than some species in its requirements, and only in very dry soils or in conditions of high acidity or alkalinity is any difficulty normally experienced. It is often stated that this species, *D. tangutica*, and its variants, require an acid soil, but we know of good specimens in alkaline soils and it seems probable that the acid loving reputation has been built up, not from their dislike of a certain amount of lime in the soil, but through a preference for humus-rich conditions.

At Highdown plants of *D. tangutica* (Farrer 271) grew and flowered well on the chalk cliff for almost 40 years and although no doubt they received a reasonable annual diet of humus, they provide an excellent example of the versatility of the species which could lead to the demise of many another daphne.

In dry chalky areas it would undoubtedly be advisable to enrich the soil with ample leaf-mould, peat or well-rotted compost prior to planting and to provide an annual mulch of similar materials—operations which are, of course, also applicable to any soils lacking natural humus.

A good deal of confusion has, understandably, occurred between *D. retusa* and *D. tangutica* in cultivation, and there are varying descriptions of their comparative growth habits given in the literature. Farrer comments that the owner of a plant of *D. retusa* "may be a grandfather before it is 2 ft. tall" whilst Lyttel records a plant as reaching 3 ft. in 10 years and a self-sown seedling 2 ft. high in 6 years! Whether or not Lyttel's plants were forms of *D. retusa* is not now possible to determine, but the plant which resembles *D. retusa* as grown now and originally introduced in 1903 by E. H. Wilson approaches more closely Farrer's description—although as usual one must allow for a little poetic licence.

The *Botanical Magazine* plate (1912) was drawn from material obtained from Veitch's Coombe Wood nursery, where plants raised from seeds of Wilson (Veitch Expedition 4439, 1903; or according to Bean, 1901) had reached 18 inches in height and as much across in nine or so years.

A more recent introduction is that by Ludlow, Sherriff and Elliot (L. S. & E. 1576) from 3700 m. (12,000 ft.) in S.E. Tibet in 1947.

PROPAGATION
(a) Seed. The bright red fruits are freely produced but rapidly devoured by birds. Fresh autumn-sown seed germinates well the following spring and we have found that seed of *D. retusa*, provided it is stored in cool conditions, remains viable for at least a year. According to Halda seed stored under conditions where it does not become too dry is viable for 2—3 years.

Self (or bird)-sown seedlings occasionally occur of both *D. retusa* and *D. tangutica*. Seedlings will flower 3—4 years after germination has occurred and, as has been mentioned in the section on propagation, are useful as grafting stocks for more difficult species.

(b) Cuttings. Both relatively soft (Group 1) and half-ripe (Group 2) cuttings root readily. A. G. Weekes of Limpsfield, a marvellous cultivator of plants, obtained 100% rooting of soft cuttings inserted in early June in a cold, sand frame. He also used the same frame to propagate *D. retusa* by leaf-bud cuttings, pulling off leaves with an axillary bud attached, an unusual achievement, although it took some time to produce a reasonably-sized plant.

(c) Grafting. Although sometimes used commercially, this method is unnecessary in view of the ease with which *D. retusa* is raised from seed or cuttings.

TYPE LOCALITY China: W. Szechuan, Tachien-lu (Tatsien-lu), 9—13,500 ft.
DESCRIPTION Much branched, dense, evergreen shrub up to 60 (rarely to 90) cm. in height and as much across; young branches at first green, then yellowish-brown, glabrous to woolly, older branches light brown, glabrescent to glabrous; leaves alternate, deep shiny green, glabrous, clustered towards the apex of shoots in old plants, sessile, oblanceolate or elliptic, apex rounded, emarginate or retuse, margins revolute, 1.5—3.5 (— 5.0) cm. long, 0.5—1.2 cm. wide. Flowers in terminal, many-flowered clusters, purple or rose outside, white sometimes tinged purple within, very fragrant; tube 8—12 mm. long, glabrous; lobes 7—10 mm. long, 4—6 mm. wide, ovate, acute. Fruit red, fleshy, subglobose, 8—10 mm. long.
CHROMOSOME NO. Not recorded.
FLOWERING PERIOD (March) April—May (in Britain) occasionally also in autumn; May—July (in the wild).

DISTRIBUTION   W. China: Yunnan, Szechuan and Kansu provinces; S.E. Tibet; Bhutan (L.S. & H. 18973). Halda also states that it occurs in upper Burma at elevations of 4,500 m., forming carpets only 5 cm. high. We have seen no specimens from this area.

HABITAT   Rocky slopes amongst scrub in open pine woods; 3,000—4,500 m.

The close relationship of *D. retusa* and *D. tangutica* has already been mentioned, and it is apparent from herbarium material that the characters used to distinguish the two are not always constant. Only when a wider range of material is available can any reasonable conclusions be reached as to their status and until that time it seems more helpful to maintain the present position.

Stocks of the two plants commonly grown under these names are readily distinguishable when seen side by side, differing particularly in habit and leaf shape. The following table may be used to separate the two as seen in gardens:

CHARACTER	D. RETUSA	D. TANGUTICA
Height	To 1 m., usually not more than 60 cm.	To 1.75 m.
Habit of branching and growth	A neat, mounded shrub with short, dense branches and slow growth.	A more upright, less branched, open shrub, with longer, more slender growths and reasonably rapid growth.
Leaves	Deep, shiny green with distinctly revolute margins. Apex normally retuse or emarginate. Leaves usually up to 3.5 cm. long and 1.2 cm. wide (occasionally to 5.0 x 1.3 cm.)	Rather dull green, more or less flat, margin not or only slightly decurved. Apex acute but also rounded to emarginate. Leaves longer, up to 6.0 cm. long and 2 cm. wide (occasionally to 7.5 cm. x 3 cm.)

Other characters used to separate the two species, including the relative hairiness of the young branches, the presence or absence of hairs on the carpels, and the shape and size of the perianth lobes, prove unreliable when a range of material is examined, and it is quite possible that the characters listed above would be less clearcut if one could see material from throughout the range of the two species.

Halda reports considerable variation in plants of *D. retusa* raised from wild collected seed (exact location unstated), both in habit and flower colour. He also refers to a "var. *yunnanensis*", a form with pale rose flowers and of compact habit which he says is often grown in England and Scotland. There appears to be no mention of this name in any other reference sources we have consulted, neither have we heard of its use in gardens in Britain.

In view of the close similarity of *D. retusa* and *D. tangutica* the latter species is considered overleaf.

169

D. tangutica Maxim. in *Bull. Acad. St. Petersb.* 27: 531 (1881).

SYNONYM *D. wilsonii* Rehder

ILLUSTRATIONS See illustration p. 181; also *Bot. Mag.* t. 8855 (1920); *Journ. R.H.S.* 78: fig. 5 (1953).

AWARDS Award of Garden Merit, (1949); A.M. (1929).

D. tangutica was first located by Przewalski, a famous Russian traveller, in 1873 in Kansu, western China, and was introduced into cultivation by Wilson from W. Hupeh during the early 1900's. The exact date of this introduction is not known, but might possibly be from the Veitch Expedition No. 637 of 1900, although Bean suggests the date as between 1908-10. Wilson's collection was at the time thought to be a distinct species named in 1916 by Rehder as *D. wilsonii*, later merged by the same author with *D. tangutica*.

Farrer in 1914 (F. 271) sent home seeds of *D. tangutica* from Kansu which, sown in October 1914, germinated the following spring at Arley Castle, nr. Bewdley, Worcs., and flowered for the first time in March, 1918. Two years later one of these plants, only 18 inches high, carried over 50 flowerheads, each about 1½ in. across. Farrer's collection was from about 3,000 m., the plants growing in open turf "in deep calcareous or vegetable mould".

D. tangutica, although slightly more robust, behaves in much the same way as *D. retusa*, and the same comments on cultivation and propagation apply. Similarly, a full description is not provided, the major differences between the two (as garden plants) being listed above.

FLOWERING PERIOD As *D. retusa*.

CHROMOSOME NO. Not recorded.

TYPE LOCALITY W. China; Kansu.

DISTRIBUTION China: Kansu, Hupeh, Szechuan; Tibet; possibly also Formosa.

HABITAT Spruce forests in shade, occasionally in open scrub; normally 2,750—3,500 m. altitude, but some collections by Rock in Kansu from 600—900 m.

Although *D. retusa*, as known in British gardens, varies little in flower colour or habit, some forms of *D. tangutica* do show variation in these characters. The most interesting of these is "*D. tangutica alba*" which is almost certainly derived from Farrer 585 with leaves pale green but approaching those of *D. retusa* in shape. It is extremely floriferous, producing axillary flower clusters all the way up the branches, the blooms opening pale pink but becoming white as they mature and age. A plant of this form at Hidcote reached about 4 ft. in height, whilst a specimen growing in a chalk garden on the South Downs has reached 2 ft. after 10 years from a cutting.

This may possibly be the semi-evergreen plant referred to in Bean (1973) as grown by Dr. Jenkin.

Another variation which Eliot Hodgkin obtained from Boothman's nursery in 1960 is still (1976) in good condition and has formed a sparse-foliaged shrub of about 3 ft. in height, with medium green foliage, obtuse at the tips, the flowers having green tubes (occasionally purple-tinted) and white lobes, pink-flushed outside and on the inner margins. This may well be originally derived from the same Farrer introduction, being of slow growth and tending to become semi-deciduous as does the Hidcote plant.

It is obvious from collectors' notes on herbarium material that flower colour varies considerably from greenish to white, pink, purplish-red and even rich purple over the range of the species. Perhaps one day we may be fortunate enough once again to obtain further introductions from China to provide some of these attractive colour forms for our gardens.

D. wilsonii in Sargent, *Pl. Wils.* 2: 540 (1916) mentioned earlier, was reduced to *D. tangutica* by Rehder in *Journ. Arn. Arb.* 9:97 (1928). Frank Knight tells us that plants grown as *D. wilsonii* were in cultivation at Werrington Park, Cornwall, and at Kew in the 1920's.

Daphne rodriguezii Texidor, in *Apunt. Fl. Esp.* 64 (1869).

SYNONYM   *D. vellaeoides* Rodrig.

ILLUSTRATIONS   Colour plate (sprig), frontispiece fig. 1.

AWARDS   None.

Although, as far as is known, *D. rodriguezii* has never been in cultivation in Britain, it is included here as attention was drawn to it in the *R.H.S. Journal* 93: 300 (1968) where Hugo Money-Coutts provided an admirable account of this species in the wild together with a detailed description.

It is not a showy plant and never likely to create a stir in horticultural circles, but if brought into cultivation would no doubt rapidly find its way into the alpine houses of enthusiasts.

Money-Coutts describes it as a "wind-swept twiggy mound of dark green on the dry rocky ground . . . like *D. petraea* but with cream flowers" and his vivid picture of its habitat suggests that in Britain it would be a candidate for the alpine house, or a nook in a covered tufa wall where the wind could reach it but where some protection from frost could be given. Even so, it would probably prove challenging to maintain in condition in view of its diet of salt spray in winter and summer-baking in its inhospitable, rocky home.

PROPAGATION

It is not possible to offer very useful advice but no doubt the methods used for *D. jasminea* would prove successful once *D. rodriguezii* was established in cultivation.

TYPE LOCALITY   Menorca, near the sea.

DESCRIPTION   Much-branched, evergreen, dwarf shrub up to 50 cm. in height; young shoots greyish, pubescent. Leaves alternate, dark, shining green above, paler below, oblong-oblanceolate, apex mucronate to obtuse, ciliate and finely toothed on the margin, 1—2 cm. long, 2—5 mm. wide. Flowers white, the buds and tube tinged green or occasionally purple, slightly fragrant, in terminal clusters of 1—4, (5); tube 5—8 mm. long, hairy; lobes 3—5 mm. long, ovate, obtuse. Fruit greenish.

CHROMOSOME NO.   Not recorded.

FLOWERING PERIOD   April—June.

DISTRIBUTION   Balearic Isles: Menorca and La Isla Colom.

HABITAT   In scrub or maquis near the sea.

D. rodriguezii was named after a local Menorcan botanist, Juan Rodriguez, who discovered it in 1866, but until the note by Money-Coutts in the *R.H.S. Journal* over 100 years later, received scant attention and was omitted from the literature even by Keissler in his monograph (1898). It was at one time included in the genus *Thymelaea*, but is clearly a true *Daphne*—although unusual in having slightly toothed leaves with ciliate margins.

Daphne x rossetii *nom. nud.* (*D. laureola* ssp. *philippi* x *cneorum*)

ILLUSTRATION   None traced

Although not a hybrid which is likely to create much of a stir horticulturally, it is interesting in being the result of a cross between two *Daphne* species belonging to different sections of the genus.

The original plant was found growing with the parents in August, 1927, in the Pyrenees near Les Eaux-Chaudes by M. Rosset, nursery manager to Henri Correvon who named it after the discoverer. The name has not been validly published, apparently, although it is used in horticultural publications and the epithet which we use here for convenience very properly commemorates the finder.

D. x *rossetii* forms a neat, low, evergreen shrub intermediate in size between the parents, rather like a dense, large-leaved *D. cneorum*, whilst in inflorescence characters it is similar to *D. laureola* but with greenish-yellow flowers suffused dark purplish-red externally.

It is not difficult to grow, thriving in slight shade in a leafy, moist but well-drained position, and apparently tolerates both acid and alkaline conditions, although less happy in dry acid or chalk soils.

As a garden plant it is not particularly exciting, although neat enough in habit and with pleasant foliage. Unfortunately it flowers rarely in most gardens. Aymon Correvon, in correspondence with Eliot Hodgkin, says that it flowers regularly in their mountain garden at 1,000 m. but sparingly at lower altitudes.

PROPAGATION

(a) Cuttings. Stem-cuttings of half-ripe wood can be rooted successfully (Group 2 p. 41).

(b)   Grafting.   Splice or saddle grafting with stocks of *D. mezereum*, *D. laureola* or *D. longilobata* may be used.

(c)   Layering is quite practical in view of the habit of *D.* x *rossetii*.

TYPE LOCALITY   Pyrenees, above Les Eaux-Chaudes, France.

DESCRIPTION (of the clone introduced by Correvon)
A low growing evergreen shrub to 15 cm. (possibly more) in height and 30—40 cm. across. Stems pale brown, glabrous. Leaves alternate, glossy, deep green, leathery, narrowly oblanceolate, acute and sometimes apiculate, wedge-shaped at base, to 3.0 cm. long and 5 mm. wide. Flowers greenish-yellow within, suffused purplish-red outside, 4—6 in axillary, peduncled heads, slightly fragrant; tube 11 mm. long, slightly pubescent; lobes 4—5 mm. long. Fruit unknown.

CHROMOSOME NO.   Not recorded.

FLOWERING PERIOD   June at low altitudes, July (Aug.) at higher altitudes.

DISTRIBUTION   Only known from the type locality.

Although only definitely recorded from the original collection there is the possibility that a plant introduced by Miss Savory may perhaps be this same hybrid. This was apparently collected before the 1939-45 war in the Vallée d'Oussou towards the top of the valley and, according to Dr. Roger-Smith, A.G.S. *Bull.* 16:66 (1948), Miss Savory found a plant of *D.* x *rossetii* in a small beechwood. In foliage and habit it was similar to *D. laureola* ssp. *philippi* but with red (!) flowers.

Desmond Clarke, in correspondence with Eliot Hodgkin over the revision of *Daphne* for Bean's *Trees and Shrubs*, suggests that a plant offered by Messrs. Marchant under this name derives from the original Correvon plant, whilst that available from Messrs. Hillier is the form said to be introduced by Miss Savory.

Marchant's (Correvon's) plant has foliage similar to that of *D. laureola* and chocolate and greenish-yellow blooms, whilst the Hillier (? Savory) plant is closer to *D. cneorum* in leaf but with greener flowers.

The "red" flowers and the habit of *D. laureola* ssp. *philippi* referred to by Roger-Smith are obviously at variance with this theory.

If the two forms are distinct clones, cultivar names could appropriately be applied to each; the problem is to get them to flower so that accurate comparisons can be made.

Daphne sericea Vahl in *Symb. Bot.* 1: 28 (1790).

SYNONYMS   *D. vahlii* Keissler; *D. olaefolia* Lam.

ILLUSTRATION   See colour plate opposite p. 30; drawing on p. 110.

AWARD   A.M. 1931.

As garden plants, the forms of *D. sericea* which are known to have been in cultivation in Britain have proved far less satisfactory than *D. collina*, being generally of more straggling habit and usually tender.

Plants cultivated as *D. sericea* have originated from Italy, Sicily, Crete, Turkey (and possibly other eastern Mediterranean localities) from sea-level to 3,000 or more feet, so it is not surprising that reports differ as to its hardiness. In Surrey plants from relatively low levels in Turkey have been killed outright in all but the mildest winters, and in Grenoble *D. sericea* (origin unstated) is cut to the ground in severe winters. In contrast, Halda states that in Czechoslovakia it is perfectly hardy, although the origin of his plants is unspecified. At Highdown, Sir Frederick Stern grew *D. sericea* well in the chalk garden although it proved an inferior garden plant compared with *D. collina*, forming a tall straggling bush and flowering sparsely. Yet in the A.G.S. *Bulletin* for 1935 there is mention of a plant of *D. sericea* 3 ft. high x 3 ft. across with over 500 trusses of flower in the garden of Dr. Giuseppi at Felixstowe.

It is evident from other accounts that *D. sericea* and *D. collina* are much confused, but their requirements for cultivation in Britain are very similar—that is full sun and a moisture-retentive, fairly rich, yet well-drained soil, moderately acid to alkaline in reaction. *D. sericea* might well succeed on a retaining wall or tufa cliff where sharp drainage and a cool moist root-run could be provided, conditions not unlike those under which it occurs in the wild.

During the spring of 1975 we found *D. sericea* in full flower growing in quantity in several localities in western Turkey, sometimes more or less dominant in areas of low scrub, but also quite frequently in scattered colonies on the outskirts of stands of *Pinus brutia* or *P. halepensis* on rocky limestone areas at altitudes between 300 and 900 m. The soil overlying the rocks was a friable and sometimes quite deep *terra rossa* with an ample cover of leafmould, sufficient to provide *D. sericea* with a cool root run with which to combat the summer drought. An interesting character, which we have not traced as being recorded previously for *D. sericea*, was the suckering habit particularly of colonies on Honaz Dag where at first we mistook the sucker shoots for seedlings as they were often a foot or two distant from the parent plant.

In some wild localities *D. sericea* can be quite spectacular, massed in spring with its intensely fragrant, deep rose blooms.

It is exceedingly variable and widespread, and it would be well worth introducing seed or cuttings of selected plants at the upper limits of its altitude range in an attempt to establish hardier clones than have hitherto been introduced.

PROPAGATION

(a) Seed. This is produced in cultivation and Halda records that it is easily propagated by this method.

(b) Cuttings. These root readily, as outlined under *D. collina*.

(c) Layering. In view of the suckering habit of some forms of *D. sericea* layering would be a useful method of increase if difficulty with cuttings or seed is experienced.

(d) Grafting has been used commercially, but for the amateur is unnecessary.

TYPE LOCALITY   Crete.
DESCRIPTION   Rather loose, much-branched, evergreen shrub up to 1 m. in height; young branches green, ageing brownish-grey, pubescent. Leaves alternate, shiny, mid-green, densely to sparsely pubescent, rarely glabrous, tending to be aggregated towards the ends of the branches in older plants sessile or shortly stalked, obovate, oblanceolate or more or less narrowly elliptic, acute to obtuse, 1—5 cm. long, 0.4—1.2 cm. wide. Flowers in terminal and sometimes also axillary clusters of 5—15, deep rose, fading to brown-buff, strongly fragrant; tube 8—12 mm. long, densely pubescent externally; lobes 4—5 mm. long, 3 mm. wide, elliptic, obtuse to subacute. Fruit fleshy, reddish or orange-brown, egg-shaped, 0.4—0.5 cm. long.
CHROMOSOME NO.   Not recorded.
FLOWERING PERIOD   April—May and occasionally again in autumn (in Britain); March—May (in the wild).
DISTRIBUTION   Italy, Sicily, Crete, S. and W. Turkey, Syria, Caucasus.
HABITAT   Rocky places, maquis and open pinewoods; 0—1800 m.

Related Species

As may be expected with a wide-ranging species such as *D. sericea*, agreement as to the specific limits is hard to find and a number of separate species have been described which fall within the range of *D. sericea* as we define it here.

D. vahlii, described in 1896 by Keissler from Crete, the southern coast of Asia Minor and northern Syria (*D. collina* var. *vahlii* Halacsy) does not differ in any appreciable way, in our view, from *D. sericea* and although the name is often applied to low-growing, densely hairy, higher altitude forms with pale flowers, they appear to represent no more than one extreme of this species with taller, less hairy, open-habited plants with deeper-coloured blooms at the other extreme in Turkey and elsewhere. As Keissler recognised *D. vahlii* var. *glabrifolia* in which the leaves are glabrous, and there are records of variation in habit, leaf and flower characters amongst specimens attributed to *D. vahlii*, it seems preferable to consider it as conspecific with *D. sericea*.

More recently the Russian botanist Pobedimov has described a new species, *D. pseudosericea*, and recognises also *D. circassica* Woronov, both close relatives of *D. sericea*.

D. pseudosericea Pobed. in *Not. Syst. Herb. Inst. Bot. Acad. Sci. URSS*, 12:140 (1950), described from the Suchum district of Abkazia in Western Transcaucasia, is distinguished from *D. sericea* according to Pobedimov "by its lighter shade of bark, by its white-dotted upper leaf surface, by its larger flowers, by its narrower perianth tube and its anthers, which are concealed in the throat". (The stamens of *D. sericea* are usually half-exserted from the throat.)

D. circassica Woronov ex Pobed. in *Not. Syst. Herb. Inst. Bot. Acad. Sci. URSS*, 12:140 (1950), also from Western Transcaucasia in the Sochinski region, is said to differ from *D. sericea* by its almost glabrous leaves, by its long perianth tube (12—13 mm. long) which is 3 x longer than the lobes (2 x as long in *D. sericea*) and by its broader almost round perianth lobes.

Obviously these two species are very similar to *D. sericea*, and some of the differences overlap those given for the range of variation of that species as we understand it. As far as is known, they have never been introduced into cultivation in Britain and it is not possible to comment in any greater detail about them.

Daphne striata Tratt. in *Arch. Gewachsk* 2: 120, t. 133 (1814).

SYNONYM ? *D. cneorum* Wahl. non L.

ILLUSTRATIONS See drawing on p. 86; also S.R.G.C. Journal 8; fig. 38.

AWARDS None.

As a garden plant *D. striata*, although floriferous and fragrant in nature, is often looked upon as a poor relation of *D. cneorum*, which it closely resembles and certainly is generally found to be far less amenable in cultivation than that species. There are numerous reports in the literature that it is a "miff", perhaps disdaining the lower elevations at which we normally try to cultivate it and being more than usually sensitive to high temperatures and dry conditions. In nature it is often a high alpine species, frequently recorded as growing in stony screes or short grassland in company with low shrubs, such as *Salix arbuscula*, *Rhodothamnus chamaecistus*, *Juniperus communis* ssp. *nana* and *Rhododendron ferrugineum*. Some reports state that it only grows on non-calcareous soils; others that it is a calcicole preferring limestone soils; yet others claim granite as its natural choice. The truth of the matter is difficult to decide without a full-scale survey of its natural habitats, but we suspect that it is indifferent to pH variations either side of neutral. It does, however, insist on a medium which never dries out completely, so that the fine roots do not suffer, and yet is sufficiently well-drained to prevent any stagnation at the roots.

Although other growers have put forward a variety of suggestions as to the most suitable conditions in which to grow *D. striata* in the garden (from a sharp scree to an avalanche!), it seems probable that moist, cool conditions with sharp "neck" drainage offer the most hope—perhaps a peat bank or bed with a slightly more open, gritty mixture than one would provide normally for peat-lovers. Our own experience of growing *D. striata* is limited, but Will

Ingwersen (1971) grew it well in a raised bed of peaty, gritty soil where it flowered profusely. Money-Coutts was also successful, finding it happiest when helped along by a dose of sequestrene.

D. striata is known to have been cultivated spasmodically since 1827 and in the A.G.S. *Bulletin* there are several records of Members finding both the usual pink and also white-flowered forms, Dr. Amsler referring to patches "as big as a tennis court" above Lautaret. Both white and pink-flowered plants have been brought into cultivation in Britain but no records of *D. striata* being grown continuously and reasonably well over fairly long periods have been traced. We should be delighted to hear to the contrary, and particularly to learn the formula for success!

PROPAGATION
(a) Seed. Several growers report raising seed collected in the wild without difficulty, but have found the seedlings very sensitive to dry conditions. We have no experience of raising *D. striata* from seed, but it is likely that early sowing and stratification would assist germination. No records of seed being produced on cultivated plants are known to us.
(b) Cuttings. Soft cuttings root under mist reasonably easily (see Group 1, p. 41), although the young plants require considerable care to establish successfully.

A lesser percentage take has been reported for more mature, half-ripe cuttings but without supporting evidence, and in view of the very limited propagating material used, it would be unwise to draw any conclusions on the optimum timing for cuttings.
(c) Grafting. Halda reports *D. alpina* and *D. giraldii* as very suitable stocks for *D. striata*, particularly for cultivation at low altitudes, presumably as the root system of these stocks is more adapted to drought or drier soils than that of the species itself.

D. mezereum also proves satisfactory, and no doubt *D. cneorum* could be used successfully in view of its close relationship to *D. striata*. Side or saddle grafting methods succeed well.
(d) Layering. Once a plant of *D. striata* has been established successfully, layering should present no difficulty.

TYPE LOCALITY   Italy, near Bolzano.
DESCRIPTION   As *D. striata* resembles *D. cneorum* so closely a full description is omitted. It differs mainly in being entirely glabrous; having slightly slender more freely-branched stems; longer, narrower leaves (5—6 times as long as wide compared with 3—4 times in *D. cneorum*); longitudinally striped, glabrous (not plain and pubescent) perianth tubes; and reddish-orange (not yellow-brown) fruits.
CHROMOSOME NO.   Not recorded.
FLOWERING PERIOD   May—July.
DISTRIBUTION   Alps of Austria, France, Germany, Jugoslavia and Switzerland; Italian Dolomites.
HABITAT   Stony screes or short grassland amongst low shrubs usually above 1,500 m. (but with an altitude range of 900 m. to 3,000 m. according to Halda). Often apparently calcicole but also occurring on acid soils.

177

Mountfort, in the A.G.S. *Bulletin* 25: 320 (1957), records in a footnote to an article by Eliot Hodgkin that he had grown *D. striata* for several years both on its own roots and grafted (stock unstated), and that in each case it proved winter-deciduous. That this might occur with unhappy grafted plants is understandable, but *D. striata* is certainly evergreen in nature. Ruffier-Lanche, however, (A.G.S. *Bull.* 26: 68 (1958) states that *D. striata* is "a true evergreen but when freshly transplanted, or unhealthy, it sheds its leaves, without being dead for all that".

Variation in flower colour from deep pink to white occurs in the wild, albinos apparently being reasonably common. If the literature is accurate, only in the Dolomites does *D. striata* overlap with *D. cneorum* which (in Farrer's words) is "reluctant perhaps to intrude on the territory of *D. striata* or disdaining such inefficient rivalry".

Daphne sureil W. W. Smith and Cave in *Rec. Bot. Surv. Ind.* 6, 2: 51 (1912).

ILLUSTRATION   *Bot. Mag.* t. 9297 (1933).

The comments on cultivation given under *D. papyracea* apply equally to *D. sureil*, a species little known in cultivation and almost certainly tender in Britain as the upper limit of its altitude range in the eastern Himalaya is only 2,000 m. (just over 6,000 ft.).

Eliot Hodgkin records receiving a plant of this species from Messrs. Hillier in 1949, and from his correspondence with Hugo Money-Coutts it appears that both raised this species from seed sometime in the late 1950's or early 1960's. Unfortunately, it is not known what happened to the resulting plants.

It seems likely, however, that seed sent by Dr. Herklots to Kew and Windsor from Nepal in 1962 was of *D. sureil*. The plants from which the seeds were taken were growing in the same region as *D. bholua*, but at lower altitudes (1,600—2,000 m.), and were smaller-growing than this latter species with white, fragrant blooms followed by the orange-red fruits, which are one of the features distinguishing *D. sureil* from *D. bholua*. Again the fate of any offspring is unknown, but as only *D. sureil* is recorded from the area in which Dr. Herklots collected it would seem reasonable to suppose the introduction to be of this species.

PROPAGATION

See under *D. papyracea* and *D. bholua*.

TYPE LOCALITY   E. Himalaya: Darjeeling District.

DESCRIPTION   Sparingly branched erect evergreen shrub up to 2.5 m. in height; young branches glabrous to downy. Leaves alternate, pale, very shiny green, rather thin and soft in texture, glabrous, distinctly petiolate, ovate-elliptic to narrowly elliptic or oblanceolate, acute to acuminate, 6—17 cm. long, 1.8—4 cm. wide. Floral bracts early-deciduous, usually falling before the buds are open. Flowers in terminal clusters of 5—15, white or greenish-white (possibly

178

rarely flushed with pale lilac) fragrant; tube 1.3—1.4 cm. long, downy outside; lobes 0.6—0.8 cm. long, 0.3—0.4 cm. wide, narrowly ovate, acute to acuminate. Fruit reddish-orange, ellipsoid, 1—1.5 cm. long.

CHROMOSOME NO. Not recorded.

FLOWERING PERIOD October—January (—May) in the wild.

DISTRIBUTION E. Himalaya: E. Nepal, Khasia, E. Bengal, Assam.

HABITAT 1500—2200 m. in mixed rain forest with *Quercus* and *Magnolia*.

For a comparison of the botanical characters separating *D. sureil* from *D. bholua* and *D. papyracea* see p. 65 under *D. bholua*.

Related Species

D. shillong Banerji described in *Kew Bull.* (1927) p. 75, is very similar to *D. sureil* and appears only to differ in the length of the perianth tube (1.8—2.0 cm. long as opposed to 1.3—1.4 cm.) and the length of the perianth lobes (0.8— 1.0 cm. as opposed to 0.6—0.8 cm.). Fruit colour is un-recorded. Further material is required to comment in detail on the relationship of *D. shillong* and *D. sureil*.

D. shillong was first collected in the Shillong District of N.E. India at Spread Eagle Falls where it grows at about 1500 m. in *Pinus khasya* forest. It is not known to be in cultivation.

Daphne x thauma Farrer in *Gard. Chron.* 52: 22 (1912).

SYNONYMS *D.* x *farreri* Hort.; ? *D.* x *leyboldii* Hort.

ILLUSTRATION *Gard. Chron.* 52: 22 (1912).

AWARD None traced.

A romantic natural liaison between the aristocratic *D. petraea* and the more plebeian *D. striata* has provided our gardens with this most attractive hybrid, located by the sharp eyes of Farrer on the Cima Tombea in 1911.

There are differing opinions as to its garden value. Bean (1973) dismisses it as a poor plant reluctant to flower, whilst Farrer found it reasonably free-flowering in his garden at Ingleborough.

Farrer's comment that it "seems to occupy more open ledges and places less bare of soil than the pitiless rock-faces affected by *D. rupestris* (i.e. *D. petraea*)" provides a possible clue, indicating that less austere conditions than are usually offered to *D. petraea* would be in order. This is certainly the experience of some cultivators, and sharply-drained scree conditions with an underlying moisture-retentive, gritty mixture rich in humus into which the roots can penetrate would be our recommendation, either for the open rock-garden or pot cultivation. Certainly there should be no stagnant moisture at the roots but neither should the drainage be so sharp that the plant is left gasping for water, even after a good soaking.

179

An open, sunny position on the rock garden or on a raised bed should be provided, and in such a situation *D.* x *thauma* forms a compact shrublet of spreading, low habit with glossy neat foliage and soft pink flowers. These are longer and larger than those of *D. striata*, but less deep in colour than those of *D. petraea*, although with the dark purplish-rose throat of this latter species. In general it is intermediate between the parents, being described either as a neater, more compact *D. striata* or a more spreading, slender growing *D. petraea*, depending on one's viewpoint.

PROPAGATION

(a) Seed. Halda reports fruiting on the plant he calls *D.* x *leyboldii* (which is stated to be of the same parentage as *D.* x *thauma*) but apparently was unable to germinate seed.

(b) Cuttings. There appears little difficulty in rooting half-ripe cuttings, just firming at the base, taken in July, the resultant plants growing reasonably vigorously on their own roots.

(c) Grafting. This is the method employed by most nurseries, using stocks of *D. mezereum*, *D. longilobata* and other species. The wood is fairly thin so the splice graft is usually preferred.

(d) Layering. Also a possibility, although we have found no reference to propagation in this way, nor have we tried it ourselves.

TYPE LOCALITY   Cima Tombea, Italy.

DESCRIPTION   A caespitose, densely-branched shrub forming mats 5—8 cm. high and 30—45 cm. across. Branches erect or slightly decumbent, greyish-brown, sparingly pubescent, seldom more than 5—7 cm. long. Leaves alternate, sessile, clustered at the tips of the branches, glossy deep green, leathery, glabrous; ovate-lanceolate with thickened or revolute margins, acute, 12—20 mm. long, 3—6 mm. wide. Flowers soft pale pink with darker pink tubes, in clusters of 5—8, fragrant; tube to 14 mm. long, downy outside; lobes to 5 mm. long, broadly ovate, obtuse. Fruit unknown to us, but reported by Halda as fleshy, yellowish.

CHROMOSOME NO.   Not recorded.

FLOWERING PERIOD   May—July (August).

DISTRIBUTION   A natural hybrid known only from Cima Tombea, Italy.

HABITAT   Limestone cliffs on open ledges.

Farrer mentions that several plants of *D.* x *thauma* were found on the Cima Tombea but does not comment on any variation. The plants now in cultivation evidently derive from his original collection in August 1911, although there is mention in Bean (1973) of a similar plant at Kew which proved impossible to propagate. Royton Heath (1969) mentions a plant on the scree at Kew with white, pink-flushed flowers which might possibly be the plant referred to by Bean. It is uncertain, however, whether this is the same clone as that introduced by Farrer and we have located no further introductions of this hybrid.

Daphne retusa (p. 167).

181

Photos: R. Elliott

Daphne tangutica (p. 170).

Daphne striata, (p. 176) in the Dolomites.　　　　　*Photo: Roy Elliott*

Lesser-known species not yet introduced or only very rarely cultivated

The following abbreviated accounts of a number of daphnes are provided for interest. The list is by no means exhaustive but contains brief details of species which may possibly be brought into cultivation in the future, as well as reference points of *Daphne* names which may occur in botanico-horticultural literature.

D. arisanensis Hayata, *Icon. Pl. Formosa* 2: 126 (1912). A large evergreen shrub, 2—3 m. in height with lanceolate or oblanceolate leaves, 5—7 cm. long, 1.5—2 cm. wide. The flowers are stated to be white (followed by yellow berries) or yellow (followed by red berries) in terminal clusters of 6—7, and apparently rather small with a tube 4 mm. long and lobes rather shorter. It is endemic to Taiwan in the higher forests at 2,000—3,000 m. Apparently related to *D. tangutica*.

D. aurea Poir. *Encyc. Suppl.* 3: 316 (1813). Very little useful information can be learned from the description about this plant except that it comes from the "Levant" and that it was called "aurea" because the leaves are golden-hairy beneath.

D. bodinieri Lev. in *Feddes Repert.* 13: 258 (1914). This has small yellow flowers in axillary clusters, and is a large shrub with long branches. The leaves are narrowly lanceolate, rather leathery and with revolute margins. It may in fact be a *Wikstroemia*, not a *Daphne*. The type locality is Kouy-Tcheou in China.

D. cavaleriei Lev. in *Bull. Georg. Bot.* 25: 42 (1915). A little-known species. We can only repeat the relevant parts of the original description, although this does not give much idea of the relationships with other species. It has oblong, acute, glabrous leaves, 7 cm. long and 2 cm. wide and fragrant white flowers in terminal clusters. It was collected in Yunnan, China at Lan-Ngi-Tsin, 2,600 m., flowering in May.

D. clivicola Hand.-Mazz., *Symb. Sin.* 7:588 (1933). This is perhaps not a *Daphne* as it is described as having five lobes to the flower. It is said to be evergreen, yellow-flowered and "like *D. aurantiaca*" but with alternate leaves. S.W. China, between Yenuen and Kwapi.

D. escalerae Pau in *Trab. Mus. Nac. Cienc. Nat. Madrid* 14:24 (1918). This species is apparently very similar to *D. mucronata*, with silvery-hairy leaves and pubescent flowers. The inflorescence is however said to be on a distinct peduncle which would serve to distinguish it from that species. It was collected in Iran at Gotvend and the Valley of Bazouft.

D. esquirolii Lev. in *Bull. Georg. Bot.* 25:42 (1915). From the description this sounds an interesting plant, for it has spikes of numerous yellow flowers produced in March before the leaves. The type locality is in Yunnan, at Mong-Kou, 2,000 m.

D. feddei Lev. in *Feddes Repert.* 9:326 (1911). The rather scanty description gives no flower colour, and states that the flowers are produced in a short raceme. The leaves are narrow, acuminate with revolute margins. It is from Kouy-Tcheou in China. Rehder (*Plantae Wilsonianae* 2:547 (1916)) suggests it is near to *D. papyracea*.

D. kabylica Chab. in *Bull. Soc. Bot. Fr.* 36:30 (1889). Unfortunately this name was given to a daphne not seen in flower, so it is difficult to say what its affinities are! However, the author said that he thought (!) the flowers were laterally produced. The green leaves are obovate and clustered at the apex of the stems, and as it is a woodland plant one wonders if it is not in fact a form of *D. laureola*. It was collected in Algeria, at Chenes and in the cedars of Mechmal.

D. kurdica Bornm. in *Beih. Bot. Centralbl.* 28, 2:498 (1911). From its description, perhaps a variant of *D. oleoides*, *D. stapfii* or even *D. mucronata*. An evergreen, the foliage covered with a bluish-white "wax", described from Kurdistan.

D. laciniata Lecomte in *Not. Syst.* 3:215 (1916).
Another yellow-flowered species with axillary clusters of flowers, having triangular lobes in var. *laciniata* and rounded lobes in var. *duclouxii*. The leaves are said to be 12—17 cm. long by 2.5—3.5 cm. wide in the typical plant but only 5—7 cm. long in var. *duclouxii*. The species occurs in Yunnan and E. Szechuan

D. libanotica Mouterde in *Veg. Arb. Levant*, 13:36 (1947).
The original description and illustration of this species suggest that it is scarcely distinguishable from *D. pontica*. The flowers are said to be yellowish with a tube 5—6 mm. long and the leaves 5—7 cm. long, 2—2.5 cm. wide. The type locality is in Syria between Ghosta and Dlepta in the region known as Kesrouan.

D. limprichtii H. Winkler in *Fedde Repert. Beih.* 12:444 (1922).
Very closely related to *D. retusa*, and the measurements given suggest that it would fall within the range of variation of *D. retusa*. It is recorded from E. Tibet at Tatsienlu, 4,100—4,200 m., which may be the same locality as that given for the type collection of *D. retusa*, although there is a slight difference in spelling.

D. martinii Lev. in *Feddes. Repert.* 10:369 (1912). This species is described as having white or yellowish-green flowers in terminal or axillary clusters. The leaves are glaucous or brownish-green, obovate or lanceolate and acute. It is from Kouy-Tcheou in China. Rehder in *Plantae Wilsonianae* 2:547 (1916) equates it with *D. feddei*.

D. roumea Meissn. in *DC. Prodr.* 14:538 (1857). A poorly known species, named from a plant cultivated in Calcutta Botanic Garden which was thought to have originated in China. It was said to be like *D. gnidium*.

D. salicina Lev. in *Bull. Georg. Bot.* 25-42 (1915). The original description of this species says that it is a willowy shrub up to 1.5 m. with white-hairy branches, and leaves 2 cm. long and 4—6 mm. wide. The flowers are produced in July and are yellow and very pubescent. The type locality is in Yunnan, at Ie-Ma-Tchouan, 3,200 m.

D. vaillantii P. Danguy in *Lecomte Not. Syst.* 2:166 (1911). This is a yellow flowered plant with a tube 5.5 mm. long and lobes 3.5 mm. long. The lanceolate leaves are leathery and 3—5 cm. long by 0.8—1 cm. wide. In the original description it is said to be a shrub of 30—50 cm. high, and very closely related to *D. tangutica* and *D. retusa*, though the yellow flowers would readily separate it from these two species. It is from Shensi Province of China, at Lou-pan-Chan, 2,700 m.

HYBRIDS

The documentation of hybrids between various *Daphne* species is poor and it is seldom possible to be absolutely certain of the parentage of hybrids like *D.* x *napolitana* which have been in cultivation for many years. In the descriptive accounts we have provided as much information as we have been able to trace on the hybrids commonly grown or referred to in the literature but include here a list of known and reputed crosses with any further information gleaned about them.

Hugo Money-Coutts made a large number of crosses in the early 1960's but unfortunately the information we have on seedlings raised is limited and the resulting plants are no longer in existence as far as we know.

Albert Burkwood also attempted to cross *D. genkwa* with various other species (around 1912) but was unsuccessful in obtaining viable seed.

In the following list the female parent (where known) is given first and the reverse crosses, which would be covered by the same name, are indexed accordingly.

D. alpina x *D. petraea*—see under *D. petraea* x *D. alpina*

D. arbuscula x *D. cneorum* var. *verlotii*—see under *D. cneorum* var. *verlotii* x *D. arbuscula*

D. arbuscula x *D. petraea*—A hybrid intermediate between the parents in habit and which has apparently not yet flowered in cultivation. Origin unknown to us, but before 1964. Plants of this cross have been grown by Eliot Hodgkin, Jack Drake, and Brian Mathew. See also *D.* 'Dr. Jenkin'.

D. aurantiaca x *D. cneorum*—A single plant raised by Money-Coutts from this cross (about 1962) was grown for a very short time at Wisley. In leaf characters it appeared intermediate between the two parents but did not flower.

D. bholua x *D. mezereum*—see under *D. mezereum* x *D. bholua* 'Gurkha'

D. x *burkwoodii* Turrill (*D. caucasica* x *D. cneorum*)—see under *D.* x *burkwoodii* in list of species. Named clones are 'Albert Burkwood', 'Carol Mackie', 'Lavenirii', 'Somerset', 'Somerset Variegated'

D. x *burkwoodii* x *D. retusa*—see under *D.* x *mantensiana*

D. caucasica x *D. cneorum*—see under *D.* x *burkwoodii*

D. cneorum var. *verlotii* x *D. arbuscula*—A hybrid raised and grown by Money-Coutts, the branches with short internodes and the leaves alternate. No details of flowers known and not apparently in cultivation now.

D. cneorum x *D. aurantiaca*—see under *D. aurantiaca* x *D. cneorum*

D. cneorum x *D. caucasica*—see under *D.* x *burkwoodii*

D. cneorum x *D. collina*—see under *D.* x *napolitana*

D. cneorum x *D. laureola* ssp. *philippi*—see under *D.* x *rossetii*

D. cneorum x *D. petraea*—see under *D.* x *hendersonii*

D. x *collina-axillaris* Jacques (*D. mezereum* x *D. collina*)—A hybrid raised, according to George Gordon in *The Garden* 9: 568 (1876), by M. Jacques near Paris between *D. mezereum*, the female parent, and *D. collina*, the pollen parent. Apparently with the habit of *D. collina* but producing its flowers (colour unstated) in the leaf axils. Said to flower "early spring". Also mentioned briefly by Burbridge (1877).

D. collina x *D. cneorum*—see under *D.* x *napolitana*

D. collina x *D. mezereum*—see under *D. collina-axillaris*

D. collina x *D. odora*—see under *D.* x *hybrida*

D. collina x *D. oleoides*. A parentage sometimes attributed to *D.* x *napolitana*—see p. 138.

D. delahayana Hort. ex. Visiani—see under *D.* x *napolitana*

D. 'Dr. Jenkin' (*D. arbuscula* x *D. petraea* 'Grandiflora'). A plant under this name was exhibited to the Joint Rock Garden Plant Committee on April 27th 1954 by K. S. West of Churt, Surrey. This may possibly be the same clone mentioned under *D. arbuscula* x *D. petraea* above.

D. fioniana Hort. see under *D.* x *hybrida*, p. 114; and *D.* x *napolitana*, p. 137.

D. x *hendersonii* Hodgkin ex C. D. Brickell et B. Mathew—see p. 112.

D. x *houtteana* Lindley and Paxton (*D. mezereum* x *D. laureola*)—see p. 113

D. x *hybrida* Colv. ex Sweet (*D. odora* x *D. collina*)—see p. 114

D. laureola x *D. mezereum*—see under *D.* x *houtteana*

D. laureola ssp. *philippi* x *D. cneorum*—see under *D.* x *rossetii*

D. x *mantensiana* Manten ex T.M.C. Taylor & F. Vrugtman (*D.* x *burkwoodii* x *D. retusa*)—see p. 126. Named clone, 'Manten'

D. mezereum x *D. bholua* 'Gurkha'. A cross made by Mr. Dummer at Hillier's in 1969. One (of three) seedlings appeared intermediate and flowered in February—March 1975. The blooms were few but similar in colour and form to *D. bholua* 'Gurkha'. The plant also resembles this parent in tending to produce suckers.

D. mezereum x *D. Collina*—see under *D.* x *collina-axillaris*

D. mezereum x *D. laureola*—see under *D.* x *houtteana*

D. x *napolitana* Loddiges (*D. collina* x *D. cneorum* (?))—see p. 137

D. odora x *D. collina*—see under *D.* x *hybrida*

D. oleoides x *D. collina*—see under *D.* x *napolitana*

D. petraea x *D. alpina*. Recorded by Mr. T. H. Lowndes in July 1975, near Passo Croce Domini, Italy at about 1800m. In its deciduous foliage and habit similar to *D. alpina;* in its pink flowers similar to *D. petraea*. A single plant growing with *D. petraea* but with no *D. alpina* in the immediate vicinity.

D. petraea x *D. arbuscula*—see under *D. arbuscula* x *D. petraea*

D. petraea x *D. cneorum*—see under *D.* x *hendersonii*

D. petraea x *D. striata*—see under *D.* x *thauma*

D. retusa x *D. burkwoodii*—see under *D.* x *mantensiana*

D. x *rossetii*. An invalidated name for *D. laureola* ssp. *philippi* x *D. cneorum*—see p. 124

D. striata x *D. petraea*—see under *D.* x *thauma*

D. x *thauma* Farrer (*D. petraea* x *D. striata*)—see p. 179

REFERENCES TO USEFUL LITERATURE ON THE GENUS DAPHNE

The following short list of references is provided of relevant botanical and horticultural accounts of the genus. It is not intended to be comprehensive but to act as a guide for those seeking further information.

Aiton, W. T., (1811) *Hortus Kewensis*, Vol. II.
Amsler, A. M., (1953) *Journ. Roy. Hort. Soc.*, LXXVIII, pp. 5-18. Daphnes.
Argles, G. K. and Rowe-Dutton, P. (1969) The propagation of Daphnes. *Nurseryman and Garden Centre* (1969) 149: 505-8; 533-6; 597-601; 630-1.
Bean, W. J., (1973) *Trees and Shrubs Hardy in the British Isles*, Vol. II, D-M.
Boissier, E., (1867-84) *Flora Orientalis*.
Burtt, B. L., (1936), *Kew Bulletin* 1936: 433-441. A note on the Himalayan Daphnes.
Domke, W., (1934), *Bibl. Bot. Heft.* 111: 1-151. Untersuchungen über die systematische u. geographische Gliederung der Thymelaeaceae.
Don, J., (1845), *Hortus Cantabrigiensis*.
Ferguson I.K. in *Flora Europeaa* (1968), Daphne in Vol. II, 256-258.
Gerard, J., (1597), *The History of Plants* (and later editions).
Gordon, G., (1876), *The Garden*, IX, 567-70. The Daphnes.
Halda, J., (1972), *Skalnicky*. Daphne.
Hamaya, T., (1959), *Bull. Tok. Univ. Forests* 50: 45-96. A dendrological mono-notes on Thymelaeaceae from Japan and adjacent regions.
Hamaya, T., (1959), *Bull. Tok. Univ*, Forests 50: 45-96. A dendrological mono-graph on the Thymelaeaceous plants of Japan.
Hegi, G., (1906-1931), *Illustrierte Flora von Mittel-Europa*.
Hodgkin, E., (1961), *Journ. Roy. Hort. Soc.*, LXXXVI pp. 481-488. Daphnes.
Keissler, K., (1898), *Botanische Jahrbucher*, Vol. XXV: 29-124. Die Arten der Gattung Daphne aus der Section Daphnanthes.
Krussman, G. (1960), *Handbuch der Laubgeholze*.
Linnaeus, C., (1753), *Species Plantarum*.
Miller, P., (1731), *The Gardeners Dictionary* (and later editions).
Nitsche, W, (1907), *Beitrage der Gattung Daphne*.
Rehder, A., (1916), *Plantae Wilsonianae*, Vol. II.
Rehder, A., (1947), *Manual of Cultivated Trees and Shrubs*, Edition 2.
Rehder, A., (1949), *A Bibliography of Cultivated Trees and Shrubs*.
Schneider, C. K., (1909), *Handbuch der Laubholzkunde*.
Winkler, G. H., (1922), *Fed. Rep. Beih.* 12: 441-445. Thymelaeaceae in Botanische Reisen in der Hochgebirgen Chinas u. Ost.-Tibets von Dr. W. Limpricht.

The following works also contain useful information on Daphnes:

Alpine Garden Society *Bulletin* (1930—)
Annals of Botany (1887—)
Botanical Register (1815—1847)
Combined *Proceedings* of the International Plant Propagators' Society (1954—)
Curtis, *Botanical Magazine* (1793—)
Flores des Serres et Jardins (1845—1880)
Gardeners Chronicle (1841—)
Journal of the Arnold Arboretum (1919—)
Journal of the Royal Horticultural Society (1812—)
Kew Bulletin (1887—)
Lindley & Paxton, Paxton's *Flower Garden* (1850-3 and 1882-4)
Loddiges *Botanical Cabinet* (1818—1833)
Notes from the Royal Botanic Garden, Edinburgh (1900—)
Paxton's *Magazine of Botany* (1834—1849)
Revue Horticole (1829—)
Sweet's *British Flower Garden* (1823—1838)
The Garden (1871?—1927)

INDEX TO DAPHNE NAMES

The following list of names is provided for easy reference to the specific and cultivar names at present in common use in horticultural and botanical literature. It does not pretend to cover the genus in its entirety, a task which could not be undertaken without many years research, but is offered as a preliminary guide for those interested in Daphnes.

The specific names accepted in this list are those which appear correct from our present state of knowledge. Some of the names given for infraspecific taxa have been retained, not because we are convinced of their nomenclatural validity or their status, but to avoid confusing matters further by transference of rank or provision of new names without carrying out the research required for proper monographic treatment. Similarly, the cultivar names which we suggest should be used may, in the future, be shown to be incorrect in some instances. The poor documentation of cultivars and the inexact application of cultivar names makes the task of unravelling the horticultural taxa involved very difficult, whilst extensive field studies of the species in the wild would be necessary to provide a reasoned revision of the genus as a whole.

PAGE

D. acuminata Boiss. & Hoh. ex Stocks, a synonym of *D. mucronata* Royle
D. acuminata Boiss. et Hoh. ex Stocks var. *kochii* Meissn., a synonym of
    D. mucronata Royle
D. acutiloba Rehder   46
D. albiflora J. Wolf., a synonym of *D. mezereum* L. f. *alba* (Weston) Schelle
D. albowiana Woron. ex Pobed.   166
D. alpina L.   53
D. alpina L. var. *petiolata* Keissler   54
D. alpina Baumg., a synonym of *D. blagayana* Freyer
D. altaica Pallas   79
D. altaica Pall. var. *longilobata* Lecomte, a synonym of *D. longilobata*
    (Lecomte) Turrill
D. altaica Steven, a synonym of *D. sophia* Kaleniczenko
D. angustifolia C. Koch., a synonym of *D. mucronata* Royle
D. arbuscula Celak. ssp. *arbuscula* 54, 57
D. arbuscula Celak. ssp. *arbuscula* forma *albiflora* Halda   57
D. arbuscula Celak. ssp. *arbuscula* forma *grandiflora* Halda   ..   57
D. arbuscula Celak. ssp. *arbuscula* "var. *grandiflora* f. *carminea*"   ..   57
D. arbuscula Celak. ssp. *arbuscula* forma *platyclada* Halda   ..   57
D. arbuscula Celak. ssp. *arbuscula* forma *platyclada* Halda subforma
    albiflora Halda   57
D. arbuscula Celak. "ssp. *septentrionalis*"   57
D. arbuscula Celak. "ssp. *septentrionalis* var. *albiflora*"   58
D. arbuscula Celak. "ssp. *septentrionalis* var.*albiflora* forma *platyclada* C"   58
D. arbuscula Celak. "ssp. *septentrionalis* forma *platyclada* B"   ..   58
D. arbuscula Celak. "ssp. *septentrionalis*" forma *radicans* Halda   ..   58
D. arbuscula Christ., a synonym of *D. laureola* L.   ..   ..
D. arisanensis Hayata   183
D. aurantiaca Diels   58
D. aurea Poir.   183
D. australis Cyr., a synonym of *D. collina* J. E. Smith   ..   ..
D. baksanica Pobed.   156
D. bholua Buch.—Ham. ex D. Don   60
D. bholua Buch.—Ham. ex D. Don var. *glacialis* Sm. et Cav. emend Burtt   64
D. bholua Buch.—Ham. ex D. Don 'Gurkha'   64
D. bholua Buch.—Ham. ex D. Don 'Sheopuri'   64
D. blagayana Freyer   65
D. bodinieri Lev.   183
D. x *burkwoodii* Turrill (*D. caucasica* Pall. x *D. cneorum* L.)   71

	PAGE
D. x *burkwoodii* Turrill 'Albert Burkwood'	74
D. x *burkwoodii* Turrill 'Carol Mackie'	77
D. x *burkwoodii* Turrill 'Lavenirii'	74
D. x *burkwoodii* Turrill 'Somerset'	74
D. x *burkwoodii* Turrill 'Somerset Variegated'	74
D. cachemireana Meissn., a synonym of *D. mucronata* Royle ..	
D. calcicola W. W. Smith, a synonym of *D. aurantiaca* Diels ..	
D. candida Wittm., a synonym of *D. alpina* L.	
D. candolleana Meissn., a synonym of *D. gnidioides* Jaub. & Spach	
D. cannabina Hook. f. (in part), a synonym of *D. papyracea* Wall. ex. Steud. emend Smith & Cave ..	
D. cannabina Hook. f. (in part), a synonym of *D. bholua* Buch.—Ham. ex D. Don	
D. cannabina Wall. (in part), a synonym of *D. papyracea* Wall. ex Steud. emend Smith & Cave ..	
D. cannabina Wall. (in part), a synonym of *D. bholua* Buch.—Ham. ex D. Don ..	
D. cannabina Wall. (in part) var. *bholua* (Buch.—Ham. ex D. Don) Keissler, a synonym of D. bholua Buch.—Ham. ex D. Don ..	
D. caucasica Pallas var. *caucasica*	77
D. caucasica Pallas var. *axilliflora* Keissler	78
D. caucasica Pallas var. *cognata* C. Koch., a synonym of *D. caucasica* Pallas	
D. cavaleriei Lev.	183
D. championii Benth.	103
D. chinensis Spreng., a synonym of *D. odora* Thunb.	
D. circassica Wor. ex Pobed.	176
D. clivicola Hand.-Mazz.	183
D. cneorum Guld., a synonym of *D. caucasica* Pallas	
D. cneorum L.	82
D. cneorum var. *abietina* Borb., a synonym of *D. arbuscula* Celak. ..	
D. cneorum L. *alba* Hort., ? an albino of *D. cneorum* L. var. *pygmaea* Stoker	
D. cneorum L. *albiflora* Hort.	87
D. cneorum L. *albo-variegata* Hort.	87
D. cneorum L. forma *arbusculoides* Tuzson	88
D. cneorum L. *argenteo-marginata* Hort., a synonym of *D. cneorum* L. *argenteum* Loddiges	
D. cneorum L. *argenteum* Loddiges	87
D. cneorum L. *aureo-marginata* Hort., a synonym of *D. cneorum* L. *variegata* Knight	
D. cneorum L. 'Carminea'	87
D. cneorum L. *elegantissima* Hort., a synonym of *D. cneorum* L. *argenteum* Loddiges	
D. cneorum L. 'Eximia'	87
D. cneorum L. *flore-albo* Loudon	87
D. cneorum L. *foliis luteo* Hort., a synonym of *D. cneorum* L. *variegata* Knight	
D. cneorum L. *foliis variegatis* Hort., a synonym of *D. cneorum* L. *variegata* Knight	
D. cneorum L. var. *grandiflorum* Lodd., a synonym of *D. cneorum* L. var. *maximum* Jacques	
D. cneorum L. var. *latifolia* Reichb. f.	88
D. cneorum L. *luteum* Hort., a synonym of *D. cneorum* L. *variegata* Knight	
D. cneorum L. forma *major* (Dippel) Schelle	89
D. cneorum L. var. *maximum* Jacques, probably a hybrid akin to *D.* x *napolitana* Lodd., q.v.	89
D. cneorum L. var. *pygmaea* Stoker	89

D. cneorum L. var. *pyramidale* Makoy, a synonym of *D. cneorum* L. var. *maximum* Jacques .. ..

D. cneorum L. var. *stricta* Hort., a synonym of *D. cneorum* L. var. *maximum* Jacques .. ..

D. cneorum L. *variegata* Knight 87

D. cneorum L. var. *verlotii* (Gren. et Godr.) Meissn. 90

D. cneorum L. var. *verlotii* (Gren. et Godr.) Meissn. forma *humifusa* (Verl. et Paz.) Keissl. 93

D. cneorum Wahl. non L., probably a synonym of *D. striata* Tratt. .. 94

D. collina Dickson ex J. E. Smith 94

D. collina Dickson ex J. E. Smith var. *neapolitana* (Lodd.) Lindl., a synonym of *D.* x *napolitana* Lodd. .. ..

D. x *collina-axillaris* Jacques A hybrid of *D. mezereum* x *collina* .. 185

D. comosa Adam., a synonym of *D. glomerata* Lam. .. ..

D. cretica Steud., a synonym of *D. oleoides* Schreb. .. ..

D. dauphinii Loudon, a synonym of *D.* x *hybrida* Colv. ex Sweet ..

D. delahayana Hort. ex Visiani, a synonym of *D.* x *napolitana* Lodd.

D. delahayi Hort., a synonym of *D.* x *napolitana* Lodd. .. ..

D. delphinii Meissn., a synonym of *D.* x *hybrida* Colv. ex Sweet ..

D. delphinium Loudon, a synonym of *D.* x *hybrida* Colv. ex Sweet ..

D. 'Dr. Jenkin' a hybrid of *D. arbuscula* x *D. petraea* 'Grandiflora'. ..

D. elisae Vis., probably a synonym of *D.* x *napolitana* Lodd. ..

D. escalerae Pau. 183

D. esquirolii Lev. 183

D. euboica Rech. fil. 155

D. euphorbioides Pusch. ex Steud., a synonym of *D. caucasica* Pallas ..

D. x *farreri* Hort., a synonym of *D.* x *thauma* Farrer; and of *D. cneorum* L. var. *verlotii* (Gren. et Godr.) Meissn, in some gardens

D. feddei Lev. 183

D. fioniana Hort. ex Dipp., probably a synonym of *D.* x *napolitana* Lodd. or *D.* x *hybrida* Colv. ex Sweet

D. fionina K. Koch., a synonym of *D.* x *hybrida* Colv. ex Sweet ..

D. fortunei Benth., a synonym of *D. championii* Benth. .. ..

D. fortuni Lindl., a synonym of *D. genkwa* Sieb. & Zucc. .. ..

D. genkwa Sieb. & Zucc. 98

D. genkwa Sieb. & Zucc. forma *taitoensis* (Hayata) Hamaya. .. 103

D. giraldii Nitsche 104

D. glandulosa Spreng., a synonym of *D. oleoides* Schreb. .. ..

D. glomerata Lam. 105

D. glomerata Lam. var. *nivalis* C. Koch. 107

D. glomerata Lam. var. *pauciflora* Meissn. 107

D. glomerata Lam. var. *puberula* Sosn. 107

D. gnidioides Jaub. & Spach. 107

D. gnidium L. 108

D. gnidium L. var. *lanata* Faure et Maire 112

D. gnidium L. forma *latifolia* Keissl. 112

D. grueningiana H. Winkler 150

D. x *hendersonii* Hodgkin ex C. D. Brickell et B. Mathew (*D. petraea* Leybold x *D. cneorum* L.) 112

D. x *houtteana* Lindley & Paxton (*D. mezereum* L. x *D. laureola* L.) .. 113

D. houttei Low, a synonym of *D.* x *houtteana* Lindley .. ..

D. x *hybrida* Colv. ex Sweet (*D. odora* Thunb. x *D. collina* Dickson ex J. E. Smith) 114

D. imerica C. Koch., a synonym of *D. glomerata* Lam. .. ..

D. indica Hort. non L., a synonym of *D. odora* Thunb. ..

D. indica Hort. non L. *foliis-marginatis* Hort., a synonym of *D. odora* Thunb. var. *foliis-variegatis* Hort. .. ..

D. indica Hort. non L. *variegata* Hort., a synonym of *D. odora* Thunb. var. *foliis-variegatis* Hort. .. ..

PAGE

D. indica Schangin, a synonym of *D. altaica* Pallas .. .. ..

D. japonica Paxton, a synonym of *D. odora* Thunb. f. *marginata* (Miq.)
Mak. (possibly the clone 'Aureo-marginata') .. ..

D. japonica Siebold ex Hort., probably a synonym of *D. odora* Thunb.
'Mazelii'

D. japonica Paxton *striata* Hort., probably a synonym of *D. odora* Thunb.
'Aureo-marginata' .. ..

D. japonica Paxton var. *variegata* Hort., a synonym of *D. odora* Thunb.
f. *marginata* (Miq.) Mak.

D. japonica Thunb., a synonym of *D. odora* Thunb. .. .. ..

D. jasminea Sibth. & Sm. 116

D. jezoensis Maxim. ex Regel.. 119

D. juliae Kos.-Pol. 93

D. kabylica Chab. 184

D. kamtschatica Maxim. 121

D. kamtschatica var. *jezoensis* (Maxim. ex Regel) Ohwi, a synonym of
D. jezoensis Maxim. ex Regel.. .. ..

D. kiusiana Miq. 151

D. koreana Nakai 121

D. kosaninii (Stoj.) Stoj. 155

D. kurdica Bornm. 184

D. laciniata Lecomte 184

D. laureola L. 122

D. laureola L. var. *cantabrica* Willk. 124

D. laureola L. var. *latifolia* (Cosson) Meissn. 124

D. laureola L. ssp. *philippi* (Gren.) Rouy 124

D. laureola L. *purpurea* Hort., a synonym of *D.* x *houtteana* Lindley &
Paxton .. ..

D. lerchenfeldiana Schur., a synonym of *D. blagayana* Freyer .. ..

D. leyboldii Hort., probably a synonym of *D.* x *thauma* Farrer .. ..

D. limprichtii H. Winkler 184

D. libanotica Mouterde 184

D. linearifolia Hart 137

D. longilobata (Lecomte) Turrill 48

D. lucida Lois., a synonym of *D. oleoides* Schreb. .. .. ..

D. luzonica C. B. Robinson 151

D. macrantha Ludlow 124

D. malyana Blecic 119

D. x *mantensiana* Manten ex T.M.C. Taylor & F. Vrugtman 125

D. x *mantensiana* Manten ex T.M.C. Taylor & F. Vrugtman 'Manten'.. 126

D. manzellii Hort., a synonym of *D. blagayana* Freyer .. .. ..

D. martinii Lev. 184

D. mazeli Carr., a synonym of *D. odora* Thunb. 'Mazelii' .. ..

D. mazelii Hort., a synonym of *D. blagayana* Freyer .. .. ..

D. mezereum L. 129

D. mezereum L. forma *alba* (Weston) Schelle 133

D. mezereum L. var. *alba* Aiton, a synonym of *D. mezereum* L. f. *alba*
(Weston) Schelle .. ..

D. mezereum L. 'Alba Plena'.. 134

D. mezereum L. var. *albida* Meissn., a synonym of *D. mezereum* L. f. *alba*
(Weston) Schelle

D. mezereum L. "var. alpina Hort." loosely applied to dwarf forms of *D.*
mezereum L. 132

D. mezereum L. var. *atropurpurea* Dipp., a synonym of *D.* x *houtteana*
Lindley & Paxton

D. mezereum L. 'Atropurpurea', a synonym of *D.* x *houtteana* Lindley &
Paxton .. ..

191

PAGE
D. mezereum L. var. *autumnalis* Hort. ex Rehd. 134
D. mezereum L. 'Bowles' Variety' 133
D. mezereum L. 'Byford's Variety' 135
D. mezereum L. 'Coppergate'.. 135
D. mezereum L. *foliis atropurpureis* Hort., a synonym of *D.* x *houtteana*
    Lindley & Paxton .. ..
D. mezereum L. *grandiflora* Jacques; see under var. *autumnalis* ..
D. mezereum L. var. *maxima* Hort. ex Schneid., a synonym of *D. mezereum*
    L. var. *autumnalis* Hort. ex Rehd. .. ..
D. mezereum L. 'Paul's White' 134
D. mezereum L. f. *plena* (Hort. ex Rehd.) Schneid., probably a synonym of
    D. mezereum L. 'Alba Plena' .. ..
D. mezereum L. 'Rosea' 135
D. mezereum L. var. *rubra* Aiton 135
D. mezereum L. 'Rubra Plena' 135
D. mezereum L. "Rubra Select" Hort. 135
D. mezereum L. *sempervirens* Hort., a synonym of *D. mezereum* L. var.
    autumnalis Hort. ex Rehd. .. ..
D. mezereum L. 'Variegata' 135
D. microphylla Meissn., a synonym of *D. jasminea* Sibth. & Sm. ..
D. microphylla Meissn. var. *angustifolia* Meissn., a synonym of *D. jasminea*
    Sibth. & Sm. .. ..
D. miyabeana Makino 151
D. mucronata Royle 136
D. mucronata Royle var. *affghanica* Meissn., a synonym of *D. mucronata*
    Royle .. ..
D. nana Tagawa, a synonym of *D. retusa* Hemsl. .. ..
D. x *napolitana* Loddiges 137
D. x *neapolitana:* incorrect spelling of *D.* x *napolitana* .. ..
D. odora Thunb. 140
D. odora Thunb. forma *alba* (Hemsley) Hara 144
D. odora Thunb. var. *alba* Hemsl., a synonym of *D. odora* Thunb. f. *alba*
    (Hemsl.) Hara .. ..
D. odora Thunb. var. *albiflora* Hort., a synonym of *D. odora* Thunb. f.
    alba (Hemsl.) Hara .. ..
D. odora Thunb. var. *albo-marginata* Hort. 147
D. odora Thunb. var. *albo-variegata* Hort. 148
D. odora Thunb. var. *atrocaulis* Rehd., a syn. of *D. taiwaniana* (Mas.) Mas.
D. odora Thunb. 'Aureo-marginata' 147
D. odora Thunb. var. *elegantissima* Hort. 148
D. odora Thunb. var. *foliis-variegatis* Hort. 148
D. odora Thunb. var. *kiusiana* (Miq.) Keissler, a synonym of *D. kiusiana*
    Miq. .. ..
D. odora Thunb. var. *leucantha* Makino, a synonym of *D. odora* Thunb.
    f. *alba* (Hemsl.) Hara .. ..
D. odora Thunb. var. *luteo-variegata* Hort. 148
D. odora Thunb. var. *luzonica* (C. B. Robinson) H. L. Li, a synonym of
    D. luzonica Robinson .. ..
D. odora Thunb. forma *marginata* (Miq.) Makino 147
D. odora Thunb. var. *marginata* Miq., a synonym of *D. odora* Thunb. f.
    marginata (Miq.) Mak. .. ..
D. odora Thunb. *marginatis* Hort., a synonym of *D. odora* Thunb. var.
    folis-variegatis Hort. .. ..
D. odora Thunb. 'Mazelii' 148
D. odora Thunb. var. *mazeli* Hemsley, a synonym of *D. odora* Thunb.
    'Mazelii' .. ..
D. odora Thunb. var. *punctata* Hemsley 149
D. odora Thunb. forma *rosacea* (Makino) Hara 150

D. odora Thunb. var. *rosacea* Makino, a synonym of *D. odora* Thunb. f.
  rosacea (Makino) Hara .. ..
D. odora Thunb. var. *rubra* D. Don 150
D. odora var. *striata* Hort., probably a synonym of *D. odora* Thunb.
  'Aureo-marginata' .. ..
D. odora Thunb. var. *taiwaniana* (Mas.) Mas., a synonym of *D. taiwaniana*
  (Mas.) Mas. .. ..
D. odora Thunb. var. *variegata* Donn., a synonym of *D. odora* Thunb. f.
  marginata (Miq.) Mak. .. ..
D. odora Thunb. var. *variegata* Hort., a synonym of *D. odora* Thunb. f.
  marginata (Miq.) Mak. .. ..
D. odorata Lam., a synonym of *D. cneorum* L. .. .. ..
D. olaefolia Lam., a synonym of *D. sericea* Vahl. .. ..
D. oleoides Schreb. 152
D. oleoides Schreb. var. *brachyloba* Meissn. 154
D. oleoides Schreb. var. *buxifolia* (Vahl) Keissl. 155
D. oleoides Schreb. var. *carminea* Hort. 154
D. oleoides Schreb. var. *glandulosa* (Bertol.) Keissl. 155
D. oleoides Schreb. var. *glandulosa* (Bertol.) Keissl., forma *puberula* (Jaub.
  et Spach.) Keissl. 155
D. oleoides Schreb. var. *jasminea* Meissn., a synonym of *D. oleoides* Schreb.
  var. *glandulosa* (Bertol.) Keissl. .. ..
D. oleoides Schreb. var. *rosea* Hort. 155
D. oleoides d'Urville, a synonym of *D. gnidioides* Jaub. & Spach.. ..
D. oleoides Tschern ex Meissn., a synonym of *D. sophia* Kaleniczenko ..
D. orthophylla St. Lag., a synonym of *D. gnidium* L. .. ..

D. paniculata Lam., a synonym of *D. gnidium* L. .. ..
D. papyracea Wall. ex Steud. emend Smith & Cave 157
D. papyracea Wall. ex Steud. (in part) a synonym of *D. bholua* Buch.-
  Ham. ex D. Don .. ..
D. petraea Leybold 158
D. petraea Leybold 'Grandiflora' 162
D. petraea Leybold "*radicans*" Hort. 162
D. pontica L. 165
D. pontica L. ssp. *haematocarpa* G. Woron., a synonym of *D. albowiana*
  Woron. .. ..
D. pseudomezereum A. Gray 122
D. pseudomezereum Tanaka, a synonym of *D. jezoensis* Maxim. ex Regel
D. pseudosericea Pobed. 175

D. rebunensis Tatew., a synonym of *D. jezoensis* Maxim. ex Regel ..
D. rechingeri Wendelbo 135
D. retusa Hemsl. 167
D. rodriguezii Texidor 171
D. x rossetii Hort. 172
D. roumea Meissn. 184
D. rupestris Facchini, a synonym of *D. petraea* Leybold .. ..
D. rupestris Facchini 'Grandiflora', a synonym of *D. petraea* Leybold
  'Grandiflora' .. ..
D. salicifolia Lam., a synonym of *D. caucasica* Pallas .. ..
D. salicina Lev. 184
D. sericea Vahl 173
D. shillong Banerji 179
D. sinensis Lam., a synonym of *D. odora* Thunb. .. ..
D. sophia Kaleniczenko 80
D. speciosissima Carr., a synonym of *D. odora* Thunb. .. ..
D. stapfii Bornm. & Keissl. 156
D. striata Tratt. 176
D. sureil W W. Smith and Cave 178

		PAGE
D. szetschuanica K. Winkler, a synonym of *D. retusa* Hemsl.	.. ..	
D. taitoensis Hayata, probably a synonym of *D. genkwa* Sieb. & Zucc.		103
D. taiwaniana (Masamune) Masamune	.. ..	151
D. tangutica Maxim.	.. ..	170
D. tangutica Pritz. non Maxim., a synonym of *D. giraldii* Nitsche	..	
D. "tangutica alba" Hort.	.. ..	170
D. taurica Kotov	.. ..	81
D. x *thauma* Farrer	.. ..	179
D. transcaucasica Pobed.	.. ..	156
D. triflora Lour., probably a synonym of *D. odora* Thunb.	..	
D. vahlii Keissler, a synonym of *D. sericea* Vahl.	.. ..	
D. vahlii Keissl., var. *glabrifolia* Keissl.	.. .. ..	175
D. vaillantii P. Danguy	.. ..	184
D. vellaeoides Rodrig., a synonym of *D. rodriguezii* Texidor	..	
D. verlotii Gren. & Godr., a synonym of *D. cneorum* L. var. *verlotii* (Gren. et Godr.) Meissn.	.. ..	
D. verlotii alba Hort., probably an albino of *D. cneorum* L. var. *pygmaea* Stoker	.. ..	
D. wilsonii Rehder, a synonym of *D. tangutica* Maxim.	.. ..	
Wikstroemia aurantiaca (Diels) Domke, a synonym of *D. aurantiaca* Diels		
Wikstroemia aurantiaca (Diels) Domke var. *pulvinata* Domke, a synonym of *D. aurantiaca* Diels		
Wikstroemia genkwa (Sieb. and Zucc.) Domke, a synonym of *D. genkwa* Sieb. and Zucc.	.. ..